"*Deliverance from Evil Spirits* is not a scientific textbook, but rather story after story confirmed with observations of authorities and biblically based theological reflections on deliverance from evil spirits. A very valuable book."

—Michael Scanlan, president, Franciscan University of Steubenville

"Francis MacNutt's *Deliverance from Evil Spirits* is a classic handbook written out of decades of experience in the ministry of healing and deliverance. Drawing on the Scriptures and church tradition, MacNutt has written by far the best book I have seen on this controversial and difficult topic."

—Vinson Synan, dean, School of Divinity, Regent University

"Francis MacNutt has written with balance and caution on a difficult subject. He attempts to carefully sort out sin, mental illness, emotional trauma and the demonic. He has the biblical knowledge, the spiritual discernment, and the years of practical experience required to do this."

—David Seamands, author of *Healing for Damaged Emotions*

"Christians seeking pastoral guidance and psychological insights in the battle against the forces of darkness will discover this book to be a treasure house of knowledge and testimony of hope."

—Barbara Shlemon Ryan, president of Be-Loved Ministry

Deliverance from Evil Spirits

A Practical Manual

Francis MacNutt

Chosen Books

A Division of Baker Book House Co
Grand Rapids, Michigan 49516

© 1995 by Francis MacNutt

Published by Chosen Books
a division of Baker Book House Company
P.O. Box 6287, Grand Rapids, MI 49516-6287

Fifth printing, March 1998

Printed in the United States of America

Library of Congress Cataloging-in-Publication Data

MacNutt, Francis.
    Deliverance from evil spirits : a practical manual / Francis MacNutt.
        p. cm.
    Includes bibliographial references.
    ISBN 0-8007-9232-7
    1. Exorcism. 2. Demonology. 3. Devil. 4. Spiritual healing.
    I. Title.
BV873.E8M33 1995
235'.4—dc20   95-5150

For current information about all releases from Baker Book House, visit our web site:
http://www.bakerbooks.com

To the Rev. Tommy Tyson,
a true friend and encourager,
who doesn't like to pray for deliverance
but who prays anyway

Contents

Introduction

At a time when evil spirits are a popular subject for movies, novels and TV talk shows, but are not a respectable topic for dialogue in seminaries or among theologians, I admit to a certain hesitation in writing about exorcism from evil spirits. As theologian Walter Wink writes:

> What does late twentieth-century Western society exclude from conversation? Certainly not sex; at least in more "sophisticated" circles, accounts of sexual exploits scarcely raise an eyebrow. But if you want to bring all talk to a halt in shocked embarrassment, every eye riveted on you, try mentioning angels, or demons, or the devil. You will be quickly appraised for signs of pathological violence and then quietly shunned.
>
> Angels, spirits, principalities, gods, Satan—these, along with all other spiritual realities, are the unmentionables of our culture.[1]

Since Walter Wink wrote this in 1986 we have seen a remarkable change. Books on angels have suddenly become bestsellers—not just in the religious bookstores but nationwide. Curiously, though, surveys taken of the American public show that, although 85 percent believe in angels, only about 65 percent believe in evil spirits (bad angels)!

Some good books on the subject of deliverance have been published but have not been widely read. One of the books that helped me in the beginning was Don Basham's *Deliver Us from Evil*,[2] although I remember his telling me, shortly before he died, how disappointed he was in the sales of what he believed

1. *Unmasking the Powers* (Philadelphia: Fortress, 1986), p. 1.
2. Grand Rapids: Chosen Books, 1972.

was his most important book. Scott Peck's *People of the Lie*[3] has been widely read. As a psychiatrist he courageously opens up the topic of the existence of evil spirits. His main desire is to let the thoughtful reader consider the possibility that evil spirits really do exist and should be recognized in psychology as a source of individual problems, as well as societal problems—such as the MyLai massacre during the Vietnam War. But he wisely limits his book to sharing evidence that evil spirits exist and influence people harmfully. He does not go into the question of how to pray for protection from evil spirits or how to rid ourselves of them.

My hope is that this book, *Deliverance from Evil Spirits*, will be widely read, and not just by people who already believe in the reality of evil spirits and pray for deliverance. My earlier book *Healing*, in its various editions,[4] has sold about a million copies in the United States and has been translated into various languages such as Japanese and Swahili, thereby reaching many people in both the Catholic and Protestant traditions to let them know about the reality of prayer for healing. Because Christian churches generally neglect to teach about deliverance, I hope this book will resurrect intelligent discussion about the need for a balanced deliverance ministry in every Christian church.

As I reread some of the personal stories I have included in these pages, I look back at how I might have reacted if I had read them thirty years ago and realize that, for a person who has not encountered the strange, mysterious world of evil, they may sound almost as incredible as aliens descending from a UFO. All I can ask as this book unfolds is that you maintain an open mind.

When we write about evil, which is only part of the universe created by God, we necessarily concentrate on the downside of life. It is like a doctor writing a book on disease, all the time knowing that his profession is really more concerned about life and health than about sickness. But someone has to write about the demonic component of life. The Gospel writers certainly did not shy away from it.

3. New York: Simon & Schuster, 1983.
4. Ave Maria Press, Bantam (now out of print), Image and Creation House have all come out with editions.

Putting out the garbage at home is only a small part of my life. I don't like to do it, but I still have to take it out to the curb once a week. And we need people in our towns to serve as garbage collectors, driving the noisy, ungainly trucks and devoting their working hours to the dirty job of disposing of our waste. Sometimes I think they deserve higher wages than bank presidents. They are absolutely necessary, and if they go on strike, whole cities grind to a halt. In the spiritual life deliverance is like that. Someone needs to do it and needs to know what he is doing.[5] In some ways I think the Church today has come upon hard times because the demonic holds sway; for a long time no one has put out the garbage.

Most of my personal and family life is devoted to the positive side of life, desiring to be a loving Christian husband, father and minister as I try to follow the beautiful, peaceful path that Jesus shows us:

> Whatever is true, whatever is noble, whatever is right, whatever is pure, whatever is lovely, whatever is admirable—if anything is excellent or praiseworthy—think about such things.
>
> Philippians 4:8

That is my great desire. Yet at times we must put on the full armor of God and take our stand against Satan by engaging in combat (Ephesians 6:12). A major reason Jesus became human was to free us from demonic influence; for Him it was no side issue, no minor ministry. His main title is *Savior* because He came to free us from evil: "The reason the Son of God appeared was to destroy the devil's work" (1 John 3:8).

If there is one thing I would like to emphasize, it is that deliverance is a ministry of love to wounded human beings. Christians who like a good fight, who like to see things in stark contrasts of good and evil, seem to be attracted by the deliverance ministry. And because of their naturally combative temperaments, they may fight against evil spirits in such a way that the injured human being, who is the battleground, is trampled

5. Because it is awkward stylistically to try to be gender-inclusive by using *he or she* for a personal pronoun, I will simply alternate, using *he* in one chapter and *she* in the next.

12

on. An old proverb says that when the elephant and lion fight, it is the ant that gets stepped on.

We are ministering to people, not demons. Deliverance is really part of the ministry of healing, and everything we say to the people we are trying to help should shine forth with love. Condemnation is reserved only for the demonic realm, not for the broken persons who come to us for help.

As Pope John Paul II said,

The Gospel, above all else, is the joy of creation. God, who in creating saw that His creation was good (cf. Gn 1:1–25), is the source of joy for all creatures, and above all for humankind. God the creator seems to say of creation, "It is good that you exist." And His joy spreads especially through the "good news," according to which good is greater than all that is evil in the world. Evil, in fact, is neither fundamental nor definitive.[6]

6. Pope John Paul II, *Crossing the Threshold of Hope* (New York: Alfred A. Knopf, 1994), p.20.

Part 1

Necessary Background
Clearing Away Misconceptions

1

How I Got Involved in Casting Out Demons

A Parable for the Church

Like all my friends who have become actively involved in casting out evil spirits, I got involved through experience, not theory. Pushing me beyond the bounds of what was theologically respectable was my desire to help wounded, struggling people. In those days in the late 1960s, the only practical instruction I received as a Roman Catholic priest came from a few Protestant friends and from my own trial-and-error experiences. Inevitably I made mistakes, through which I hope I have learned some valuable lessons.

Praying for deliverance has been very different from my experience in the healing ministry. I can honestly say I have known thousands of people who seem to have been healed through prayer. Not all were healed physically, but even those who were not were blessed spiritually. But in my ministry of deliverance, so closely connected with healing, I know a few persons I was unable to help, either because of my ignorance, or because I did not have time to follow through, or because I attacked the most obvious problem, the demonic element, when a positive building up or inner healing was needed first.

15

We are all aware, I think, of the problems involved in deliverance ministry. It is the most dangerous ministry I know—not only for the exorcist, as Malachi Martin observes in *Hostage to the Devil*,[1] but for the sufferer who needs to be freed. We need to learn how to pray for deliverance without repeating the same old mistakes so that the oppressed will be freed in increasing numbers. But refusing to help hurting people by restricting, or even forbidding, exorcism is far worse than the mistakes we make, for it abandons multitudes of the oppressed to suffer for the rest of their lives or, worse yet, to commit suicide when they see no hope of ever getting better. I see no reason, as we learn more and rely more on the Lord for guidance, to be overly fearful. Every minister or priest should be able to help hundreds of people through deliverance prayer.

Although I love to pray for healing and see the joy on people's faces as they experience the love of Jesus washing away their pain, I have also discovered that healing prayer is not always enough. I might be conducting a healing service in a chapel, for example, praying quietly for the people who come forward asking for physical healing, when suddenly, with no outward provocation, a man's face contorts and he shouts out something like, "We hate you!" On one occasion a young woman tried to strangle me, and several times I have seen people reach for their throats as if to strangle themselves. Over the years a number of bizarre occurrences like these have taken place. There are not many, to be sure; but usually when we pray for a sufficiently large number of people, several erupt with disturbing behavior. (Just two nights ago a woman started screaming and her face contorted grotesquely when I started to pray at a healing service of about four hundred people in a United Methodist church.)

Sometimes when I continue praying, the person falls to the ground, then starts rolling around and shouting, reminiscent of individuals in the Gospels like the epileptic demoniac: "When the spirit saw Jesus, it immediately threw the boy into a convulsion. He fell to the ground and rolled around, foaming at the mouth" (Mark 9:20).

We might pass these off as psychotic episodes, except for puzzling factors that simply do not compute, such as:

1. New York: Reader's Digest Press, 1976. Later printed as a Bantam paperback.

1. At other times these persons act normally. Often this is the first time something like this has ever happened to them.
2. The atmosphere is usually not highly charged emotionally. These incidents occur during a quiet service characterized by love and gentle prayer. If these are hysterical outbursts, what could be their cause?
3. When these people say something, it is often spoken in the plural: "*We* will kill you!" Where did the *we* come from? Sometimes they roar like lions or bark like dogs. How do we explain that?
4. Usually these tormented people have not seen others behave like this, so where have they learned it? It amazes me that demonized people all over the world behave in the same ways when we pray for them.

I tried over the years to figure out what to do when these bizarre episodes took place. Most of my ministry in those early days was ad hoc. What *do* you do, after all, when you are praying with a person for healing and she starts screaming at you and topples over in convulsions? How do you help a person like that? Do you just send her home the way she came? Where are we supposed to learn what to do?

On those occasions when I was praying for such a person, I would take her, along with a prayer team, to a side room. After a period of prayer, during which I would command the spirits to depart, they would seemingly leave, often through coughing or some other external manifestation. Afterward the person would almost always say that she had felt the tormenting entity leave.[2] And she would appear to be at peace and often radiantly transformed.

I noticed several unusual things. Paradoxically we on the team usually felt exhausted while the freed person appeared full of life, exhilarated and joyful. Also, these liberated persons could often remember nothing that went on from the time they came forward in line until the process was over and they were freed. It was as if the demonic spirits had taken over for a time,

---

2. This sense of total relief, of "It's completely gone," is significantly different from what we see in inner healing, where there is usually a process that takes place in stages over a period of time.

even speaking through the person. It was like a possession, but a temporary one, during which the person had apparently been submerged, which was why she could not remember anything that had happened. These scenes reminded me of the story of the Gerasene demoniac, in which the "Legion" shrieked out until Jesus sent them into the pigs. Then at last the wild man rested, in his right senses (Mark 5:1–20).

I tried to steer clear of all these difficulties by emphasizing the love of Jesus in the healing services we held, because I did not think I knew enough to pray for deliverance. (Out of the mouth of one of the first persons who ever asked me to pray for deliverance came these embarrassing words: "You can't drive us out; you don't have enough experience!") But in 1972 a case was thrust upon me that forced me to learn more.

Roberta

A young married woman (let's call her Roberta) came to me seeking advice during a conference. She had a history of mental illness and had spent much time in hospitals. She wanted my help yet was not eager for me to pray. Later, when she came to my office and allowed me to pray for her profound depression to lift, no evident healing took place.

I noticed two strange things about her appearance: She had a beautiful but haunted face and rows of patterned burn marks arranged neatly up and down her arms like tattoos. She had inflicted them on herself, she told me, by sticking a lighted cigarette to her flesh. When I asked if that had not hurt, she answered, "No!" The lack of pain seemed strange but I ascribed it to some mysterious kind of psychological blocking out. She also told me she liked to wander around in cemeteries, and felt most at home in settings that reminded her of death. She left my office pretty much the way she came; I simply did not know how to help her.

A few months later some of her friends brought her to where I was speaking at a large conference. At that point I began to suspect I might be dealing with something more than a mere psychological problem. Every time she started to approach me to talk, she turned around again and disappeared into the crowd. Her friends finally calmed her down and brought her forward to tell me how, as a young girl, her father had consecrated her to an evil spirit in a satanic ritual in Brazil. She had become a priestess of Satan. But now that she was in the United States she was trying to live a normal life. She asked me to free her.

Realizing I was in over my head, I introduced her to a leader at the camp who had a lot of experience in praying for deliverance. Aside from my own lack of experience, I did not have much time to spend with her because I was a main speaker and 350 other people were attending the camp. I told her I would be available to start the prayer, but that my friend would do the actual casting out. She pleaded with me to stay and lead the entire deliverance prayer, but I felt that my more experienced colleague would do better at praying for her deliverance.

So around ten o'clock one night I initiated the prayer, then turned the session over to the other leader, who took over and prayed vigorously for several hours while I watched. Finally, around two in the morning, I decided to leave since I was scheduled to speak the next morning and was becoming exhausted. It seemed like wisdom for me to leave and retire to my cabin to get some rest.

Before dawn I was awakened by a knock at my cabin door. A man told me to get up, that Roberta had tried cutting her wrists. I stumbled to my feet and got dressed. But what could I possibly do that I had not already done? Nevertheless, they brought Roberta over. She asked if we could talk. So we sat down on the doorstep of my cabin as the sun came up. She told me she had just called her husband two hours away to come pick her up and take her home. Then she threatened to commit suicide when she got there.

Is Satan using guilt to keep me up night and day? I thought.

"You're a priest," she went on pointedly, "and you don't even believe in who you are. You're the only one in this camp who has the spiritual power to free me. I came to you, and you turned me over to somebody who can't do it."

This hit me hard. Suppose God did want me to pray for her? If it was the devil, on the other hand, what better way to wipe me out as a speaker than get me trapped the way my friend was trapped last night? By telling me I was the only one who could pull it off, was she just appealing to my vanity?

I finally promised to try to help her, provided that she, in turn, did everything possible to cooperate. She agreed. And as a first step she confided that she had been consecrated to a particular demon mentioned in the Bible, and that a Scripture verse had been pinned to her when she was consecrated to Satan. She was not familiar with the Bible, but asked in her accented English if there might not be a book named "Jope."

"That sounds like Job," I said.

"That's it!"

By the time of our appointment the next morning, she had spent hours preparing and had found her verse, Job 18:14: "He is torn from the security of his tent and marched off to the king of terrors."

"King of Terrors is the one I was offered to," she said.[3]

For the next hour I led her through repentance and forgiveness of sins, then asked her to renounce all her involvement in the occult realm. After that I prayed to break any curses and cast out the King of Terrors. The beautiful conclusion came when she consecrated her life to Jesus Christ, was baptized in the Holy Spirit, prayed in a tongue and interpreted it herself.

"Just as Satan has been using you for his purposes," went the interpretation, "I will now use you for My own glory."

At the end of our prayer time, which was quiet and lasted about an hour, Roberta looked different, not to say transformed. Her original reason for coming to see me, as it turned out, was her shock when one of her daughters had asked her if she was a devil. Also, she had been addicted to various drugs, which I had not known about when I prayed, and yet the addiction was broken during our prayer. Thereafter she was able to begin a radically new life with her husband and children.

Roberta's story is a parable of what is happening to the Church in a variety of ways. Here are two lessons that spoke to me then and still speak to the Church today.

The Human Need

The first lesson that leaps out from Roberta's story is that I was forced to take action simply because I was confronted by an immediate, deep human need—a case of life and death—and no

---

3. The King of Terrors is a Ugaritic god of death. Some current translations, such as the NIV, downplay the element of personal evil by lower-casing *king of terrors*; but the New Jerusalem Bible capitalizes it: *King of Terrors*.

one else was there to help. Ignorant as I was, I simply could not stand by with folded arms and watch her move toward destruction. I did not know much but finally decided to risk praying.

This is the way most of us get involved in praying for deliverance. We are the only ones around, so we finally decide we have to do something. It is possible we will make mistakes, but it seems certain that the results will be disastrous if we do nothing.

I want to share, in this connection, the illuminating results of a small survey I made following a pioneering seminar on deliverance held for 132 priests and two bishops in 1978 at Mt. Augustine Retreat House in Staten Island, New York (which has long since closed its doors because of the priest shortage). Fifty-eight responded to the questionnaire.

To the question "How did you learn about the need for the deliverance ministry?" the largest number (26) said they had learned about the need not from their training but from their own experience.

"It just happened at retreats," one said.

"Through conducting healing services," said another.

Or, "A psychiatrist sent them to me."

Or, "Demonic problems began to surface in our prayer groups."

Another five priests said that tormented people had started coming to them for help. Two more said they discovered it as a need among their parishioners. Three even admitted that their own personal need for deliverance had opened them up to this ministry.

Like me, most of them had not been taught to cast out evil spirits; they simply found that there was an imperative need to help suffering people tormented by demonic oppression. None of them had learned about it in seminary.

Of those who had *not* discovered this need through experience, nineteen first learned about deliverance through reading or hearing tapes, and another nine learned through hearing about it from friends. Like me, they all had been taught to believe in Satan and formal exorcism, but at a distance and not as something they themselves might get into.

For most of us, I think, learning about deliverance begins not as some cosmic intellectual question about the cause of evil, but as a puzzling pastoral dilemma about how to help this person standing in front of me who seems to be under demonic attack.

I see the need for deliverance now as a common, not a rare, problem. (More about this later.) Deliverance affects the well-being of the Church and must be addressed because multitudes of hurting people are looking for the help that can come only through prayer for deliverance. If people are suffering from psychological problems, fine; they can receive help through counseling and prayer for healing. But if the source of the problem is demonic, they will not be notably helped through ordinary psychological intervention. Also, many victims of Satanic Ritual Abuse are now surfacing and asking publicly (through TV talk shows, for example) why the Church is not there to help.

These wounded people are crying for help, just as Roberta was, which forced me to confront the issue. The Church will either have to take action or continue in denial, asserting that the problem of satanic oppression is either rare or unreal.

Forcing Afflicted People to Seek Help from the Wrong Sources

The second lesson that leaps out from Roberta's story is that just as I tried to turn her over to someone else—an action that at the time I considered wise and prudent—I think most of us have been trained to seek help for difficult cases from anyone but ourselves. By and large people who need deliverance come first to their minister or priest. The minister often refers them to a psychiatrist. If the problem is emotional, the psychiatrist should be able to help; but if the problem is demonic, the sufferer will probably not be helped, and may well end up institutionalized—out of harm's way but also out of commission, perhaps for a lifetime.

Roberta's rebuke—"You're the only one who can help me. Don't you believe in who you are?"—can be addressed to thousands of ministers and priests, while we rest contentedly, having given the afflicted person the phone number of a local psychiatrist and confident that we have done the best we could. But how can this help when most counselors and psychiatrists do not operate out of a frame of reference that enables them to recognize the presence of the demonic even when it is there? It is not in *their* training, either.

Many patients, including those in mental hospitals, can be cured or helped through prayer for inner healing or deliverance. This proposition, admittedly, is impossible to prove; I simply present it as a heartfelt belief.

I once prayed for a young woman who had been confined in a mental hospital for twelve years, suffering from schizophrenia. After two hours of prayer for healing and deliverance, the glazed look in her eyes left and she was able to converse in a normal way. Several weeks later the doctors recognized a dramatic change in her behavior and released her from the hospital. I could cite many more examples from a steady stream of supplicants (ever since I first stumbled into the deliverance ministry more than twenty years ago) unable to find help from psychotherapy or from those who are ministers of religion who had not learned to deal with the demonic. My great desire is to encourage Christians to learn more about deliverance—and then, when necessary, to pray for it. My interest is not academic; to me the issue is life and death. ("If I don't get help, I'm going to end it all!") Some people *will* die, spiritually or even physically, if no one is there to free them from the torment that may drive them to kill themselves.

Ministers of the Gospel need to stop passing the buck by denying that demonic oppression exists or by simply referring people to psychiatrists or counselors when what is needed is deliverance. Counseling and medication may also be needed; and we should by all means cooperate with mental health professionals. But ministers must not continue to deny responsibility *in their own field.* When my wife, Judith, a psychotherapist, worked on staff in an excellent psych unit in Boston, she had some patients she believed needed prayer to free them from oppression, patients she referred to their chaplains. But the chaplains, she found, knew as little about spiritual warfare as she did. They were good at encouraging people and were a helpful adjunct to counseling, but were unable to help in the spiritual realm, their own chosen field, where the patient needed them most.

A Woman Who Found Help

Here is a story with a happy ending that comes from an educated woman who sought help unsuccessfully from both a psychiatrist and a priest. In her desperation she finally found deliverance from an unexpected source.

Dear Francis,

Never before have I written to someone I knew only from reading his book. . . .[4] I pray that you may be able to give me the advice I need. Only in the last five weeks have I put a tag on my trouble, and I still have a problem using words that sound out of the Dark Ages and go against my educational background.

About three years ago I began to reach for a closer relationship with God. At the same time I became chronically depressed and actually suicidal. I didn't understand and talked with my priest and told him I needed help. I am 37 years old, well-educated and analytical. I majored in psychology, and hated to admit it but something was wrong with me, and a mental health center seemed the answer. I began psychotherapy, worked hard and did all the right things, but still felt no better—nothing changed inside me. I was being driven. My doctor couldn't understand why we couldn't change things. There is a voice in my head (we called it a parent-tape then) that said I couldn't live. Two years ago I tried twice in one week to kill myself. I went from intensive care to the psychiatric unit of the hospital. I told my doctor and also my priest that it wasn't me; I didn't want to feel that way. But I sounded crazy so I stopped saying it.

I prayed and prayed but felt even worse.

At this time God sent Sister _____ into my life; she is an intelligent, well-read, down-to-earth woman. She said that perhaps I should pray for deliverance. Finally, to please her, I agreed, so we went to see a couple for prayer. While there I realized for the first time in my life the evil I am dealing with. I was asked to renounce all my occult activities. It sounded simple (I had long ago relegated them to the level of the unnecessary), but I found them extremely difficult to renounce. I have had a voice in my head since I was about three years old. It was in *my* head, so I assumed it was me, even though I knew it wasn't. It told me what to do and how; I felt it took care of me. It told me how to make things happen and how to read the future or see the past. I told fortunes

---

4. She had read the chapter on deliverance in my book *Healing*.

when I was older, but people were frightened because I could tell so much. I am what Sybil Leak calls a born witch.

After these people prayed with me it was quiet, but I could still feel its presence and knew it wasn't gone.

The next week was awful. This thing no longer pretended to be my voice or me. It attacked me almost continually. I was desperate, so Sister and I went back again to pray with the couple. This time it was very hard. I could not talk and they physically restrained me. The voice kept saying, "Make the 'connection'; let me do it. They can't hold you if you do; they don't know how." I was so afraid someone would be hurt that I didn't let go, and we didn't expel it.

This brings me to my problem. I am trying to be rational in the light of my twentieth-century upbringing, but I know this is a very powerful demon who is tormenting me. I want to be free; I want to give my whole will to God. I will try deliverance again, but only if I feel I am protected. I don't want to be part of an exhibition that leaves me the same way afterwards. I feel like a battleground. I have talked to my priest and he is sympathetic. He tells me to go to confession, but it is not enough. I need help. Can you give me any advice?

This is really a question asked of the whole Church, isn't it? How can we help people who, in desperation, write or phone even from distant places? Here we have what I now see as a common pastoral case: an intelligent person who has already turned to both traditional sources of help, the Church and psychiatry, but who has gotten no help from fine, well-intentioned priests and doctors.

How many ministers or priests do you know to whom you might turn for deliverance prayer?

So desperate was this woman that she telephoned me several times to see if I could see her. I just could not. The only thing I could think of was to refer her to a priest I knew who lived fifty miles from her home.

Two weeks later she wrote again:

Dear Francis,

As soon as I mailed my letter to you the demon began to push and torment me harder than ever. My friends took me to the emergency room because I had overdosed. The sister in charge of the psychiatric unit asked me if I was trying to separate myself from the voice by killing myself. I felt the only way I could separate from it was to die. My psychiatrist came and told me I had to be admitted. I refused because I knew I could not get the help I needed in a hospital.

When I finally traveled to meet your friend, Father _____, I liked him at once. He is intelligent, well-read and very pleasant. I talked with him and was open and honest. He seemed to avoid the subject of the voice and the demon. After talking and talking, Father said in essence that I was a nice, confused lady who needed a psychiatrist. That hurt, not because I hadn't heard it before, but because I hadn't come all the way to a distant city to hear it. Then I asked him point-blank about the voice. He was very distressed but said he thought the voice was mine.

I cannot describe to you how I felt. I felt God was being very cruel. I had bitter tears running down and told him I didn't know what to say except that I knew the voice wasn't me. "How do you know?" he asked.

She went on to describe how she roamed around in desperation that night, until at last she ended up in a retreat house to see a sister she knew. Another sister in the retreat house ended up helping her:

I wasn't sure if she thought I was sane or not, but she was nice. I must have looked as if I were about to leave, because she asked me to stay while she got her Bible. She sat still, looking at the Bible for a moment, then looked at me and said, "The Lord wants me to pray with you."

I wasn't surprised; after all, she is a nun. First we prayed together, then she read Mark 9:14–29 [the healing of a boy with an evil spirit] and said, "I believe that's how it is with you." I agreed and she said, "Let's pray." She began praying that God would be with us and guide us. Then I started to realize she was praying for deliverance. Her voice was very low and she didn't look at me. She took authority, bound the spirit, and commanded it to leave and never return. I felt the evil spirit, but that little room was full of God. Sister was open and God was pouring through her. I was not afraid. I let go completely and the demon left. God held me very gently. I told Sister it was gone. She looked at me and her eyes were full of tears. She said, "Let's go to the chapel and thank God and praise Him."

There the sister who is my friend saw me and commented that I looked different.

"It's gone," I told her.

"When did that happen?"

"Just now. Sister prayed for deliverance."

"I didn't know she could do that."

Well, I don't know if she had ever done that before; I didn't ask. But I think she is beautiful to let the Lord use her in such a special way.

It feels strange, but good, just to be me. The voice and the connection in my head are gone. Thank you for helping me! God used you, too.

All this is to God's glory.

Peace!

I am writing this book, then, to answer the question I have faced in my own ministry: How do you help people like this woman and like Roberta? If we are not to send them home the way they came, but to offer them the kind of help they need, we need biblical and practical guidelines. I am writing to share what I have learned.

In the next section we will discuss the existence of evil spirits and what different kinds we may expect to find.

Part 2

The Existence and Kinds of Evil Spirits

2

Do Demons Really Exist?

The Scriptural Evidence

Two hundred years ago few Christians questioned whether Satan and the demonic realm were real. There would have been no need to write a chapter like this.

Even as recently as 1972, Pope Paul VI, reaffirming the age-old understanding of Scripture (and human experience), wrote:

> It is contrary to the teaching of the Bible and the Church to refuse to recognize the existence of such a reality . . . or to explain it as a pseudo reality, a conceptual and fanciful personification of the unknown causes of our misfortunes. . . .
>
> That it is not a question of one devil, but of many, is indicated by various passages in the Gospels (Luke 11:19–20; Mark 5:9). But the principal one is Satan, which means the adversary, the enemy; and with him many, all creatures of God, but fallen, because of their rebellion and damnation; a whole mysterious world, upset by an unhappy drama, of which we know very little. . . .[1]

To decide whether demons exist, we need to look at the two basic sources of such a belief: sacred Scripture and our human experience. In this chapter we will look at the scriptural evi-

---

1. "Deliver Us from Evil": General Audience of Pope Paul VI, Nov. 15, 1972. Reported in *L'Osservatore Romano*, Nov. 23, 1972.

dence for the existence of demons. Then, in the next chapter, we will share human experience relating to their activity.

As we read through the Gospels we cannot help but be struck by the extraordinary numbers of references to Jesus confronting Satan and the whole realm of demons. A major theme in the New Testament is the clash between the Kingdom of God and the kingdom of Satan. The climax of human history, in fact, occurs when God, in Jesus, overpowers Satan and frees the human race from Satan's dominion.

Nor do I propose that the ministry of exorcism is simply one minor ministry among many that need to be resurrected in today's Church, but that Jesus' ministry of deliverance is central to an understanding of the Gospel: "The reason the Son of God appeared was to destroy the devil's work" (1 John 3:8).

The entire New Testament shows that Jesus was not primarily a Teacher (although He was an extraordinary Teacher) but that His chief title is *Savior* or *Redeemer*. The traditional title *Savior* means, of course, that He actually saves us; He rescues us from a real danger, from something evil.

Again, Christian tradition says that the evil that weighs down the human race is a force so powerful that our own unaided humanity cannot successfully overcome it: "For our struggle is not against flesh and blood, but against the rulers, against the authorities, against the powers of this dark world and against the spiritual forces of evil in the heavenly realms" (Ephesians 6:12). It is precisely because the evil in the world has a satanic origin that we cannot simply overcome it by better Christian education or church programs; we need a Savior. Without a Savior our world is lost.

Another traditional way of saying this is that we need *grace*, God's help. In fact, the early Church had to condemn a heresy, Pelagianism, that taught that our human efforts were in themselves enough to bring us salvation.

The basic evils that Jesus came to confront were

- Sin
- Sickness
- Affliction by evil spirits

- Nature out of control (e.g., the storm at sea that Jesus rebuked)
- The last enemy of all, death itself

So when Jesus began His public ministry, He preached good news—that is, the Gospel: "The time has come. . . . The kingdom of God is near. Repent and believe the good news!" (Mark 1:15).

The flip side of preaching that the Kingdom of God is at hand is preaching that the kingdom of Satan is being destroyed. For that reason Jesus' first act of ministry in Mark was casting out an unclean spirit from a man He met in the synagogue. This spirit "shook the man violently and came out of him with a shriek. The people were all so amazed that they asked each other, 'What is this? A new teaching—and with authority! He even gives orders to evil spirits and they obey him'" (Mark 1:26–28).

This was a *teaching*, then, and not just an action to free a suffering man. The teaching was that the kingdom of evil, which up to this point had held sway over the human race, was being destroyed and that the Kingdom of God was at hand.

This is what we pray for, of course, in the Lord's Prayer: "Thy Kingdom come, thy will be done, on earth as it is in heaven" and "Deliver us from evil." A still more accurate translation, according to many Scripture scholars, renders it, "Deliver us from the *evil one*" (that is, Satan).

Consequently, delivering people from evil spirits is, along with forgiving sins and healing the sick, an essential part of the Gospel. To the extent that we no longer realize the reality of the supernatural power of the demonic realm—against which we are powerless in our own unaided humanity—we no longer sense the need for a Savior, for Jesus Christ. Even for many professing Christians, Jesus has become simply an excellent teacher of values, among many other teachers, like Confucius and the Buddha. This is a major problem with the New Age movement: It fails to recognize the reality of the supernatural dimension of evil, and affirms that human beings are good and have tremendous untapped potential for growth if only they can discover how good they are and rid themselves of shame. Consequently, there is in the New Age system of thought no real need for a Savior; they see Jesus simply as a good man bringing a wonderful message of love for the human race.

The Jesus of Scripture, by contrast, is clearly presented as the Savior, the One who rescues us from sin, sickness and domination by evil spirits. The very name *Jesus*, in fact, given to Mary through the message of the angel Gabriel (Luke 1:31), means "God saves." For the Hebrews, a person's name was more than a name; it was meant to signify one's mission in life. Jesus' mission was to save the human race. Peter summed up Jesus' entire public ministry, as he preached to the household of Cornelius (the first Gentiles to come into the Church), by stating that they had already heard "how God anointed Jesus of Nazareth with the Holy Spirit and power, and how he went around doing good and healing all who were under the power of the devil, because God was with him" (Acts 10:38).

This renewed emphasis on preaching that the Kingdom of God is at hand, and that Satan's kingdom is being destroyed, helps us understand why Pentecostal and charismatic churches are growing at such an extraordinary rate in the developing world.[2] Because people there experience the reality of evil spirits and the power of witch doctors and shamans (see the next chapter), they respond readily to preaching and ministry that promise to set them free. The explosive growth of the Vineyard movement, which grew in fifteen years from a home prayer group to five hundred churches under John Wimber's leadership, again reflects the hunger of ordinary people to hear a message of Good News that stresses the Kingdom of God being at hand.[3]

Because of the multitudes of sick and oppressed, Jesus shared His authority as the Son of God with His disciples; and every time He sent them out to preach, He "gave them authority to drive out evil spirits and to heal every disease and sickness" (Matthew 10:1; see also Luke 9:1; Luke 10:9, 17). It is as if the Twelve and the 72 would not have been able to preach the Good News unless they were also able to back up their message by showing that the Kingdom of God truly was at hand by casting out evil spirits and healing the sick.

Let's look now at more of the scriptural background for the deliverance ministry.

2. See C. Peter Wagner's books, such as *Spiritual Power and Church Growth* (Lake Mary, Fla.: Creation House, 1986).
3. See John Wimber's book *Power Evangelism* (San Francisco: HarperCollins, 1986).

Evil Spirits in the Old Testament

One of the fascinating differences between the Old and New Testaments is that, while there is a great deal of exorcism of evil spirits in the New Testament, there is very little of it—even little *mention* of evil spirits—in the Old. "Nowhere in the Hebrew Old Testament does Satan appear as a distinctive demonic figure, opposed to God and responsible for all evil," writes Dennis Hamm, S.J., a professor of Scripture.[4]

Perhaps the best-known mention of Satan in the Old Testament is in Job, but even here Satan is really a title: "the satan," "the accuser." Furthermore, he is part of the heavenly court—a kind of prosecuting attorney. Rather than being a personage with a capital S, he simply fulfills the function of being "the accuser." (*Satan* became a proper name only in St. Jerome's Vulgate translation around the year A.D. 400.)

Similarly, "the satan" is mentioned again in Zechariah 3. As the accuser (again, in God's presence) he is ready to challenge Joshua's fitness to be high priest.

One of the few mentions of an evil spirit in the Old Testament is when David was enlisted in Saul's court to play the harp when Saul was tormented by an evil spirit:

Now the Spirit of the Lord had departed from Saul, and an evil spirit from the Lord tormented him. Saul's attendants said to him, "See, an evil spirit from God[5] is tormenting you. Let our lord command his servants here to search for someone who can play the harp. He will play when the evil spirit from God comes upon you, and you will feel better."

1 Samuel 16:14–16

And that is precisely what happened: Whenever David played upon his harp, "Relief would come to Saul; he would feel better, and the evil spirit would leave him" (1 Samuel 16:23). It sounds like the phenomenon we often find during times when people

4. Dennis Hamm, S.J., "The Ministry of Deliverance and the Biblical Data," *Deliverance Prayer*, edited by Matthew and Dennis Linn (Ramsey, N.J.: Paulist Press, 1980), p. 51.

5. In the Old Testament the earliest authors apparently want to ascribe everything that happens, even evil, to God's power. Nothing escapes God's causality.

are singing and praising God: Someone in the congregation feels something "lift off and leave."

The description of David playing his harp and freeing Saul temporarily from his black moods is about as close as we get to actual deliverance in the Old Testament.

We also read about the prophet Micaiah telling King Ahab about a vision he had of the heavenly court in which the Lord asked for volunteers to deceive Ahab. One of the spirits volunteered by saying, "I will go out and be a lying spirit in the mouths of all his prophets" (1 Kings 22:22). All the false prophets had foretold that Ahab would be victorious, and Ahab wanted to follow their advice, but somehow they realized that only Micaiah, who predicted disaster, was right. The leader of the false prophets even intimated that the spirit who had lied to him had then gone to Micaiah: "Which way did the spirit from the LORD go when he went from me to speak to you?" (1 Kings 22:24). It is not clear, then, that this spirit was really an evil spirit. It was at least a spirit sent by God to carry out the divine will by inspiring Micaiah with the truth, just as it had filled the false prophets with lies.

Then, in 1 Chronicles 21:1, a "satan" incited David to take up a census of Israel, although in 2 Samuel 24:1 the same incident is ascribed to God, who was angry at Israel and incited David to take up the census. (The passage in 1 Chronicles was written before the one in 2 Samuel and perhaps reflects an unwillingness to ascribe evil to God.)

We can see then, that there is little in the Old Testament to give us a comprehensive understanding of the demonic realm. Certainly there is not much that resembles a deliverance ministry.

Jewish Literature Just Before the Birth of Jesus

Just before Jesus arrived upon the scene we have the so-called intertestamental literature. The book of Daniel from this period was accepted into the Bible by the early Christians, but the majority of books were not, the most important examples being the Book of Jubilees and 1 Enoch.

These apocryphal books contain many stories about the genealogy of bad angels and how these angels corrupt human beings. 1 Enoch 6 takes the Genesis account[6] about "the sons of God" taking as their wives "the daughters of men" and elaborates it into a story about angels lusting after women. It describes how from these unions a race of giants emerged.

The fascination with the origin of angels was condemned by Paul as a distraction: "Do not let anyone who delights in false humility and the worship of angels disqualify you for the prize. Such a person goes into great detail about what he has seen, and his unspiritual mind puffs him up with idle notions" (Colossians 2:18).

Much of our popular understanding about how angels and evil spirits originated and how they engage in combat (such as in Milton's *Paradise Lost*) comes from these apocryphal books. Many popular books about angels today contain some of these fanciful stories, and it is important to separate what may be simply human imagination from the little that is contained in Scripture.

The New Testament

When we come to the New Testament we see an enormous change—numerous references to evil spirits. Here their existence is assumed, and we read many accounts about how they harm and dominate people. Especially we see the example of Jesus and His disciples who spent much of their time freeing God's people from their baneful influence.

The Gospels offer both *general* and *specific* descriptions of Jesus' freeing demonized people. Among the general descriptions, here is a typical example: "When evening came, many who were demon-possessed were brought to him, and he drove out the spirits with a word and healed all the sick" (Matthew 8:16).[7]

6. See Genesis 6:1–4.
7. Similar general passages are found in Matthew 4:24; Mark 1:32, 34, 39; 3:11; 6:13; Luke 4:41; 6:18; 7:21. Translations stating that the people were "demon-possessed" illustrate what I say elsewhere in this book—that translators tend to talk about "possession" when the Greek says merely that they "had a demon"—a larger frame of reference that includes people who were not totally possessed.

This kind of passage summarizing Jesus' threefold ministry of preaching, healing and deliverance is often used by the Gospel writers as a transition from one major section of the Gospel to another. Matthew uses a general section about Jesus' exorcising many people, for example (4:23–25), as a transition between Jesus' preparation for ministry (ending with His temptation in the desert) and the Sermon on the Mount (5–7). These repeated summary passages make it harder to ignore the central message of the Gospels: Jesus came to teach, to heal and to free us from the influence of evil spirits.

In addition to these generalized summaries, the Gospels contain seven specific accounts of Jesus casting evil spirits out of individuals:

1. The man in the synagogue tormented by an unclean spirit (Mark 1:21–28; Luke 4:31–37)
2. The blind and mute demoniac (Matthew 12:22–29; Mark 3:22–27; Luke 11:14–22)
3. The Gerasene demoniac (Matthew 8:28–34; Mark 5:1–20; Luke 8:26–39)
4. The Syrophoenician woman's daughter (Matthew 15:21–28; Mark 7:24–30)
5. The epileptic boy (Matthew 17:14–21; Mark 9:14–29; Luke 9:37–43)
6. The woman with a spirit of infirmity (Luke 13:10–17)
7. The mute demoniac (Matthew 9:32–34)

Three of these incidents appear in all three synoptic Gospels, which indicates their importance. The sheer volume of material in the Gospels that describes these exorcisms indicates the importance the evangelists ascribed to Jesus' ministry of deliverance.

In Mark, the shortest Gospel, we find no fewer than thirteen references to a personified Satan or to casting out demons. These include four exorcisms worked by Jesus as well as four references to His disciples' ability to perform them. In fact, Jesus was angry when the disciples were unable to free the epileptic demoniac and rebuked them for their failure: "O unbelieving generation, how long shall I stay with you? How long shall I put up with you?" (Mark 9:19). His disciples were so embarrassed that they waited to get Jesus in private to ask why they had failed. He told them that this kind of spirit (apparently stronger than most) could be driven out only by prayer and fasting (Mark 9:29).[8]

As Dennis Hamm writes:

> To remove the thread of the exorcism ministries of Jesus and the disciples would be to destroy the fabric of Mark's account. Moreover, it would not be . . . honest to take literally language of the New Testament about a Holy Spirit (*pneuma hagion*) and to psychologize the language referring to an unclean spirit (*pneuma akatharta*).[9]

We see the same emphasis in Matthew and Luke on Jesus' ministry of casting out demons. They present it in the graphic terms of eyewitness accounts, describing people falling to the ground, rolling in convulsions, shrieking, with spirits speaking through their mouths—the same extravagant phenomena we see today when we pray for the oppressed.

Charles H. Talbert, one of the foremost commentators on Luke among biblical scholars, states that Luke set forth the program for Jesus' total mission for His life during His inaugural sermon in the synagogue in Nazareth (Luke 4:16–27). It was a state-of-the-union address in which Jesus declared His threefold mission: preaching, healing and exorcism.[10]

When Jesus quoted the section of Isaiah 61 that describes a mission of "[proclaiming] freedom for the captives and release for the prisoners," Talbert says He was identifying Himself as an exorcist. Luke, writes Talbert, "depicts Jesus as an exorcist and healer and then in 4:43 seems to identify this activity with his preaching the good news of the kingdom."[11] Furthermore, the purpose of Luke in writing Acts was to show that the early Church continued Jesus' mission of preaching, healing and casting out evil spirits.

---

8. Some of the earliest manuscripts contain only the words *by prayer* without adding *and fasting.*

9. Hamm, p. 62.

10. Charles H. Talbert, *Reading Luke: A Literary and Theological Commentary on the Third Gospel* (New York: Crossroad, 1992), p. 56.

11. Ibid., p. 55.

John the Evangelist does not describe any particular deliverance, but instead presents Jesus' ministry globally as a direct confrontation with and victory over Satan and his work: "The reason the Son of God appeared was to destroy the devil's work" (1 John 3:8).

Embarrassment About the Supernatural

Nevertheless, despite the clarity of all these passages, many theologians and preachers profess a profound skepticism as to whether we should take accounts of people being tormented by Satan and other evil spirits in a literal way. They explain their position by saying that people in Jesus' day believed in evil spirits, as do many primitive people today. Jesus, born into that culture, accepted their superstitious beliefs, as did Matthew, Mark, Luke and John.

In those days, for instance, people thought epilepsy was caused by demons. So the Gospel writers describe the epileptic boy Jesus prayed for as being tormented by evil spirits. Similarly, primitive people believe that an insane person is possessed by evil spirits, so naturally the Gospel writers describe the Gerasene man, running wild among the tombs, as "possessed." Many Gospel commentators in our day prefer a natural psychological explanation and believe that we understand these behaviors better than the people of Jesus' day. The Gerasene "demoniac" was actually a psychotic suffering from severe paranoia. And so on.

It is true that, with the advance of medical science, we know a lot more today about the natural causes of illness. We are embarrassed, on the other hand, to talk about any possible supernatural causes of illness. In our day the diagnosis of disease is made on the natural level, while the supernatural and preternatural causes are left out.

You can find a good example of this in one of our more popular Bible commentators, William Barclay, who goes back a generation and is relatively conservative. I appreciate Barclay's writing personally and use his books for my own spiritual reading. Yet I find, in terms of my own experience, that he understands neither healing nor deliverance. It is as if Barclay is embarrassed by the healing and deliverance stories in the Gospels, so he talks about all kinds of side issues to avoid the main point of these passages.

About Jesus being accused of casting out spirits by the power of Beelzebub, for instance (Matthew 12:22–29), Barclay states:

> One of the most interesting things in the whole passage is Jesus' saying, "If it is by the Spirit of God that I cast out demons, then the kingdom of God has come upon you" (v. 28). It is significant to note that the sign of the coming of the Kingdom was not full churches and great revival meetings, but the defeat of pain.[12]

Barclay cannot bring himself to say that the sign that the Kingdom of God has arrived is that the kingdom of Satan is being destroyed. Instead he has to change the defeat of Satan to the defeat of pain.

Barclay's own attitude, moreover, comes out clearly in passages like this:

> When people believe in demon-possession, it is easy [for them] to convince themselves that they are so possessed; when they come under that delusion, the symptoms of demon-possession immediately arise. . . . When a person under such a delusion was confronted with an exorcist in whom he had confidence, often the delusion was dispelled and a cure resulted. In such cases if a man was convinced he was cured, he was cured.[13]

Barclay never carries his reasoning to its logical outcome by stating openly that Jesus was Himself subject to delusion and superstition, but he states flatly that demon possession *is* a delusion and that people are cured simply through the power of suggestion. In relation to Jesus' own understanding of the exorcism, we are left to draw our own conclusions:

> It may seem fantastic to us; but the ancient peoples believed explicitly in demons. . . . To this day anyone can think himself into having a pain or into the idea that he is ill; that could happen even more easily in days when there was much of what we would call superstition, and when men's knowledge was more primitive

12. William H. Barclay, *The Gospel of Matthew*, Vol. 2, Revised Edition (Philadelphia: Westminster Press, 1975), p. 39. (First published in 1957.)

13. Ibid., p. 35.

than it is now. Even if there are no such things as demons, a man could be cured only by the assumption that for him at least the demons were the realest of things.[14]

I quote Barclay precisely because he is middle-of-the-road and represents the common view of many educated Christian scholars. The established wisdom of mainline theologians and Scripture commentators is that demon possession and exorcism come out of a primitive, superstitious worldview that we have fortunately escaped, but which Jesus, a man of His day, accepted. In this, either He did not realize that evil spirits were a superstitious fiction of the naïve people of His day, or He simply went along with these fictions. Seldom is any writer so bold as to say directly that Jesus was deluded; they limit themselves to intimating that we ourselves are deluded if we believe that the demonic world is real and, in particular, if we pray to free people from demons. So they deride demon-chasing and "seeing a devil in every bush."

Rediscovering the Power of the Supernatural

Indeed, the skeptics are right: There *is* a real danger of seeing a devil in every bush. But have these critics ever found a devil in *any* bush? Have they ever had to cast out a demon, or are they using exaggerated language because they think any belief in the demonic realm is (as Barclay wrote) "fantastic to us"?

A basic principle of Scripture interpretation is that we should accept what the writer says in its literal sense unless there is strong evidence that we should understand the passage in a symbolic or metaphorical way. A symbolic understanding of Jesus' driving out demons argues that these exorcisms are metaphors for His victory over evil, pictured in a way that would appeal to a Christian of the first century. But where is the evidence to convince us that there are no demons? On what basis should we interpret Jesus' exorcism ministry in a symbolic or poetic way?

The reason is the acceptance by the Western world, beginning with the eighteenth-century Enlightenment, of a rationalistic, scientific worldview that assumed there is no reality beyond the natural, material universe. If something cannot be

14. Ibid., Vol. 1, p. 321.

measured and observed in a laboratory, it does not exist. This materialistic worldview has so affected Western Christianity that we automatically regard the work of the supernatural with skepticism and rule out the world of angels and demons with no further need for discussion.

Writes Charles Kraft, professor of anthropology and intercultural communication at Fuller Theological Seminary:

> It is interesting (and discouraging) to note that even though we are Christians, our basic assumptions are usually more like those of the non-Christian Westerners around us than we would like to admit. . . . Even though there is a wide discrepancy between the teaching of Scripture and the common Western assumptions, we often find ourselves more Western than scriptural.[15]

> Western societies passed through the Renaissance, the Reformation, the Enlightenment, and a wide variety of ripples and spin-offs from these movements. . . . The result: God and the Church were dethroned, and the human mind came to be seen as Savior. It is ignorance, not Satan, we are to fight.[16]

Chuck Kraft writes as an evangelical who went through a drastic change in his own worldview caused by his experiences on foreign mission fields, and through attending John Wimber's classes at Fuller Seminary. In African missions he discovered a worldview much like that of the New Testament, in which people experienced the reality of evil spirits and demanded that missionaries perform exorcisms and divine healing. If the missionaries did not respond, they returned to their witch doctors. Kraft and many other evangelical Christians are returning to a lively belief in the supernatural and are attempting to restore this belief, as well as belief in prayer for healing and deliverance, to the Christian academic world and the life of the seminaries. (As yet they are still the minority.)

That Christians should rediscover the power of the supernatural is not surprising. What surprises me is that the medical

15. Charles H. Kraft, *Christianity with Power* (Ann Arbor, Mich.: Vine Books, 1989), p. 26. Dr. Kraft's book is a fascinating description of his own change from a typical evangelical theologian who did not believe in healing or deliverance to a professor who now not only teaches about a confrontation with the demonic world but prays actively with his students.

16. Ibid., p. 31.

world seems to be even more open than Christian academia to this vision. We find Scott Peck, a psychiatrist, writing openly about his newfound belief in the world of evil spirits and the need for exorcism,[17] and many doctors are similarly rediscovering prayer for healing. Some of these studies about "alternative" medicines venture into areas that are problematic for Christians, but their research is opening up the medical-psychological model of disease to the possibilities of divine healing and deliverance.

A new worldview is opening up, too. Take, for example, Dr. Larry Dossey's book *Healing Words* in which he, too, describes the fact that our

> Western materialistic beliefs exclude the possibility of prayer-based healing. Because our modern scientific paradigm, or world view, has no place for healing at a distance, it can be more convenient to ignore the evidence for spiritual healing—the "if-it-can't-occur-it-doesn't-occur" approach. . . . The possibility that non-material forms of healing might exist is virtually unthinkable.[18]

Dr. Dossey is a medical doctor whose book summarizes the nearly three hundred studies that have been done to show the effectiveness of prayer. Dossey's book (among many others) describes a remarkable convergence of forces indicating that the worldview we find in the Gospels is more "scientific" than the worldview of Newtonian scientists and of nineteenth-century theologians, who taught that rational people could no longer believe in supernatural healing or the existence of evil spirits.

Jesus' mission of healing and deliverance is as timely today as it has ever been and calls us to take another look at His ministry in a more direct and literal way.

I just read a thoughtful article by a Roman Catholic priest, John Markey, O.P., who reflects on his experiences as a student and teacher. He remarks that

> Having both taken and taught religion classes for the last 25 years, I can attest that the most perplexing problem for post-Vat-

17. M. Scott Peck, *People of the Lie: The Hope for Healing Human Evil* (New York: Simon & Schuster, 1983).

18. Larry Dossey, *Healing Words* (San Francisco: HarperCollins, 1993), p. 201.

ican II Catholic students is the existence of evil. For my generation it is a genuine source of disbelief and agnosticism. . . . This is not a new question—indeed, it is as old as the Bible itself. But in our time a new answer has emerged. It is not that God is not all-loving and all-knowing, but that in some way or another, God is not all-powerful. God is compassionate and caring but is simply unable to effect change in the situation. . . .

But while few people will actually voice it, there is something wholly inadequate with this view of God. For one thing it does not seem to be the God of Scripture; for another, it turns God into a visitor to the sick—nice to have around, but what you really want is a cure, not just sympathy and good intentions. In its own way, this response to the problem of evil has contributed to the sense of nihilism that in fact pervades much of the culture in which I was raised. There is a general sense, I believe, that the world is out of control and no one is in charge or capable of taking charge. . . . The individual either gives up hope of any great change or transformation (because not even God can do that) and concentrates instead on personal transformation; or one so resents God's weakness and inaction that God is simply ignored and discounted. . . .

The "problem of evil," therefore, presents a conundrum for my contemporaries. The task of theologians, teachers and preachers of our time will be to confront this issue in all its complexity and develop a new articulation of the providence of God that can move people beyond the piety of denial, the paralysis of agnosticism and the politics of victimization and blame.[19]

But suppose the answer is already there? As Markey says, the scriptural view is that God does have the power to conquer evil.

A Biblical Worldview of Evil

The scriptural worldview is that there has been a Fall and that the human race is broken and wounded. Furthermore, evil in the world is bigger than we are; it is basically supernatural and Satan is behind it. Our enemy is stronger than we are. Our struggle is not just against the human forces of evil, but against principalities and powers.

19. John Markey, "The Making of a Post-Vatican II Theologian: Reflections on 25 Years of Catholic Education," *America* magazine, Vol. 171, No. 2 (July 16, 1994), pp. 19–20.

Precisely because of the enormity of this vast evil, we need a Savior to rescue us. In the fullness of time God so loved the world that He sent His only Son, Jesus Christ, the One who was anointed with the Holy Spirit and God's power, to free us from the dominion of the devil (Acts 10:38). Freeing us in this way required God's power, which Jesus shared with His disciples (Matthew 10:1; Luke 9:1; 10:1, 9). Later the entire community of believers was filled with this power at Pentecost (Luke 24:49; Acts 2:1–4). The early Church, filled with power by the Holy Spirit, proceeded to preach the Good News, demonstrating it by healing the sick and casting out evil spirits.

All this is the traditional teaching of Christianity. But we cannot really understand it unless we come to grips with certain realities:

1. Evil is something we cannot overcome by simple human good will and teaching. Evil is, at its root, demonic and too great for us to overcome.
2. It is for this purpose that Jesus came: to overcome evil.
3. Evil cannot be overcome just through teaching ethical values, but by the power of God, which is given to us by the Holy Spirit.
4. Through prayer—prayer for healing and prayer for deliverance—we become channels for Jesus to heal and to free people (as well as institutions and societies) from the evil that weighs them down.

When we rediscover the active power of the Holy Spirit in our lives, we see that God is not powerless, but simply waiting for us to receive what is already there. He will not (ordinarily) act without our cooperation.

But when we come to believe in Jesus' saving power to overcome evil, then our good intentions and good advice are transformed into the Good News that Jesus came to announce:

"He has sent me to proclaim freedom for the prisoners and recovery of sight for the blind, to release the oppressed, to proclaim the year of the Lord's favor."

Luke 4:18–19

That, in Jesus' own view, is why He came to live among us—a view that is summarized and demonstrated repeatedly throughout the New Testament.

Do we find this view of the demonic realm reinforced by our human experience?

3

What Is the Evidence
of Human Experience?

First we must admit that the demonic world cannot be seen, measured or placed under a microscope. We are dealing with an unseen, mysterious world of fallen spirits. A spirit, by definition, is a "non-material" being. This has always been recognized by people of all cultures. So how do we find scientific proof that demons exist?

We do not, nor do we expect to. Every evidence we have indicating the presence of a demon is bound to be ambiguous since we do not see the evil spirit itself, but only what it causes people to do. These effects of its presence, moreover, can be explained in some other way.

Once, for instance, I was casting out some spirits in a dramatic deliverance. The spirits were speaking back to me in a husky voice through a lovely, witchlike lady dressed in black. I asked a friend of mine, a thoughtful theologian, to come in and watch this dramatic proceeding, in hopes he would be convinced of the reality of demons. Afterward he commented, "How can you be sure she isn't just a psychotic exhibiting multiple personalities?"

The honest answer is that on the human level—the level of reason and science—you cannot be sure. The voices might be a sign of Multiple Personality Disorder. MPD, in turn, can be caused by either demons ("If you believe in them," Barclay might say) or by underlying psychological problems or by both.

How in the world can you tell the difference, since by definition the demonic realm is unseen, and since all you can see is some external activity that can be explained by a natural cause?

So, from a rational point of view, I could not prove to my friend that spirits were speaking through the woman dressed in black. But why do so many people today rule out the influence of the demonic world as a possible explanation for strange behavior and speech? The main reason for our skepticism is that scientific rationalism, the predominant worldview since the so-called Enlightenment of two hundred years ago, has now become the dominant worldview of Western Christians. If something cannot be seen, measured or proven through reason, it simply does not exist—or at the very least should be doubted.

Consequently, Westerners find it hard to believe in angels or in Satan. As Dr. Charles Kraft states:

> Though many Westerners retain a vague belief in God, most deny that other supernatural beings even exist.... Indeed, unlike most of the peoples of the world, we divide the world into what we call "natural" and what we call "supernatural." And then we largely disregard the supernatural.[1]

The difficulty, clearly, is how we can show that the spiritual realm of angels and demons really exists when we can neither see them nor prove them by reason. Yet Jesus *assumed* the existence of a spirit world—so much so that a major theme of His preaching highlighted the clash between two kingdoms: the Kingdom of God and the kingdom of Satan.

The question is which worldview is the true one—the worldview of Jesus or our own contemporary worldview? By what right do we ignore or reject the New Testament passages that describe how Jesus cast out evil spirits in favor of a more culturally acceptable view of reality that denies the existence of a personal demonic realm? Kraft points out that the more "respectable" denominations (such as the Presbyterians, United Methodists and Episcopalians) by and large preach a belief system that is like that of our secular society.[2] While preachers do not usually at-

1. Charles H. Kraft, *Christianity with Power* (Ann Arbor, Mich.: Vine Books, 1989), pp. 26–27.
2. Ibid., p. 59.

tack the traditional Christian belief in Satan, they let the subject die through benign neglect, or else talk about exorcism as a red herring that diverts attention from the real problems of evil in our society, such as war and poverty.

Admittedly, war and poverty are greater concerns than the possibility of one person being demonized. But it is not an either-or issue; it is a both-and. If demons do exist and do harm people, then we need to deal with the victims' suffering, too. To throw out the deliverance ministry because the greater issues of evil are war and poverty is as ridiculous as demanding that we get rid of physicians and dentists because they deal only with an individual's cancer or one pitiful rotting tooth rather than the specter of nuclear holocaust! If more people, moreover, especially political leaders, could be freed from demonic influence—leaders like Adolf Hitler—our world would be vastly improved in the larger areas of war and poverty.

I think the skeptics' real problem with deliverance is simply that they believe exorcism is unreal, a vestige of ancient superstition, and the sooner we get rid of it, the sooner we can concentrate on the real issues of evil. So our question is basically one of truth: Are evil spirits real?

In Western Culture

My own experience backs up the scriptural worldview as true, for although we cannot see the spiritual world with our physical eyes, other evidence makes it easy to accept Jesus' work of casting out evil spirits as a literal, rather than poetic, description of reality.

I have been amazed at the positive response whenever I ask Christian groups whether they have had experiences with angels. The first time my eyes were opened to this was fifteen years ago as I was directing a question-and-answer session during a conference of about three hundred people. A man stood up and said hesitantly that he thought he had seen an angel recently and wondered if that was possible or if he was deluded. I asked if anyone else had encountered an angel, guessing that maybe two or three people would raise their hands. To my great surprise, two-thirds of the group lifted their hands.

My wife, Judith, who is planning to write a book on angels, has had a similar response. She is frequently asked by churches to give talks about angels (she also sees them from time to time); and when she asks whether any of the listeners has had an experience with one, she, too, is astonished at how many claim to have had such an encounter—usually the majority, even of teenagers.

Clearly this kind of "seeing" is not a physical seeing, something that could be measured or captured on film. It is a spiritual vision. As in the case of the celebrated near-death experiences, people are hesitant to share these angelic visitations, fearing that their friends—ministers, even—will think they are suffering from hallucinations. And yet when I have visited non-European cultures, the people are open to sharing their dreams and visions and consider this normal. "Your young men will see visions, your old men will dream dreams" (Acts 2:17).

Beyond that, many ordinary people have told me they have, at some time, encountered a demonic personality, not just the evil we all encounter every day but a personified evil. At a recent conference on the subject of deliverance, for example, about two-thirds of a group of 250 people believed they had actually met up with demonic spirits. Admittedly, this conference was selective since it was attended by people interested in the demonic, but in other conferences I have found that usually at least half the group testify they have actually encountered evil spirits.

Throughout the earlier centuries of Christianity these spiritual experiences were common. Only in the past few centuries, under the influence of the Enlightenment, have Christians come to question the reality of such experiences. Yet demonic encounters remain frequent; it is just that people are ashamed to own up to them.

The ironic thing is that while the predominant Christian fashion is to profess skepticism, the secular world is fascinated with spiritualism, the occult and even Satanism. In most bookstores I visit, the occult section is twice the size of the religion section. Fueled by a desire for supernatural experience, moreover, many people in this counter-Christian movement routinely experience the reality of the spirit world. From Dr. Kraft:

A friend of mine was chatting one day with a woman who had recently been converted to Christianity out of the occult. While in bondage to Satan, she had the gift of being able to "see" the amount of spiritual power different people carry with them. She told my friend that she had been able during that time to spot Christians "a mile off" because of the amount of power they carried! . . .

A similar story comes from the experience of a fourteen-year-old girl I'll call Lisa. While in rebellion against her parents and her Christian upbringing, Lisa became involved with a popular rock group. Reportedly, she was invited by one of the stars of the group to join them after the concert for partying, drugs and sex. As Lisa attempted to go backstage, however, she was stopped by a woman who forbade her to pass. The woman identified herself as a witch and told Lisa that no Christians were allowed in the gathering. When Lisa asked the witch how she knew she was a Christian, she was told, "I saw it on you."[3]

While I myself have never "seen" an angel or a demon (they, too, are angels), I know and trust many friends who claim to have had such visions, and find their statements credible. Similarly, some of my colleagues who help me minister tell me they see demons when we are praying for people, and can often identify the evil spirits' names and nature.

Later, when we come to talk about the gift of discerning spirits, we will discuss this in greater depth. Suffice it to say here that I personally know and trust a few friends who tell me privately they can sense the presence of evil spirits, and I have learned to trust the accuracy of their perceptions.

In Non-Western Cultures

It is not just individuals who claim to experience the world of spirits; it is entire cultures. The majority of the people of the world, in fact, not only believe in the supernatural but experience it. It is hard for Europeans and North Americans, living in a culture in which most educated people find it difficult to believe in angels and demons, to realize there is another point of view and that most of the world finds it hard to fathom why we are so ignorant about the spirit world.

3. Ibid., p. 125.

In every culture except the European (and those influenced by the European, such as our own), I have found that ordinary people have a lively appreciation of spiritual bondage and the reality of demonic forces. They are waiting to hear the good news that they can be freed by the power of God; and when they hear that someone is casting out evil spirits, they come in droves. I met one priest in India who had a unique pastoral problem: So many people came to him for deliverance—five hundred in two years—that it created havoc with his schedule of teaching in the seminary.

In our contemporary understanding of Christianity, we impose a heavy cultural overlay of rationalism: While we think we are bringing these other "less enlightened" cultures into Christian truth, what we are really doing is converting them to a Western (that is, Western-since-Descartes) view of humanity and the world, which is prejudiced against a number of spiritual practices we label as superstitious. One of the "superstitions" our missionaries want to eradicate is the belief of these people in the presence and activity of evil spirits.

Preliterate Cultures

The people of every culture I have visited, except the European, are eager to share their experiences of a spiritual world that oppresses them. Nor do they understand why many missionaries seem to have less belief in these demonic forces than they do. The missionaries, meanwhile, are trying to educate the people not to fear this dark world of "spirits." If only they will accept our more advanced, scientific worldview (so we think), they will become like us and no longer be tormented by an irrational fear of demons.

One of the reasons why we have not succeeded in bringing the Gospel to many cultures is simply that we do not fully understand what Jesus Christ came to bring. We have turned the Good News into Good Advice.

To give a few examples:

In 1974 I received an invitation from a group of Catholic missionaries to come to Nigeria. These dedicated missionaries had decided that the native seminarians were superstitious and needed to be enlightened. Because the seminarians were afraid of witch doctors putting curses on them, the authorities brought in a psychologist from the local university to explain to the students that they should not worry, that there were psychological explanations for what was going on.

The Nigerian seminarians told the psychologist he had been working with white people too long. All they knew was that if somebody back in their village got angry and put a curse on them, they would wake up sick the next morning. This sickness could not have been caused by the power of suggestion, the Nigerians told the psychologist, because no one had forewarned them about being cursed. They had found out about the curse only *after* they came down sick. So the psychologist left, having failed to convince the young African seminarians.

That, in fact, was one of the reasons our team was invited to visit Nigeria for six weeks—to see if the seminarians might be right.

There was another thing we found in Nigeria. We would be praying with a group when suddenly a man would fall down in the aisle and start displaying the signs that often indicate the presence of a demon. The Nigerians understood immediately what was going on. If the man began convulsing and shouting in a strange language, the Nigerians would stand and applaud until the deliverance was over. Some of the European missionaries, meanwhile, were heading toward the door, shaking their heads at what they saw as a throwback to the primitive religion from which they were trying to rescue the people.

Many of these Nigerian Catholics also attended *Aladura* (Pentecostal) churches to get free of the demonic influences they experienced in their lives. The missionaries themselves told us that these *Aladura* churches were growing at an explosive rate.[4] Within two miles of the seminary in Ibadan where our team gave a conference, they had discovered some 72 *Aladura* churches!

Although the missionaries looked on the Nigerians as prone to superstition (and there did seem to be many elements of superstition in their culture), the Africans understood the biblical worldview far better than we did, and seemed more in touch with some basic spiritual realities. Western churches have come

---

4. Much the same thing is going on today in Latin America, especially in Argentina, Chile, Brazil and Guatemala, where traditional Catholics are flocking to Pentecostal churches.

to recognize their pride in imposing European church architecture on African peoples and have mostly repented of it. But in a far more important realm, they are still imposing their Western spiritual bias. These Africans know by experience the reality of an evil power that destroys, and of witch doctors with the power to heal. Unless Catholic and mainline Protestant missionaries exhibit a greater power, the Nigerians will flock to the *Aladura* churches or will continue to revert to their native witch doctors in time of need.

Sophisticated Cultures

Not only do preliterate cultures fear the activity of demons, I found, but advanced, sophisticated cultures as well. Around the world, in fact, there seems to be a common, natural religion based on experiencing the activity of evil spirits, which manifest themselves everywhere in much the same way.

In Japan, for instance, where Shinto and Buddhist beliefs today remain as part of the Oriental cultural tradition, people still hold a lively belief in the need for exorcism. I read an account while visiting in Japan of how Shinto priests were called on to drive evil spirits out of a vast public housing complex in Tokyo, where 32 persons had committed suicide in a six-year period by jumping from the tops of the apartment buildings.[5] The American reporter who wrote this up suggested that psychologists should perhaps be called in, or that the apartments should be made more hospitable. But the sophisticated Japanese believed that evil spirits were causing the suicides, and responded by calling in their Shinto priests to cast them out.

Another unusual aspect of Japanese life, not publicized in the United States, is the extraordinary growth of the so-called "New Religions." Although fewer than one percent of the Japanese are Christians, some fifteen percent now belong to these New Religions, the fastest-growing religious interest in Japan. Most have sprung up since World War II, and although they are centered on God, most of them are not Christian. They focus on healing and deliverance, indicating that the people themselves feel a great need for healing and deliverance, and that perhaps the basic preevangelism of Christianity (as it was in Jesus' own ministry) should be healing and deliverance. In default of our belief in

5. *Japan Times,* July 30, 1978.

healing and deliverance, the field has been left open to anyone (like proponents of the New Religions) who offers to fill this basic need.

To investigate this I went to a center of one of the healing religions known as *Mahikari No Waza* (the "Art of Spiritual Purification") and observed a large room where various members of their group were praying one on one for people who needed healing or deliverance. The literature they gave me opens with this statement: "What do you think if you are told that your life is partly controlled by some invisible force?"

In thirty years' time several hundred thousand Japanese have converted to this group founded by Kotama Okada, whose initial conception of his mission is quaintly described as follows (misspellings included):

> At five o'clock in the morning, February 27, 1959, Great Saint Kotama Okada, a Japanese, was revealed by God, the Creator: "Rise up, name yourself Kotama (literally, Jem of Light). Hold your hand up and purify the world. The world will become more and more bitter and severe for the human beings." Great Saint Kotama Okada started holding his hand over people soon after the revelation, and he found a dying man come to life again, the paralyzed started to walk, and the blind began to see, just like Sakyamuni or Jesus Christ performed miracles, God ordered the Saint, "Go and save the human beings, distributing the Light of God, and give the power of Mahikari No Waza to everybody who wishes to obtain it."

In the pamphlet from which this excerpt is taken are several descriptions of how adherents of the sect were freed from the spirits of the dead, together with a picture of a young woman minister praying for a possessed man whose body is jumping off the ground with a "movement which is impossible to make normally."

During that same visit to Japan I had the opportunity to visit the Roman Catholic archbishop of Tokyo, who admitted that the Catholic plan of evangelization might have been faulty in that it was aimed at winning over the intellectuals and ruling class, who were expected in turn to change the rest of the nation. Yet in more than a hundred years few had been converted, and those few were not particularly zealous to share the Gospel.

This stands in marked contrast to the rapid spread of the three hundred New Religions. Their members are enthusiastic promoters of their expanding programs, while the successes of Christians are relatively meager. (Some members of the Emperor's family, for example, are educated in Catholic schools.)

Relinquishing the Field to Witch Doctors

Because our rationalistic worldview does not allow for a practical approach to freeing people from demonic influence, most Christians in the developing world (as I said in the last section) will go to an independent Pentecostal church in time of need. If they do not know any Pentecostals, they often return to the world of witch doctors to receive exorcism.

When I was in Venezuela, the missionaries there estimated that eighty percent of Venezuelans go to a witch doctor or *curandero* when they feel oppressed. The same holds true in New York, Miami, New Orleans and other U.S. cities with large Hispanic or Haitian populations. Many Caribbean Catholics in Brooklyn are as much at home in voodoo services as they are at Sunday Mass. The main purpose of voodoo services is to hex enemies and heal relatives and friends.

> When Haitians become sick, they believe that their priests can invoke spirits to cure diseases caused by magic. When they are hospitalized in Brooklyn's Kings County Hospital and are not getting well, they are often advised by fellow Haitians, including medical doctors, "Go back to your country. See a special houngan or mambo [witch doctor], as only they can cure you of your illness."[6]

The author suggests that voodoo is no more of a problem than leprechauns are for the Irish. The attitude that sees voodoo as a harmless superstition reflects the cultural bias of many educated Christians. Priests and ministers may discourage their people from attending voodoo services or going to a *curandero* or spiritualist, but if they do not regard these visits as dangerous, the people will continue going there for healing and deliv-

6. Hugh Cassidy, "Saturday Night Voodoo; Sunday Morning Mass," *U.S. Catholic,* July 1978, p. 36.

erance. Regrettably, many of the clergy not only do not exercise the deliverance ministry to which they have been called, but do not even believe in it. In Africa I found that when someone was sick in a Christian hospital, the family was often allowed to call in a witch doctor to perform incantations over the patient.

A fascinating research article, "'El Duende' and Other Incubi,"[7] describes the disbelief of priests and bishops that causes the "possessed" to seek help from non-Christian sources. El Duende is a particular familiar spirit believed in some Latin American countries to haunt young girls and their families. The author, a physician, Carlos A. Leon, interviewed twelve families that reported cases of demonization to the hospital where he worked in Colombia. What concerned Dr. Leon was that psychiatry did not seem to help these patients, nor did ordinary religious practices like receiving a priest's blessing. The only real help these girls were offered came from occult healers.

The case histories concerning the efforts of the priests and church people to heal indicate real unbelief on their part. They, like the sons of Sceva in Acts 19:14–16, did not know how to handle the puzzling behavior. Dr. Leon remarks,

> Requests for exorcism were formulated in several instances, but never granted; the present position of the local clergy concerning these cases seems to be one of extreme caution if not outright skepticism. When priests came to help, they only offered some blessings and prayers. On the other hand, spiritualists were anything but reluctant or hesitant.[8]

One of the cases was that of Ursulina. Her family believed that El Duende wanted to take possession of Ursulina and carry her off to his realm, so they sought help to protect her from this fate.

> The family first approached the parish priest right after Ursulina had been troubled by the Duende at Mass. He advised them to go to the bishop and ask him to appoint an exorcist for the case. The bishop reacted by sending two nuns to investigate the case and make a report. During their visit the Duende displayed frantic activity: whistling, scratching, and hitting Ursulina; singing ob-

    7. Carlos A. Leon, M.D., "'El Duende' and Other Incubi," *Archives of General Psychiatry,* Vol. 32, February 1975, pp. 155–162.
    8. Ibid., p. 158.

scene songs; passing flatus; and making profane remarks about the visitors who, in spite of not seeing or hearing him, were terrified by all the gesticulations and wild activity exhibited by the girl. . . . Her family decided that Ursulina had to go to confession and communion. Then, all hell broke loose: the Duende dragged Ursulina by the hair through the house. . . . The girl was in such a state the following morning that the priest refused to confess her and ordered her relatives to take her to the psychiatric hospital.[9]

In short, Ursulina got the runaround: Priest went to bishop; bishop went to nuns; nuns dropped out; family went back to priest; priest sent family to psychiatrist.

After she was discharged uncured by the hospital, Ursulina was taken to a group of spiritualists who taught her to communicate with spirits. She later became a gifted medium and the center of a cult.

This is a good example of a general problem. Just as I tried to pass off Roberta to someone else, Ursulina's pastor referred her to the psychiatrists. When they were not able to help sufficiently, her family thought they had only one recourse: to go the occult route.

In an amazingly similar case, a woman came to Barbara Shlemon Ryan, who has long been active in the healing ministry. Although Barbara had never heard of the El Duende tradition, the woman described being oppressed by an unusual-looking apparition that corresponded exactly to the description of El Duende: a little pot-bellied figure with dark complexion and large white teeth, dressed in red and black, wearing a large, tall hat and pointed boots.

Psychiatry Discovers Satan

The article about El Duende hints at a significant recent development: More and more psychiatrists and psychotherapists are coming to discover the existence of Satan.

Dr. Morton Kelsey has written a fine history of the practice of healing in the Church and gives the reasons for its near demise, in spite of all the scriptural injunctions to heal the sick. He be-

9. Ibid., p. 160.

60

lieves that medical doctors are more open to healing prayer than the clergy.

> ...A similar meeting was called by a large Western hospital which has a department of religion and health. A selected group of clergy and medical men were invited to meet together and discuss the topic. All but one of the physicians responded, and 80 percent of them came, while barely 50 percent of the clergy even answered the letter, and less than 30 percent of them attended the meeting.
>
> My wife, Barbara, and I have been in many different church groups over the last twenty years. Except for Pentecostal seminaries, we have found that, of the hundreds of Christian seminaries, less than half a dozen offer any courses in the religious dimensions of healing. In most seminaries the subject is dismissed with scorn.
>
> ...The "orthodox" Christian, whether liberal or conservative, has ... little or no interest in physical or mental healing through orthodox means.[10]

My own experience in speaking to clergy about Christian healing has been different from Dr. Kelsey's, in that I have spoken to thousands of priests and ministers about healing and have found them generally to be open and receptive. (Deliverance and exorcism are another matter.) But, like Dr. Kelsey, I have found a growing degree of receptivity among psychiatrists and psychotherapists brought about through their own experiences. For this coming year, for example, I have accepted invitations to speak to the staffs of medical institutions in Georgia, Ohio and Quebec.

The best-known example of this increasing openness is the celebrated author and psychiatrist, M. Scott Peck. In *People of the Lie* Peck states flatly that he has come to see that some people are truly evil.[11]

In the beginning Dr. Peck did not believe in the devil or in exorcism,[12] but now he believes in Satan because of his own experience: He has seen the face of evil.[13] Dr. Peck agrees that you

10. Morton Kelsey, *Psychology, Medicine and Christian Healing* (San Francisco: HarperCollins, 1988), p. 3.
11. M. Scott Peck, *People of the Lie* (New York: Simon & Schuster, 1983), p. 10.
12. Ibid., p. 178.
13. Ibid., pp. 182–183.

cannot *prove* the existence of Satan; like conversion to God, it requires personal experience.[14] For him that experience came by participating in two exorcisms:

> As a hard headed scientist—which I assume myself to be—I can explain 95 percent of what went on in these two cases by traditional psychiatric dynamics. . . . But I am left with a critical 5 percent I cannot explain in such ways. I am left with the supernatural—or better yet, subnatural. . . .
>
> When the demonic finally spoke clearly in one case, an expression appeared on the patient's face that could be described only as Satanic. It was an incredibly contemptuous grin of utter hostile malevolence. I have spent many hours before a mirror trying to imitate it without the slightest success. I have seen that expression only one other time in my life—for a few fleeting seconds on the face of the other patient.
>
> . . . The patient suddenly resembled a writhing snake of great strength, viciously attempting to bite the team members. More frightening than the writhing body, however, was the face. The eyes were hooded with lazy reptilian torpor—except when the reptile darted out in attack, at which moment the eyes would open wide with blazing hatred. Despite these frequent darting moments, what upset me the most was the extraordinary sense of a fifty-million-year-old heaviness I received from this serpentine being. It caused me to despair of the success of the exorcism. Almost all the team members at both exorcisms were convinced they were in the presence of something absolutely alien and inhuman. The end of each exorcism proper was signaled by the departure of this Presence from the patient and the room.[15]

Like Dr. Kelsey, Dr. Peck found a marked resistance in getting help from church authorities. Because the team could not find a monastery or convent willing to serve as a site for the exorcism, they eventually had to end up in a private home.

> It would have been much easier for all concerned if the institutional Church had been more open to offering its sponsorship, blessing and service. While there was cooperation from some Church authorities in both cases, the more general response of the Church was to try to avoid any involvement. The Church's

14. Ibid., p. 184.
15. Ibid., p. 195–196.

fear of repercussions in such cases is both natural and realistic but not necessarily humane.[16]

The recent rise in the number of cases of Satanic Ritual Abuse (SRA) has also caused many psychotherapists to take a second look at whether there really is a demonic world. As a result, psychiatrists, counselors and people experienced in deliverance are openly discussing Satanism and learning from one another. No longer is it true to think that all of what we used to call possession is simply mental illness, and that the psychiatrist is the only professional competent to help a psychotic. A priest or minister may be needed. (More on SRA in chapter 17.)

Also—a wonderful development!—there are now a number of counselors and a few psychiatrists who pray with their patients for inner healing and, on occasion, deliverance. One was my friend the late Dr. Conrad Baars, a Christian psychiatrist, who described the deliverance of one of his patients:

> Some years ago I became the "victim" of such a spirit in one of my patients, a woman religious with severe obsessive-compulsive neurosis and deprivation neurosis. In our therapy sessions this woman developed an uncanny ability to arouse my anger. This, of course, is not too uncommon, but what concerned me was my inability to control it. This had never happened before, or since, but in this case session after session ended with a loud exchange of angry remarks and the patient storming out of the room in tears.
>
> Finally, after weeks of my wondering what was happening, and why I could not handle my anger in a calm, professional manner, the sister expressed her own concern with this development in what was once a consistently pleasant, friendly physician-patient relationship. She told me she liked and respected me greatly and had no reason to be angry with me, but she knew exactly what to do or say that would make me lose my temper. It seemed, she added, that there was something in her that made her do or say these things.
>
> With her permission, I consulted Fr. Francis MacNutt, O.P., who happened to visit me around this time. On his recommendation we prayed over my patient for deliverance. She was indeed delivered of several spirits that left her quietly and without much objection. None of them identified themselves, nor were

16. Ibid., p. 202.

they instructed to do so, but if one of them had, I am certain it would have used the word "anger." There was a dramatic change in the patient's behavior and appearance from then on. Never again did her words or facial expression reveal any feeling of anger or hate toward me.[17]

Another remarkable case of deliverance was written up in the *Archives of Sexual Behavior* and entitled "Gender Identity Change in a Transsexual."[18] These authors describe the change of a transsexual (whom they call John) through exorcism. The remarkable part of this case was that John suffered from a psychological disorder that normally resists all treatment. They had tested John thoroughly and decided that the best thing was to encourage him in his determination to have a sex-change operation. In preparation for surgery John changed his name to Judy, had his facial hair removed through electrolysis and his breasts enlarged through estrogen. The date of the operation was set.

But on the insistence of a Christian friend of his, John visited another doctor, who told him his real problem was "possession by evil spirits." John consented to a three-hour exorcism session during which 22 evil spirits purportedly left him. After this session John felt affirmed in his masculine identity and discarded his female clothing. At a subsequent prayer session the enlargement in John's breasts subsided almost immediately.

The doctors tested John for the next two and a half years and were amazed that he showed a clear reversal of gender identity—something they had never seen in their own practice or heard about in psychological literature. They concluded their report by stating:

> What cannot be denied, however, is that a patient who was very clearly a transsexual by the most conservative criteria assumed a long-lasting masculine gender identity in a remarkably short period of time following an apparent exorcism.[19]

17. Conrad Baars, M.D., *Feeling and Healing Your Emotions* (Plainfield, N.J.: Logos International, 1979), pp. 204–205.

18. Gene Abel, M.D., David Barlow, Ph.D., and Edward Blanchard, "Gender Identity Change in a Transsexual," *Archives of Sexual Behavior,* Vol. 6, No. 5, 1977, as quoted in Baars, pp. 205–206.

19. Ibid., p. 206.

In all this excitement revolving around the topic of exorcism, we see the happy prospect of the religious community encouraged by the psychological community to rediscover part of its Christian heritage. Until that happens a host of suffering people will not receive the help they need from the Church to break free of the chains that bind them. They may then become bitter and angry or fall into despair.

This is especially true of those who have entered satanic groups and want to break out. They are often terrified to ask for help because of their fear of retaliation from Satan (or the coven) if they try to cut free. They are also afraid they may meet a priest or minister who does not believe them or does not know how to set them free.

One disturbing private interview was shared with me by Dr. Timothy O'Higgins, who was instrumental in helping a witch of the third degree break loose from her bondage in a coven that had been desecrating churches and offering blood sacrifices in its rites. She approached several priests for help who were not sure whether to believe her. Her reaction was to retaliate against them in various ways. Part of the interview went as follows:

Q: You told me earlier that one of the reasons why you were engaged in that incident was because you were angry with the Church?

A: Any church.

Q: Where did this anger originate?

A: From their not believing it was real.

Q: And your anger was first directed against St. _____'s parish?

A: Yes.

Q: And the prayer group there?

A: I wanted to split them up and cause division.

Q: That was three years ago?

A: Yes; and I did.

Q: How did you cause division?

A: Put thoughts in people's minds . . . like, "This stuff isn't for real. What's in it for me?" Gossip about each other—not being secretive about each other when they should have been. . . . I directed my anger at priests.

Q: What priests?

A: There were two of them, actually; one was in the city of
_____. Now he's gone. . . .

Q: How did you manifest your anger against him?

A: I got at his weakness, which was sex.

Q: How did you do that?

A: He was showing me an apartment which he was going to
help me try and rent. . . . I was mad; I wanted to get him frustrated. Finally, when I saw he could not contain himself any
longer, I broke away. Then he had a problem to deal with. . . . I
didn't care how he was to deal with it, and I was satisfied.

Q: Why were you angry with him?

A: Because he wouldn't believe me.

Q: And who was the other priest that you were angry with in a
special way? How did you show your anger against him?

A: I just started putting crazy ideas into his head, about men
and relationships with men, wondering if he was cut out to be a
priest. I was trying to disillusion him, and I wanted him to leave
here very badly . . . and he did.

Q: What would you say if someone said that you were crazy?

A: I would say, Maybe so, but I know what I'm talking about. If
they say I'm crazy, they had better back off, because they are in
the line of fire. I know what is real and what isn't. I know what
I've been into, and they don't know what they are talking about.
If they had seen and felt the power that I have, they wouldn't be
saying that.

Q: What power do you have?

A: I'd rather not have it.

Q: What power is it?

A: The power of destruction and the power to help.

Q: The power to help?

A: The power to help is white magic; the power to destroy is
black magic.

Q: Some people say that magic is only superstition.

A: Then they don't know what they're talking about; they are
going by what someone else has said. I know for one that it is not
superstition, that it is real. I have seen what it can do. It can hurt
real bad sometimes. [Here she describes an instance of human
sacrifice.] That was before they believed me, but now that they
believe me I have hope.

Q: So now you want the Church to get involved?

A: I don't care how they work it out. I want help. I can't do it by myself. If there were not people helping me the past couple of weeks, I would not be here talking. I would already be dead.

So, just as Roberta was saying to me, "Don't you believe in who you are?" this former witch (and countless other people) are asking the churches, "Why can't you help us? Don't you believe in what God has called you to do?"

The Power of Evangelization

This brings us to a major point: *The Gospel is not meant merely to teach doctrine, but necessarily includes the power to free, to save and to heal.* After preaching in thirty countries, I believe that peoples of every culture are waiting to hear the message of Christ's salvation. Whenever we preach that God, in love, sent His Son, Jesus Christ, to free the human race from sin and evil, people respond eagerly.

In the days when I taught homiletics in seminary, I thought the preacher's problem was to figure out how to make the Gospel relevant to the needs of contemporary people. Now I realize the Gospel is in itself relevant, that it *does* appeal. But I was not preaching the Gospel fully because I did not fully understand the need for the power to heal and free people from evil spirits. Basically I saw myself as a teacher and did not experience the Spirit's power that Jesus always gave His disciples when He sent them out to preach:

> When Jesus had called the Twelve together, he gave them power and authority to drive out all demons and to cure diseases, and he sent them out to preach the kingdom of God and to heal the sick.
>
> Luke 9:1–2

Only when we are able to free the oppressed and heal those suffering from the curse of sickness can we really preach Christ's basic message: The Kingdom of God is at hand and the kingdom of Satan is being destroyed.

4

Should We Call It *Possession*?

Whenever we talk about praying to liberate the oppressed from evil spirits, most people think immediately that we are talking about *possession*. And if they happen to believe in the reality of it all, they think of the proper antidote for possession: exorcism.

I would like to state flatly that this way of thinking blocks rather than helps our understanding. Here is why.

In the first place, possession, when it truly exists, is rare. Everyone agrees about this. So if possession is all we need to worry about, most of us can avoid getting involved and refer the occasional case of possession to higher church authorities. Something as severe and dangerous as exorcism requires not us but experts.

The problem is, while the need for exorcism is rare, the need for deliverance is common. Ask people experienced in the deliverance ministry (who seem fairly well-balanced) how many in the general population need deliverance, and they will tell you they believe that many of the people you pass on the street need some kind of deliverance. My wife, Judith, estimates that in the days when she was counseling clients as a psychotherapist, she ended up praying with about a third of them to be freed from the influence of evil spirits.

I personally have never met anyone who seemed to be totally possessed. Scott Peck comes to the same conclusion:

It is because there is a struggle going on between an intact human soul and the infesting demonic energy that Martin correctly states[1] that all cases of what we call possession ought more properly to be referred to as "partial possession" or "imperfect possession."[2]

But even if it should prove that some people are totally possessed, we still have a major pastoral problem if only one person in a million is possessed, while three hundred thousand in a million need deliverance. It is as if doctors decided to treat only patients with terminal cancer and refused to deal with all other sickness. If you refer someone complaining about a demonic presence to Roman Catholic authorities, for example, they will test for possession by asking about such rare and extraordinary symptoms as the patient being lifted off the ground (levitation) or speaking a foreign language that he or she has no natural way of knowing (the demonic counterfeit of the gift of tongues). If you cannot prove that the person is possessed, as evidenced by the kind of weird phenomena we saw in the movie *The Exorcist*, the Church will not call on an exorcist or perform an exorcism. When these criteria are used, thousands of people are denied the help they desperately need.[3]

Clearly the word *possession* implies that Satan has taken over and possesses the very core of a human personality. But this is not ordinarily what we find. We find more often that one area of the victim's life is invaded. Derek Prince has compared demonization to criminal influence in a city: While the center of the city, including city hall, may be free and under governmental control, a few back alleys and side streets are controlled by criminals. Most people we meet who need deliverance seem to be good people, not evil people. Most of them are Christians and go to church on Sunday, but in some part of their lives they

1. Malachi Martin, *Hostage to the Devil* (New York: Readers Digest Press, 1976), p. 442.

2. M. Scott Peck, *People of the Lie* (New York: Simon & Schuster, 1983), p. 191.

3. Recently in some dioceses, priests who are trusted by their bishops have been appointed as exorcists to perform the kind of deliverance I describe in this book. Roman Catholic thought on deliverance tends to concentrate on exorcisim and permission to perform it, granted by a bishop to a priest. Two fine books from a Catholic perspective are *Deliverance from Evil Spirits* by the Rev. Michael Scanlan, T.O.R., and Randall Cirner (Ann Arbor, Mich.: Servant Publications, 1980) and *Spiritual Warfare for Catholics* by the Rev. Jeffrey Steffon (Ann Arbor, Mich.: Servant Publications, 1994).

are not free. They will tell you that they seem compelled to act in ways contrary to their inmost desires.

A better word for what people commonly experience is *demonization*. Another good word is *infestation*. In fact, the Greek word used in the New Testament can best be translated as "to have a demon" or "to be demonized" rather than "to be possessed." This correct translation makes all the difference because it is quite possible to have a demon yet not be possessed.

Unfortunately, we have no good word in common English usage to describe this ordinary phenomenon. Some writers aware of the problem use the word *oppression* for what we are talking about, but *oppression* derives from the Latin verb meaning "to press down upon." Demons do oppress people, but "pressing down upon" comes from outside, not from inside. Here we are talking about demons somehow getting inside people and affecting their attitudes or actions, yet not possessing them.

City hall is not infested by criminals, but some side streets are.

Different Levels of Oppression and Infestation

We find different levels of demonic activity in our lives.

Demonic Activity Outside of Us

The first level, which we all experience, comes from demonic activity on the outside of us.

Temptation

Temptation is common to us all. We certainly do not need demons to tempt us, since the world, the flesh and the pride of life cause us enough problems. But just as Jesus was confronted by Satan in the desert, so evil spirits can work on and aggravate our existing weaknesses. Being spirits, they can touch on our imaginations and make our ordinary human temptations worse.

Physical Attacks or Obstructions

Occasionally some people experience actual physical attacks or obstructions coming from outside. We often read that holy people (like the famous curate of Ars, St. John Mary Vianney, who lived in France 150 years ago) were harassed by apparitions in the middle of the night or even thrown around the room and bruised by Satan. It is commonplace in the lore of exorcism that cars break down for no apparent reason while the exorcist is driving to the place chosen for the exorcism.

Emotional Oppression

Third, there is what we might call emotional oppression, which comes when our spirit and emotions are weighed down by heaviness or depression. Many human psychological factors produce depression, but sometimes we find a demonic force bearing down on us to slow us up or prevent us from acting— something like a 280-pound football player sitting on us to keep us from getting up. The effect—heaviness or depression—is the same, but the cause is what we have to question: Was it some really bad news, or something we ate, or do we have to contend with an evil spirit oppressing us?

Dr. Scott Peck wrote a perfect description (in a passage we quoted in the last chapter) of what oppression feels like: "What upset me the most was the extraordinary sense of a fifty-million-year-old heaviness I received from this serpentine being. It caused me to despair of the success of the exorcism."[4]

Demonic Activity from Within Us

All the above come primarily from outside. But spirits often attack people from inside. Being demonized in this way has many levels, starting with a light form of infestation—in which the spirits can easily be run off when the person goes to a place where there is a strong presence of the Holy Spirit, and especially where people are praising God—all the way up the scale to possession. Even then the very center of the personality may still be free.

Demonization

It sounds strange to say that demons, which are spirits, can be *in* people, but that seems to be the case. How it happens is a mystery, but a truly demonized person experiences the evil presence within. Then, during prayer for deliverance, the demon seems to touch the person from inside—causing pain or contortions, for example, in some area of the person's body. If

4. Peck, p. 191.

the infestation is severe, the voice may become so constricted that the person cannot say the name of Jesus Christ. In the most severe infestations, the spirits actually take control and speak or act through the person's voice or body.

The afflicted person almost always feels it when the evil spirit leaves (this is true more than ninety percent of the time) and can tell you, if there is more than one spirit, when *all* of them have left. This is an extraordinary phenomenon that we find in all parts of the world. It is all the more impressive when we consider that most of these people, even if they have read some books on deliverance, have never learned that people *can* experience when the spirits leave and when they have all left! Typical is a letter I received recently:

> When you prayed for the spirits of Grief and Rejection to leave in the name of Jesus, I felt something move through my body each time and out both arms, which were raised in prayer. It was awesome. At the same time I became aware of great peace all through my body.

Whether spirits are in or out (or both) is another of those areas we cannot *prove*. It is a question of our human experience. But the idea of demonic activity from within corresponds to the way Jesus and His disciples talked about it.

When Ananias and Sapphira held back part of the selling price of their property from the early Christian community, for example, Peter said, "'Ananias, how is it that Satan has so filled your heart that you have lied to the Holy Spirit and have kept for yourself some of the money you received for the land?'" (Acts 5:3). Peter could have been speaking metaphorically, of course. But when John, referring to the Last Supper, wrote, "As soon as Judas took the bread, Satan entered into him" (John 13:27), it sounds like a description of something that really happened.

Possession

The different levels of possible demonic activity in our lives culminate in the worst-case scenario of possession.

Here I need to add that it often happens, when we pray for someone demonized but not possessed, that the spirits seem to take over in a last-ditch effort to avoid eviction and temporarily possess the person. Up to the point of praying for deliverance, we are clearly talking to the person. But during the prayer, the person's face changes and contorts, the voice shifts and starts to spit out threats in the plural *we* ("We will kill you"). Often this is the first time in the person's life that this has ever happened, or the first time she has become aware of how severe the infestation really is. Usually she cannot remember afterward what she did or said during the period the evil spirits took over. It is like a blackout—a "lost weekend" experience, a brief episode, a mini-possession.

Permanent, total possession is rare, but this kind of brief, transitory possession is, in my prayer experience, fairly common.

Which brings up a familiar question.

Can a Christian Have a Demon?[5]

The argument goes that if a Christian is filled by the Holy Spirit, there is no room for an evil spirit; that would be a contradiction in terms. The celebrated David DuPlessis, "Mr. Pentecost," held this view, and in the 1970s refused to minister on the same platform with several well-known preachers who performed group exorcisms in Christian gatherings.

Clearly you cannot be filled with the Holy Spirit and at the same time be fully possessed. But can Christians be demonized—have some part of their being infested with evil spirits?

It is difficult to answer this question scripturally because there were no Christians until after the death of Jesus, or perhaps until Pentecost. So the only books of the Bible that might deal with Christians being demonized are Acts and the epistles, which do not deal much with deliverance. Yet we have the example of Judas, who was one of Jesus' closest followers: "As soon as Judas took the bread, Satan entered into him" (John 13:27). Furthermore, Ananias and Sapphira were part of the early Christian community.

But even if Scripture does not lead to an inevitable conclusion that Christians can be demonized, experience leads me to believe that many people who have trusted Christ as their Sav-

5. Don Basham wrote a book by this title (Monroeville, Pa.: Whitaker Books, 1971). In it he gave good arguments why he believed (and saw in his own experience) that a Christian *can* have a demon.

ior do suffer from an inner demonic presence while they are try-ing hard to live a Christian life. It is no more inconceivable that they may harbor a demonic presence than that they are filled with the Holy Spirit and still commit serious sin. In recent years we have seen dramatic evidence that Christian leaders and preachers have been capable of not just minor lapses but major sins. As the apostle John wrote, "If we claim to be without sin, we deceive ourselves and the truth is not in us" (1 John 1:8).

The answer, regarding both our sinning and our harboring evil spirits, is that the center of our spirit may be indwelt by God's Holy Spirit, while outlying areas—"the cravings of sinful man, the lust of his eyes and the boasting of what he has and does" (1 John 2:16)—are still not fully conquered by the power of the Holy Spirit. To some extent most of us have not fully sur-rendered our lives to the Lordship of Jesus. Paul described our painful situation:

> What I do is not the good I want to do; no, the evil I do not want to do—this I keep on doing. Now if I do what I do not want to do, it is no longer I who do it, but it is sin living in me that does it.
> Romans 7:19–20

And if sin lives within me and robs me of my freedom of ac-tion, is it inconceivable that an evil spirit might not also be in-festing that corner of my being? The city hall of my village may be clean and uncorrupted, but how about the streets with the bars, brothels and pawnshops?

To summarize: We should use the word *possession* only when it really fits—for the rare Charles Mansons of this world. The best nouns to use are *demonization* or *infestation*. The best verbs to use are *to be demonized* (the scriptural term) or *to be infested*. There are various levels of demonic activity, rang-ing all the way from temptation and other outside attacks; to demonization, in which we are influenced from the inside; on up to possession, in which we are under compulsion to per-form evil.[6]

---

6. Danny Rolling, a serial murderer notorious in our area during the time this book is being written, has ascribed the driving force for the sadistic murders of college stu-dents to two personal demons whom he knows by name.

But how can we tell if we are just being hit by human problems (some of them pretty fierce) or if we are really being influenced by demons? Am I like the medical student who has just read through *Gray's Anatomy* and suddenly worries about suffering every disease in the book? How can I tell if demons really are present?

5

How Do We Know
If an Evil Spirit
Is Really Present?

J ust as diagnosis (discovering the nature of the patient's sickness) is the beginning of all medical treatment, so discernment (the ability to diagnose spiritual sickness) is the starting point for all healing prayer.

Since evil spirits cannot be seen but only experienced as they affect us, their presence is bound to be problematic and ambiguous. We cannot see them with our physical eyes, nor can we prove their presence (as we saw in the last chapter). This leaves us with a problem: How do you tell if the person asking for help is really troubled by an evil spirit or (since the symptoms of demonic infestation are often the same as the symptoms of psychological sickness) suffering from a psychological problem?

You may find both, of course. The person may be suffering from a psychological problem as well as demonic interference. Usually, in fact, you will find it a both-and rather than an either-or situation.[1]

1. This makes the procedure followed by church authorities of sending possible possession cases to the psychiatrist for evaluation a questionable one. The person should undoubtedly see a psychiatrist or counselor, but if he does need that kind of treatment, it in no way means that he does not also need deliverance. It is like sending all cancer patients to a psychiatrist for evaluation. They may need help with their fears, but that will not treat the cancer itself.

How to Tell When a Person Needs Deliverance

How can you tell when deliverance is needed? There are several ways.

When the Tormented Person Is Aware of the Spirits

The first and most common way we find out that a person needs deliverance is that he tells us. Affected people usually know not only that something is wrong, but that their problem might be caused by evil spirits.

We do not necessarily believe what people tell us, of course. I remember a high school student brought to me by a group of priests who said he exhibited all the signs of demonic infestation when they prayed for him. Fortunately Dr. Conrad Baars, the Christian psychiatrist, was visiting me at the time and sat in on the interview. In a skilled way Dr. Baars asked the boy a number of questions. Finally, after an hour, the boy admitted he had faked all this behavior because he was lonely and wanted to attract attention.

People genuinely afflicted by evil spirits are usually loath to talk about their problem and are often afraid even to tell their friends or counselor, much less their minister or priest, because they fear they will be written off as unbalanced or, worse yet, psychotic.

I have found, though, that many people really seem to experience evil, either from within themselves (demonization) or from without (oppression), and they do need help in being freed.

They experience evil in all sorts of ways. Some hear voices, which typically impel them toward suicide or hate (especially hatred of themselves): "Drive your car off the road into that tree! Now!" "You're no damn good. You are condemned to hell forever." "You belong to me and you will never escape." These are common messages I hear from the afflicted again and again.

Others see visions or have nightmares that seem more real and convey more terror than ordinary nightmares. Still others feel impelled to do things they would never ordinarily think of doing.

No matter how this demonic control manifests itself, a significant number of people will tell you—if they feel you will listen and can help—that something is radically wrong and that they believe evil spirits are involved.

We realize, of course, that they may be wrong; they may simply be deluded or they may be hallucinating and suffering psychotic episodes. They may be more in need of a psychiatrist or counselor than of someone who can pray for their deliverance.[2] It goes without saying that we need to understand this and not take everything people say at face value. But we need to be open to the person who asks for help, believing he is under demonic attack.

It usually takes courage for people to tell us they think they may be under demonic influence. Do not subject them, first of all, to skepticism or, worse yet, scoffing. You will need to sort out whether their conviction is true. But take it seriously. If you begin by reacting skeptically, they will probably clam up.

Many of the deliverances we perform start out with a conversation in which the victimized person gives us the right discernment about where the problem lies.

When You Observe Symptoms of Demonization

For me this has been the most common way I have discovered the need to pray for deliverance: The person I am praying with starts to act in a strange way that indicates an evil spirit is present. I have already described some extreme examples, such as when the person reaches for your throat to strangle you. But there are many other signs that you may be confronted by a demonic presence.

The strongest signs are bodily contortions, changes in the voice and changes in facial expression.

Bodily Contortions

We read in the New Testament about such phenomena: "The evil spirit shook the man violently" (Mark 1:26) and "He would cry out and cut himself with stones" (Mark 5:5).

At times—for instance, when the spirit of death is present—the person grows rigid, especially around the fingers. Other

2. The psychiatrists and counselors I work with also believe in prayer for inner healing and deliverance and include prayer as part of their practice.

people may arch their spines backward, while still others roll on the ground. One man started leaping around like a tiger and jumped up on the back of the couch as if to pounce on me. (I commanded him in the name of Jesus not to jump and he was immobilized.) Another man got down on all fours and started roaring like a lion, while at the same meeting a woman dropped off her chair and started slithering on the floor like a snake.

These examples may sound bizarre to someone who has never seen someone being freed from the effects of witchcraft, but they happen frequently in our ministry. Fortunately, most of the bodily contortions we see are not so violent.

The Voice

Sometimes the *tone* of the person's voice changes. A woman may start speaking in a husky voice like a man, or a mild-mannered person may begin speaking in a snide, insulting tone of voice.

Sometimes the *content* of what the person says changes and indicates the influence of a spirit. I have already mentioned that the person may start speaking in the plural *we* instead of *I*: "We are not going to leave."

When the voice changes, the content usually changes, too. In Japan a woman who did not speak English said, in English, to a priest on our team who was praying with her, "I'd like to sleep with you."

The Face

Perhaps the most common external indication of demonization comes when the person's facial expression changes. It is as if you are no longer looking at the same person you started talking to. The old saying "The eyes are the windows of the soul" becomes especially meaningful. It is as if the evil spirit is peering out at you. The eyes become filled with hate, mockery, pride or whatever the nature of that particular spirit is. Now that the evil spirit has surfaced, you are no longer directly in touch with the person you have been praying for.

Sometimes the eyes roll upwards, so that all you can see are the whites of the eyes—a weird effect. (This seems to be the spirit's way of avoiding looking at you, in an effort to keep the victim from making contact with you and getting help.)

Other Clues

Some of these dramatic examples are evident only in a person who suffers from severe demonization. Again, notice that all these signs are ambiguous; psychological problems can account for many similar extraordinary gestures. Yet when you see these signs, be aware that you may be watching the effects of demonic activity and may need eventually to pray for the person's liberation, or refer the person to someone with more experience.

A significant aspect of these strange activities is that they occur consistently. Facial expressions, bodily contortions and vocal statements caused by evil spirits are remarkably similar, even though most of the people we work with have never read in detail about such activity or seen it in anyone else. (In the United States we see the same symptoms as in Africa or Japan.) It is one more indication that we are truly dealing with demonic forces.

When Judith worked in Jerusalem she became convinced of the reality of the demonic world when she saw contortions, together with vocal and facial changes, in many of the people she prayed with, regardless of whether they came from Christian, Jewish or Muslim backgrounds. (Later, in fact, a spirit speaking through a woman we were praying for in Florida said to Judith, "I met you before in Jerusalem!")

Some other signs of demonic presence include unpleasant smells and, above all, cold. When the Holy Spirit is present we often experience heat. (I usually need to take off my sweater when we pray.) But when an evil spirit is present the room grows cold.

After you have had a certain amount of experience in the deliverance ministry, you will learn to recognize many of these familiar signs of demonic presence. They enable you to say to yourself, *I think we're faced with an evil spirit here.*

A Special Caution

A special area of concern is Multiple Personality Disorder (MPD, also known as DID, Dissociative Identity Disorder), which subject I touch on more in chapter 17. Since the external symptoms of the need for deliverance are ambiguous, we must ask what is causing the symptoms, a psychiatric disorder or a demon. If we are not sure, we need to proceed gently and with caution.

> Rolling eyes, voice changes, twitches, or marked shifts in facial
> expression could indicate either. . . . Exorcists likely have not
> known enough about MPD to tell the difference. . . .Christians
> who have had years of experience in deliverance work say they
> knew all along that certain entities seemed like demons initially
> but didn't respond to exorcism like demons do.[3]

The worst thing you can do, if the person does have various personalities (needed in order to survive), is try to cast them out. Just this week an MPD client visited here devastated and confused because a female minister had sat on her physically and tried to perform an exorcism. This kind of well-meaning but ignorant ministry further fragments the person and gives exorcism a bad name in the psychiatric and counseling professions.

If anger emerges unexpectedly and the person you are working with suddenly acts like an entirely different personality, how can you be sure what you are working with?

The most accurate way of diagnosing the presence of an evil spirit is through the gift of discerning spirits (which we will discuss next). Apart from that, I encourage you to read a reputable book about MPD that takes into account the reality of the need for deliverance. One such book is *Uncovering the Mystery of MPD*, in which Dr. James Friesen writes:

> It can be easy to misdiagnose dissociations. When a different al-
> ter takes executive control of the body, the process is often ac-
> companied by a change in posture—a twitch, a blink, or a black-
> out, for example. It is understandable that some people could
> misinterpret the postural change as an evil spirit taking control.
> Whenever such a dissociation is treated as possession, I would
> call that religious abuse. . . . Alters cannot be erased, and they
> cannot be cast out. Life takes a plunge if that is attempted. Reli-
> gious abuse can cause even more hurt than therapeutic abuse.[4]

3. James Friesen, Ph.D., *Uncovering the Mystery of MPD* (San Bernardino: Here's Life Publishers, 1991), p. 246.
4. Ibid., p.107.

Clearly, whenever possible you should get to know the person you are going to pray with and really listen to what he says. Do not force him to interpret his experience according to your understanding. MPD clients have been victims of severe trauma (usually in childhood) and can be set free from demons of trauma if you pray for Jesus to heal them of these traumas. This gentle approach, if you are not sure what you are dealing with, bypasses the problem of getting involved too quickly in a direct confrontation.

The Gift of Discerning Spirits

One of the gifts the Holy Spirit gives us to build up the Christian community is the ability to discern spirits. This gift of recognizing spirits is the seventh of the nine spiritual manifestations listed by Paul in 1 Corinthians 12:8–10. Discernment is the God-given ability to know, on occasion, whether an evil spirit is present. This gift enables us to distinguish whether a person (or his actions) is influenced primarily by

1. the *Holy* Spirit;
2. *natural*, human, psychological or created causes;
3. an *evil* spirit.

Without discernment, when we are faced with the signs we have been talking about (signs like changes in the voice), we must try to deduce the presence of a spirit from what people say or how they act. We are merely using our minds to argue from an effect (for example, a man convulsing on the ground) to the possible cause. We can make a good guess about the diagnosis, but unless God helps us in some way, we can never be certain what we are dealing with.

When a person has the gift of discernment, on the other hand, he is able to come closer to certainty. The only difficulty is that this wonderful gift of discernment does not seem to be fully developed in many people.

In general, we need not accept the discernment of a person unless we know him well—one of the reasons we need an established Christian community and colleagues we know and trust.

In talking to friends whom I believe have this ability to discern spirits, I find that discernment operates on two levels:

1. the ability to recognize the *presence* of an evil spirit;
2. the additional ability (at a higher level) to know the *identity* or name of the evil spirit.

Recognizing the Presence of a Spirit

Simply being able to recognize that a spirit is present is a considerable spiritual gifting. This ability comes to people in all sorts of ways. Just as a fairly large number of people "see" angels, a number can also see evil spirits (fallen angels). Some of my friends see the spirits with a kind of spiritual vision in ministry situations when they start praying for guidance or healing.

Different people sense the presence of evil spirits in different ways. One evangelist has learned that when he feels the hair on the back of his neck stand up, a demon is present. Another friend, Dr. Robert Lindsey, long-time pastor of the Narkiss Street Baptist Church in Jerusalem, has come to recognize that when his right earlobe tingles in a certain way, an evil spirit is present. Still another friend smells an unusual, unpleasant odor when evil spirits are around. When St. Catherine of Siena visited the papal court in Avignon, France, she was overwhelmed by the stench she found there, and attributed the odor to sin and demons rather than to natural causes. Other people simply sense in some inexplicable way that an evil spirit is near.

Some of these ways of discerning, as you can see, are highly singular and require some experience to interpret rightly. But those who detect evil (like a smoke detector warning us of fire) say there is something unusual in the way they sense evil that alerts them to the fact that it is not a purely natural phenomenon. If you *smell* the presence of evil, for example, it is like nothing you have ever smelled before; it is as distinctive as the smell of Limburger cheese.

Regardless of the form that discernment takes, it certainly helps to be able to walk into a situation (sometimes one that appears innocent) and know immediately that something evil lies beneath the surface. At the very least, you are being warned to watch out, to be wary about what this person says or does. At most, God may be calling you to pray for a deliverance that will free the sufferer.

Discerning the Identity of the Spirit

If it is a great help to know when an evil spirit is present, it is even more useful to know the spirit's nature and identity. The clearest discernment seems to come, again, through spiritual sight, "seeing" what the spirit looks like, combined with a direct spiritual insight into its name or nature. Knowing the spirit's name (for example, the spirit of lust) seems to give us a power over the spirit that helps us cast it out.

When I am praying for a person for healing, it helps to have someone by my side who has the ability to discern spirits. If the person I am praying for starts to exhibit behavior indicating that a spirit is present, I will ask my colleague to tell me what we are dealing with.

Like all gifts of the Spirit, this one needs to be tested. I do not have to believe every person who tells me he discerns that a particular evil spirit is present. Again, this is one of the reasons we need a community in which we have time to recognize and test the gifts that the Holy Spirit gives to different people to benefit the Church.

Some may have a strong gift of prophecy, healing or discerning of spirits but contaminate it, if they are immature in its use, with elements of their own prejudice, self-interest or religious background. A prophetic message may, at least in part, be from God but mixed with personal opinion, because the person has listened to his own heart and desires and has mistaken that for the Lord.

Thus, unless we ourselves have the gift of discernment, it is important to know the people we work with. I know several people whom I trust because of our past common experience; they always seem to be right on.

The people I know who not only recognize when an evil spirit is present, but can identify the spirit's identity or nature (e.g., "A spirit of death is in this room"), receive this information in a variety of ways. Some "see" the spirits and recognize them from having seen and identified them on previous occasions. Others pick up a kind of spiritual or mental apprehension of the spirit's identity, perhaps through a thought or word that comes to them, like *hatred*.[5]

Learning the identity of the spirit we are facing is helpful because it gives us a clue as to how the spirit entered the afflicted person. This avenue needs to be closed through either repentance or inner healing. If you find you are dealing with lust, for example, the person probably needs to repent of past behavior. If you discover that rejection or grief is the spirit coming to the fore, it is likely that inner healing is needed to heal the traumas of rejection and grief that have left a spiritual wound. A tormenting spirit has moved into that wound and continues to inflame it.

An authentic ability to discern spirits given by the Holy Spirit is the quickest, most accurate way of getting the diagnosis we need to decide how best to proceed. The key word here is *authentic* because, at least according to my experience, a finely tuned, mature gift of discernment is relatively rare. The reason for this, I believe, is that churches have neglected the deliverance ministry, and those people God might have called into a deliverance ministry have not had a chance to exercise or grow into their spiritual gifts.

Zealous Christians who *have* gotten into deliverance, on the other hand, have usually received insufficient instruction or oversight to direct a balanced ministry. The most common problem we find is that some ministers of deliverance know little about psychology and are unable to tell whether a person needs inner healing or deliverance or both. Right now, for example, a psychiatrist friend is treating a client who went to a ministry that tried to cast demons out of her. When she got no better, they thrust her further into the pit of self-hatred by blaming her for not getting well. Such unbalanced ministry has given exorcism a bad name in the medical and counseling professions, as well as in the mainline churches.

But the answer to abuse is not to shut down the deliverance ministry. The answer is not *no* use but *right* use.

5. I have sometimes wondered if the way we pick up on this spiritual information is connected in any way with the psychological makeup God has given us. In the Myers-Briggs system, for example, a sensate person might "see" a spirit, while an intuitive person might simply receive an impression or idea, without any picture.

The problems that turn up (and everyone has heard about them) simply serve as an excuse for denial by many Christian ministers unwilling to recognize a more important problem: that many people suffer from demonic infestation and that there is an enormous vacuum in pastoral practice because most churches are not dealing with demonic infestation.

Yet even without a clear gift of discernment, the ordinary signs indicating that an evil spirit is present are often sufficient to allow us to minister with practical certitude.

Here I should mention that it was only after I was baptized in the Holy Spirit in 1967 that I began to see demonic manifestations in the people I was praying for. It was certainly not that I was any holier; it was as if the level of my ministry was turned up a notch. The power of the Holy Spirit started expelling the evil spirits that, up to then, had not really been threatened.

The steps I encourage you to take, then, are these:

First, if you have not received the baptism of the Spirit, study about it, then pray to receive it.[6] The empowering of the Holy Spirit enables us to minister deliverance more effectively. In addition, it brings with it those charismatic gifts essential for a fully rounded deliverance ministry—gifts like healing and the discerning of spirits.[7]

Second, I encourage you to look carefully, when you pray with people, for signs of demonic activity, without jumping to conclusions. Also, listen carefully to what people tell you. They are usually fearful about sharing any demonic visitations they have experienced (as I have said); but if they find you are open to hearing about them, you may be the first person they have ever dared to share with. Since they are usually ashamed to talk about their unsettling experiences, believing that a person influenced by evil spirits must be an evil person, it is important for you to know—and let the victim know—that most sufferers from demonic infestation are *good* people who have aligned

---

6. The last chapter in this book deals with receiving the baptism of the Holy Spirit.

7. In Malachi Martin's *Hostage to the Devil*, he recounts the history of five actual exorcisms. One of his points is that the priests who performed the exorcisms were pretty well chewed up in the process. I personally believe the reason they suffered as much as they did was that they had not received the baptism of the Spirit and relied too much on the written text of the exorcism, rather than expanding it through the use of the charismatic gifts.

themselves with Jesus Christ and are thus particular targets for the enemy.

Third, if you find that a person does seem to have a demon or be oppressed, you need to decide whether you should pray with him or suggest that he go to someone else with more experience. Even if we have experience, some situations are far more difficult than others (e.g., victims of Satanic Ritual Abuse who exhibit multiple personalities), and we should not hesitate to refer them to someone more gifted or experienced than ourselves in the deliverance ministry.

In the next chapter we will deal with the broad categories of evil spirits you may encounter and their basic ranking in the hierarchy of spirits.

6

The Different Kinds of Evil Spirits

Now that we have discussed different ways of telling whether a demon is present (preferably through the gift of discernment), and of finding out what kind of demon is present, we are ready to talk about the different kinds of evil spirits we may discover.

Just like us, the spirits have names. A demon's name is especially important because it indicates its nature and purpose in life. When you know that my name is Francis, it does not tell you much about me. But if a spirit identifies itself as *envy*, you know something about how that spirit influences the person.

The names of some of the good spirits, the angels, are well-known: Gabriel, Michael and (in Hebrew tradition) Raphael. The evil spirits have names, too, beginning with Satan or Lucifer. And just as the angels are ranked in a hierarchy of majesty and spiritual power, with archangels, cherubim and seraphim the most important, so, too, the evil spirits have their own levels of power under the leadership of Satan.

It helps us to identify the spirits by name and rank for several important reasons:

1. The identity of the spirit gives you a clue as to how it influences the person to whom you are ministering. This is most important in knowing both how to minister and how to proceed during the necessary follow-up.

2. If the spirit is higher up in the hierarchy of spirits, it usually requires exorcists who have more than ordinary spiritual authority to cast it out; and it usually takes more time than when you are dealing with lesser spirits. You may not have an easy time of it.

3. Knowing the spirit's name somehow gives you additional power over the spirit.

One of the most fascinating aspects of the deliverance ministry is that we find different categories and types of spirits. The most common types seem to be clustered in four major groups.

Spirits of the Occult

Most spirits in the first group have unusual personal names such as Beelzebub, Pasuzo or Antichrist. These odd names usually indicate that the spirits are in the higher realms of the evil spirits' hierarchy.

These types of spirits usually move into people's lives through their direct involvement in the occult. (More about this in the next chapter.) They represent a relatively small percentage, perhaps only ten percent, of the spirits we encounter, but they are the most difficult, dangerous group—the true demons from hell.

Spirits of Sin

A second large category of spirits are characterized by names signifying a human vice or sin. We frequently encounter spirits, for instance, that identify themselves by such names as *lust, hatred, murder* or *envy.* These names are not exactly personal names but represent the sins or weaknesses that the spirits seem to induce and, in some mysterious way, feed on. It is as if the person's sinning has, over a period of time, built a kind of home that the spirit can enter and feel welcome in while it tempts or aggravates any natural weakness to which the person has already surrendered.

We find every human sin represented in this group of spirits, all the way from relatively minor vices like vanity to major ones like murder. One of the more fascinating aspects of these spirits is that some of them are very specific. For instance, I have run into not only spirits of hatred, but such particular spirits as *hatred of men*. (I met this one in the daughter of a prostitute.) Not only do we encounter generalized *lust* but also a more specific unclean spirit called *pornography*. The evil spirits seem to make clear distinctions between different kinds of vice, almost as if they had taken a theological dictionary and outlined precise categories of human weaknesses that they were going to work on.

People who have long been involved in deliverance ministry are aware of clusters of spirits that seem to aggravate a victim's major weakness. Frank and Ida Mae Hammond list 53 groupings of evil spirits. As one group under *paranoia* they include *jealousy, envy, suspicion, distrust, persecution, fears* and *confrontation*.[1] These are aspects of the paranoid personality that any psychiatrist might come up with. The curious thing is that these specific aspects of paranoia are targeted by the demonic realm[2] and discovered by Pentecostal ministers who have no background whatever in psychological studies.

And what is the nature of these spirits that they should zero in on such human activities? Do they just delight in tormenting people and taking away their freedom; is that all they get out of it? Or is there something in their personalities that finds enjoyment in working through a human body to accomplish something they cannot do in their own spiritual form? Does a spirit of hate, for instance, not only get satisfaction from driving a man to commit murder, thus trapping him and guiding him toward hell, but have its own personal evil enjoyment in slaughtering and killing? When hate is a spirit, can it work out its destiny only by influencing a human being to wield a knife or fire a gun into another human being?

Since these spirits enter a habitation built by sin, the cure and casting out of these spirits necessarily means that the human

1. Frank and Ida Mae Hammond, *Pigs in the Parlor* (Kirkwood, Mo.: Impact Books, 1973), p. 114.
2. Here it should be mentioned that Fr. Richard McAlear and Betty Brennan, who have had much experience in deliverance, say that most of what we call different evil spirits are actually what they call "aspects" of a particular evil spirit. For example, rather than one main spirit, *paranoia*, surrounded by a cluster of seven other spirits, such as *jealousy*, there is one evil spirit named *paranoia*, which has seven aspects to it.

host has to turn away from sin and repent. (More about this in chapter 15.)

Spirits of Trauma

It is here that we find the most common need for deliverance. Strangely, these spirits do not invade us because of our own personal sin, but because of the wounds caused by fallen creation or by the sins of others. Through our weakness, through our wounded emotional past, evil spirits can attack us.

It is very much like a physical wound: If the skin closes over the wound before it has been cleaned out, an ugly infection gets into the body and starts growing. Not only the original wound causes the festering infection but also the filth that got in with it. Sometimes these infections become life-threatening, pouring into the bloodstream, while others eat up tissue and bone, developing into gangrene or osteomyelitis.

Similarly, in our psychological history, what began as a tiny emotional wound, if it is not opened up to the light, can close over and become a permanent personality disorder. That emotional wound can also serve as an entrance to spirits of trauma that come to dwell there and aggravate it, preventing it from healing.

This frequently brings about an infestation of evil spirits, not because of personal sin, but because of the generalized fallen human condition—what Christian tradition has called original sin. Most deliverance prayer, in fact (as we said earlier), is to free good people, sometimes very good people, from the results of what happened to them in childhood when they were weak and unprotected. A certain amount of infestation happens even before birth, while the baby is still waiting to be born.

I would estimate, from the experience of our ministry and from talking with people familiar with deliverance ministry, that perhaps two-thirds of deliverance prayer aims at ridding people of various spirits of trauma.

This all sounds totally unfair—and it is! Satan, the destroyer, has no more pity for children or the weak than the Nazis did, or any harsh, militaristic regime today that routinely tortures people in order to intimidate and rule. Satan reigns over a kingdom governed by terror, sucking up as much power as possible. He does not fight fair. And Satanists who kidnap children for their rituals play according to their own sadistic rules. All this simply highlights our need for a Savior, who can free us from Satan's kingdom and bring us into the Kingdom of God.

One of the pioneers in resurrecting the deliverance ministry in the last generation was Don Basham, who described how he came to find that his own small daughter Laura needed deliverance. Don and his wife, Alice, thought they had lost Laura and were exasperated when they found that Laura had simply wandered off and was playing in her friend's garage while they were searching the neighborhood frantically. When they discovered her, Alice cried out, "We thought we would never see our Laura Anne again!" at which point Laura began to wail in terror. Her parents tried to console her, but she continued to wail.

At bedtime Laura told Don she could not sleep. When Don asked why, she answered, "'Cause every time I start to say my prayers, something inside of me makes fun of my prayers."

Reluctant as I was to think it, it sounded precisely like the activity of some demonic, mocking spirit. What a frightening idea, that such a thing could invade my own child!

I tried to sound casual as I made the suggestion to Laura. "You know, honey, that sounds a little like it might be an evil spirit."

"Uh-huh."

"Want to get rid of it?"

Laura nodded. I was grateful that the children knew about the ministry I was getting into and accepted it quite naturally. . . .

From what Laura had said I had assumed the spirit's name would be mockery, but to my surprise, when I commanded it to name itself, Laura answered firmly, "Fear." As I ordered the spirit of fear to come out, Laura grabbed herself across the midriff. Then she straightened up.

"I felt it leave," she said matter-of-factly. "I'm fine now. G'nite, Daddy." And she snuggled down against her pillow. . . .

"Daddy?" Laura's sleepy voice reached me at the door. "I think I know when that old spirit came in."

"You do? When?"

"Well, you know this afternoon when you and Mommy were so mad at me? And you said you might never see me again? Daddy, I got *so scared!* And I've felt something laughing ever since." . . .

This was how I began to explore, quite by accident within my own family, the ways in which an evil spirit can gain entry into the system. What happened with Laura, I felt, was that because of the afternoon's trauma, a crack appeared in her natural defenses. As a child of God she was ordinarily protected from such invasions. Actually, however, it must work out often for us that because of some disturbance—a shock, an illness, an accident—our normal defenses are let down. Obviously it doesn't take long for an evil spirit to take advantage of the situation, get in and start doing its dirty work.[3]

Again, how do we know that Laura was not just afflicted with a normal but powerful experience of childhood fear? Well, she was—and that is usually all there is to it. But sometimes, as Don Basham indicated, a spirit seems to enter through the trauma, the emotional wound, just as a speck of dirt or contagion might enter when I puncture my foot with a nail. The sign of a spirit present was that Laura herself felt something inside her. Then, too, when Don prayed she felt it leave, and afterward fell asleep.

Can you prove that a spirit of fear was there? No. The only sure indicator we have (as we said in the last chapter) is the gift of discerning spirits. Aside from that, though, we can deduce its presence from external signs—in this case, Laura telling her dad about what she felt inside.

We will discuss more about spirits of trauma in chapter 14. For now, suffice it to say that, unfair as it is, most of the evil spirits we encounter seem to enter with trauma, and most of that trauma takes place in childhood, or even before that, in the womb.

Ancestral (Familiar) Spirits

The last category of spirits we commonly encounter are named by ordinary, everyday, personal names like George or Susan. These spirits are mysterious in origin. There are two very different theories explaining who they are.

The first theory is that they are simply masquerading as the souls of the dead, so as to excite people's curiosity about de-

---

3. Don Basham, *Deliver Us from Evil* (Grand Rapids, Mich.: Chosen Books, 1972), pp. 125–126.

parted relatives, and hence to entice them into communicating with the dead through séances and other forbidden activities.

If this is true, then these evil spirits are to be treated like any other category of evil spirits and simply cast out. Most Christians of evangelical background prefer this understanding of familiar spirits.

The second theory is that these familiar spirits are truly the dead who are not at rest. In this case we should treat them not as evil spirits but as departed spirits who need prayer to commend them to Jesus, so that they might be set at rest and cease their wanderings.

Here, of course, we see some relation to the tradition of ghosts, haunted houses and other mysterious phenomena that excite curiosity and form the subject matter of many of our horror films. Here, too, we apply a long Christian tradition of praying blessings and exorcisms for places where these fearsome hauntings and visitations take place.

This second theory, that these familiar spirits are truly departed spirits that need to be set at rest, is perhaps best known through Dr. Ken McAll's book *Healing the Family Tree* [4] Dr. McAll, a psychiatrist and former missionary to China, believes that many of his formerly "incurable" patients are the victims of ancestral control. By drawing up a family tree with the patient, he tries to identify the relative or ancestor causing the patient harm. Then he cuts the bond between ancestor and patient through a prayer service (in a sacramental tradition, this would be a Communion service) that commits the departed spirit to Jesus and cuts the living person free.

One way for you to avoid having to decide which of these two beliefs is true, when a familiar spirit is troubling a person—that is, "Is this an evil spirit that needs to be sent to the Abyss, or is it simply a misguided human spirit that needs be set to rest?"—is simply to say to the spirit, "I command you to go to Jesus Christ, for Jesus to deal with you in His justice and mercy." With this kind of prayer you are safe in letting the Lord work out the theological questions, while you free the person asking for help from the influence of a departed (or evil) spirit.

4. Ken McAll, *Healing the Family Tree 4* (London: Sheldon Press, 1982, revised edition, 1984).

Following a section on curses and one on preparation for the ministry of deliverance, we will discuss each of these categories in detail—*occult spirits, spirits of sin, spirits of trauma* and *familiar spirits*—and tell how you can free people from the influence of each one.

Curses and the Power of False Judgment

7

Falling Under a Curse

If coming under demonic attack or being infested by a demon is not a currently acceptable concept in most mainline Christian churches today, the idea of being cursed is seen as even more superstitious and primitive, even in many fundamentalist or conservative churches that claim to be based solely on Scripture. Certainly in my own seminary training, freeing someone from a curse was never seen as a skill we needed to learn about.

So I have spent years learning more about the traditional practice of being freed from curses—traditional not only in early Christianity but in all religions. Hardly a week has gone by in recent years that I have not had to pray for someone affected by a curse, exchanging that curse for a blessing.

The following is a present-day example. It took place in England in 1990 when I was speaking in a church filled with six hundred people. After my talk that evening on how to pray for physical healing, I asked if anyone would like the whole church to pray for healing from the kind of sickness that we could tell on the spot had been healed. My purpose was to encourage the people to pray for the sick, showing them how simple it is. Half a dozen people raised their hands and I chose a man about forty years old.

He came up to the front of the church and told us he felt a little sheepish because he did not have a life-threatening sickness like cancer, yet he would be able to tell if he were healed because he had a ringing in both ears (tinnitis) and pain in his right ear. He also told us he was the Anglican vicar of a nearby church.

Our team gathered around as we led the whole church in prayer for him. After a few minutes we asked if the ringing and pain were gone.

"No," he said.

So we prayed once more. Again we stopped to ask, and again he reported that nothing had changed.

I decided to pray a third and last time. Again he told us quietly that his ears continued to ring.

My experience has been that when we pray publicly, if we are really following the Spirit's leading, some perceptible degree of healing almost always takes place. Also, it is disheartening, as you can imagine, when you are trying to encourage people to believe in God's desire to heal and nothing seems to happen. We know, of course, that not everyone we pray for is instantly and visibly healed, but in this kind of public demonstration, the percentage of healing is, for whatever reason, extraordinary.

I was thinking there might be a spirit of infirmity blocking the healing when one of the members of our team, Mrs. Anne Bloch, leaned over and whispered to me, "Francis, I think there's a spirit of infirmity here."

What do you do in a situation like this? Here is an Anglican priest in front of a large congregation, many of whom would be surprised (to say the least!) if you told them an evil spirit was present— in their priest, no less.

What I did was pray under my breath commanding the spirit of infirmity to depart. As soon as I did, the pastor bent over and started coughing with the violent hacking that often accompanies the expulsion of a demon. We continued praying quietly, hoping the deliverance would end quickly. On the contrary, his violent coughing continued, so I stopped and sent the pastor and four of our team back into the privacy of the sacristy to continue praying where he would not be needlessly embarrassed.

The next night he came back and announced to the congregation that the ringing had stopped completely and the pain in his right ear was gone.

Here is what happened. The team ministered to him that first night for an hour in the sacristy, then for several hours the next day in his home. He told the team that he and his family had been serving as missionaries in Africa, where the ringing and pain had first started. Even more serious, their son had developed an intense rash spreading across his abdomen that the doctors were unable to diagnose. In time he lost about a quarter of his body weight. The missionary was advised to take his family back to England or risk the boy's life, so they retreated. The boy's rash had subsequently disappeared but the pastor's problems had remained.

After hearing this story and praying for discernment, our team discovered that local witch doctors had put the family under a curse to get rid of them. Even so, the priest had no suspicion about what had caused his problems. So when the team prayed with discernment, the Lord freed him from three spirits, one of which was the spirit of infirmity that had been directed against him by the witch doctor's curse. And he was freed.

This kind of freeing deliverance is, in my experience, not at all rare. The surprising thing is that so few churches consider the possibility of the curse as a real pastoral concern, when so much traditional pagan religion not only believes in it but concentrates on seeking blessings and avoiding curses through the rituals of their native priests (shamans). The Christians in these areas still seek help instinctively, believing in the power of the curse. It has been estimated that the majority of Hispanic Catholics in Latin America (and in the United States, too) seek help from Santeria, voodoo or other such groups when they feel cursed.

I met a woman in a thriving, fervent Christian community in Colombia whose son who had fallen prey to a mysterious ailment. The woman had made an appointment with a *spiritista* living in that Christian community to seek help. The *spiritista* informed her that another family in the community had gotten angry at her and paid the *spiritista* to put a curse on her family. So the mother paid the *spiritista* to remove the curse, and the boy was healed instantly.[1]

It was ironic that the *spiritista* was paid by two women to curse and to unbind the same curse—all in a fine Christian community where there had been no teaching on these sub-

---

1. Demonic powers can heal by simply removing the evil they have inflicted on people.

jects, nor prayer for healing and deliverance. (This has since changed.)

The Evidence of Scripture

Our abandonment of teaching on blessings and curses is all the more extraordinary when you consider what a prominent place it occupies in the New as well as the Old Testament. Certainly Scripture's main emphasis is on God's goodness and blessings coming on those who do His will, rather than on evil and curses. Blessing is mentioned in Scripture some 410 times. Still, cursing in its various forms is mentioned 230 times.

One of the reasons given for Jesus' death on the cross was the transformation of the curse on the human race into a blessing:

> Christ redeemed us from the curse of the law by becoming a curse for us, for it is written: "Cursed is everyone who is hung on a tree."
>
> Galatians 3:13

Large sections of the Bible give lists of curses that descend on those who disobey God's commandments. Moses, for example, divided the tribes of Israel into two groups and had six tribes stand on Mount Gerizim to pronounce the blessings of God on those who follow His commandments. Then the other six tribes stood on Mount Ebal to pronounce curses on the disobedient (Deuteronomy 27:12-14).

The Levites proclaimed the curses in a loud voice, beginning with this:

> "Cursed is the man who carves an image or casts an idol—a thing detestable to the LORD, the work of the craftsman's hands—and sets it up in secret." Then all the people shall say, "Amen!"
>
> Deuteronomy 27:15

In the next chapter Moses listed the blessings showered on the obedient, followed by a longer and very graphic list of curses. Among them:

> The LORD will send on you curses, confusion and rebuke in everything you put your hand to, until you are destroyed and come to

sudden ruin because of the evil you have done in forsaking him. The LORD will plague you with diseases until he has destroyed you from the land you are entering to possess. The LORD will strike you with wasting disease, with fever and inflammation, with scorching heat and drought, with blight and mildew, which will plague you until you perish. The sky over your head will be bronze, the ground beneath you iron. The LORD will turn the rain of your country into dust and powder; it will come down from the skies until you are ruined.

Deuteronomy 28:20–24

This list of disasters goes on and on: Your enemies will defeat you; your carcasses will lie unburied; you will be afflicted with boils and tumors; you will go mad; your wife will be ravished; another nation will take everything that belongs to you. These sufferings dramatize what the forces of evil will do to us once God's protection is removed through our disobedience.

The book of Numbers devotes three chapters (22–24) to the fascinating struggle between Balak, the Moabite king, and Balaam, the local prophet. Balak tried to bribe Balaam to curse the Israelites who had arrived at the border of Moab: "Now come and put a curse on them for me. Perhaps then I will be able to fight them and drive them away" (Numbers 22:11). Balaam had sense enough to know he should not "go beyond the command of the LORD my God" (verse 18). Still, King Balak persisted in trying to lure Balaam into joining the Moabite side.

Only Balaam's donkey could see the angel God sent to block the way, and it balked three times. Balaam beat the donkey until at last Balaam also saw the angel and was convinced it was better to turn back and face Balak rather than incur God's wrath. After that, each time King Balak commanded Balaam to curse the Israelites, Balaam would open his mouth only to bless: "May those who bless you be blessed, and those who curse you be cursed!" (Numbers 24:9).

These and countless other Scripture passages reveal the truth that words can convey spiritual power for either good or evil, beyond mere human utterance.[2]

Nor is this simply an Old Testament concept left behind in New Testament times. Remember, for example, the mysterious

---

2. A curse is defined in my Webster's as "a prayer or invocation for harm or injury to come upon one."

incident of Jesus cursing the fig tree (Mark 11:14); the next day Peter was startled to see that the curse had worked and that the fig tree, in one day, had withered to its roots (verse 20). In the early Church we find Paul cursing the sorcerer Elymas, who was trying to turn Sergius Paulus, the proconsul, against Paul.

> . . . Paul, filled with the Holy Spirit, looked straight at Elymas and said, "You are a child of the devil and an enemy of everything that is right! . . . Now the hand of the Lord is against you. You are going to be blind, and for a time you will be unable to see the light of the sun." Immediately mist and darkness came over him, and he groped about, seeking someone to lead him by the hand. When the proconsul saw what had happened, he believed. . . .
>
> Acts 13:9–12

Here again we see that early Christian preaching presented the Gospel primarily as an active struggle between the Kingdom of God and the kingdom of Satan—a conflict in which Jesus brings us victory because He bears God's power to overcome evil. At first glance it might seem that Paul was not acting in a Christian way, calling Elymas "a child of the devil," then striking him blind. But then we notice that the blindness was only for a time; the curse was to stop Elymas' interference and, Paul hoped, to lead to his conversion. The purpose of witchcraft is to gain power; and Elymas, a man greedy for power, discovered a power stronger than his own. It was an argument Elymas could understand. Also, the effectiveness of Paul's curse led to the pro- consul's conversion—a conversion story people in Africa today would understand better than most of us, since they know by experience the power of witchcraft.

The curse on Elymas is clearly a New Testament exception, since Paul taught that we should bless those who curse us and return blessings for evil (Romans 12:14); furthermore, when James and John wanted to call down fire on the Samaritans who refused them hospitality, Jesus rebuked them (Luke 9:52–55). (No wonder He nicknamed them "Sons of Thunder"!)

Whenever we wish evil on others, in the worldview of the Bi- ble, our words may carry not only the human freight of anger and ill-wishing, but a spiritual power to block or hurt people.

Our Own Experience

The power of evil spirits invoked by cursing is a primary component of most native religions. The ability of witch doctors to impose curses, hexes and spells, and to lift them off, gives them power and respect based on fear. When Christians do not understand their own religion, they are at a disadvantage in trying to convert pagans, who may better understand the reality of spiritual warfare.

Recall the Nigerian seminarians I mentioned in chapter 3 who refused the Western idea that witchcraft was simply superstition. This recognition is true not only in Africa. Many people in the United States have been cursed in some way and, when we pray, they are dramatically (or at times quietly) freed. Several who have come out of satanic covens in the Jacksonville area have revealed to us that my family and I, as well as others on our staff, have been targeted by name by some of the local covens. They pray for us in their own way, which is to direct curses at us. (Consequently we pray daily for protection.)

An example of an "ordinary" deliverance from a curse is contained in a recent letter I received from a pastor for whom we prayed. His church is in an area of the country heavily populated by devotees of witchcraft, and he believed a curse had been directed at him by a local coven. His presenting problem was depression, so severe as to lead him to think of giving up his pastorate. Ordinarily we would have prayed for healing and perhaps encouraged him to receive professional counseling, but we decided he did need to be freed from a curse. Here is how he describes what happened:

> The most interesting thing to tell you folks has to do with my own well-being and that of the church. The result of your prayers was not very dramatic, but rather, within a couple of hours, I just felt O.K. I don't mean that in the sense of mediocre—like grade C. I mean it in the sense of normal or at peace or healthy. Something that was oppressing me was simply not there anymore. Not only has that effect continued to this day, but there has been a steady growth of energy and a renewed interest in ministry—and activities outside of ministry. It is marvelous! I don't know what happened, but whatever it was, I praise the Lord for it.

A fascinating example of a belief in curses survives, even in our sophisticated society, in the world of theater. An old tradition remains that those who act in Shakespeare's great tragedy *Macbeth* are likely to suffer disaster. You remember that *Macbeth* features three witches who cast curses as well as prophesy the future. In one scene we find them cursing the sailor-husband of a woman who has insulted them. The first witch promises:

> I'll drain him dry as hay;
> Sleep shall neither night nor day
> Hang upon his pent-house lid;
> He shall live a man forbid.
>
> Act I, Scene III

Then there is the famous scene of the witches brewing their cauldron of evil, a concentrated potion of cursing:

> *Second Witch.* Adder's fork and blind-worm's sting,
> Lizard's leg and howlet's wing,
> For a charm of pow'rful trouble,
> Like a hell-broth boil and bubble.
> *All.* Double, double toil and trouble;
> Fire burn and, cauldron bubble.
>
> Act IV, Scene I

Driven by the witches' prophecies that Macbeth will become king of Scotland and that no man born of woman can kill him, Macbeth and Lady Macbeth conspire to kill Duncan, the legitimate Scottish king. But in the end evil and destruction recoil on them both. Lady Macbeth goes mad and Macbeth is killed in battle.

The entire tragedy centers on evil and its terrifying power to destroy. The power of darkness is overcome by the good nobles; and Macbeth's dark power is contrasted with God's power manifested in England's saintly king, Edward the Confessor:

> *Malcolm.* A most miraculous work in this good king;
> Which often, since my here-remain in England,
> I have seen him do. How he solicits heaven,
> Himself best knows: but strangely-visited people,

All swol'n and ulcerous, pitiful to the eye,
The mere despair of surgery, he cures.

Act IV, Scene III

Shakespeare contrasts God's healing and blessing, coming through good King Edward, to the demons' influence over the evil King Macbeth; although modern productions usually leave out as irrelevant the description of Edward the Confessor.

An actress with years of experience in the New York theater world tells me that even today many think a curse is attached to this great tragedy of Shakespeare. A history of disasters befalling actors and directors of *Macbeth* is so well-known that many theater people are afraid of being involved in the production of this play. Not only do many believe in an active curse touching actors in the play, but some believe that the very word *Macbeth* bears bad luck, so they will speak about "the Scottish play" or refer to Lady Macbeth as "the Scottish queen." It is fascinating, too, that if certain actors happen to mention the name *Macbeth*, they believe they can ward off the curse by quoting *Hamlet*: "Angels and ministers of grace defend us."

How Do We Know If Someone Is Cursed?

Whenever we try to decide whether a person has been demonized, the visible evidence is ambiguous. The only sure way of knowing about these things—since the cause is in the spirit realm and therefore invisible—is when the minister of deliverance has a true gift of discernment. But the effects of a curse can still often be observed, so that we can say, "Probably this person, or this family, is under some kind of curse."

Derek Prince, who has amassed years of experience in praying for deliverance, lists seven signs indicating that a person or family may be suffering from a curse:

1. *Mental or emotional breakdown.* Derek's experience leads him to believe that chronic depression usually has its source in some kind of occultic activity—either the person's own involvement or that of an ancestor. You do not need to believe that most depression can be traced back to a curse, but it would be wise to consider, when you are try-

ing to help someone suffering from depression, whether a curse might be the root cause.

2. *Repeated or chronic sickness*, especially if it is hereditary. This is particularly true if physicians can find no adequate cause for the illness.

3. *Barrenness and a tendency to miscarry.*

4. *Breakdown of marriage and family.*

5. *Continuing financial insufficiency* when a person's salary and education indicate that she should be financially solvent, yet she never seems to be able to pay her bills.

6. *Being accident-prone.*

7. *Family history of unnatural* (e.g., suicide) *or untimely deaths.*[3]

None of these very human problems is enough in itself, of course, to prove the presence of a curse. It is only when several signs are present, or when one sign is particularly severe, that you may suspect a curse has been inflicted. Even then you can be certain only through the guidance of the Holy Spirit. Yet we need to be aware that many Christians who should be enjoying life are living under a curse.[4] We should note, too, that these seven categories correspond to the list of curses we read in Deuteronomy 28.

Let's take just one example. Almost everyone in the United States realizes that the breakdown of family life, especially the alienation of children from their parents, is at the root of many of our problems. Human factors account for much of this: greed (with one or both parents spending too much time at work), infidelity, adultery, racism (leading to minority families suffering from the rage of failed hopes). Yet we need to recognize that, along with natural, human problems, the force of a curse may underlie many of the problems destroying our society. As Deuteronomy predicts: "Your sons and daughters will be given to another nation, and you will wear out your eyes watching for them day after day, powerless to lift a hand" (28:32); and "You

3. Derek Prince, *Blessing or Curse: You Can Choose* (Grand Rapids, Mich.: Chosen Books, 1990), pp. 45–58. If you want to know more about the topic of blessings and curses, I recommend this book.

4. Ibid., p. 38.

will have sons and daughters but you will not keep them, because they will go into captivity" (28:41).

The literal fulfillment of these prophecies occurred, of course, when the Israelites were marched off into Babylonian captivity; but Derek Prince believes this curse is being worked out today when parents see

> their sons and daughters taken captive by a rebellious subculture devoted to drugs, sex, satanic music and every form of the occult. . . . We need to see it as the outworking of a curse, which is responsible for the agonies of strife-torn homes, broken marriages and disintegrated families. Perhaps the most accurate word to describe the force responsible for these results is *alienation*. It comes between husbands and wives, parents and children, brothers and sisters, and all others who should be united by the bonds of family. Its goal is the destruction of the family.[5]

This dissension and the breakup of family life has hit our churches. In newsletter after newsletter, pastors and evangelists report the unprecedented destruction of churches and clergy marriages. Just yesterday I received a newsletter from our friends Harry and Ruth Fullilove, who are Lutheran missionaries. Ruth writes:

> As we have been traveling here, there and everywhere these last years, we have been in church after church that has been divided, dissected and almost destroyed. (Some have had to close down.)

Friends of mine in direct contact with what goes on in satanic covens in various parts of the country report that these covens target clergy marriages and churches, and direct curses to destroy them, in two ways:

1. Creating dissension in churches.
2. Dividing marriages through lust and adultery. In addition to directing curses at the churches and families of their leaders, sometimes they actually send a member of the coven to stir up criticism and division within the church or to seduce the pastor or pastor's spouse.

---

5. Ibid., p. 52.

Again, human weakness can account for many of our failings. But we also need to be aware of the reality of spiritual warfare and the need to pray for protection—and perhaps to be freed from the effects of a curse. For this reason our family prays daily for protection. More on this in a minute.

Curses that Come on Us from Outside

"Like a fluttering sparrow or a darting swallow, an unde-served curse does not come to rest" (Proverbs 26:2). The New King James translation of Proverbs puts it, "A curse without cause shall not alight." In other words, we remain free from curses unless there is some reason for the curse to settle on us. So whenever we need to remove a curse, it helps to know its cause so we can pull it out by the root.

The causes for curses that come on us from outside, through no fault of our own, fall into two general categories:

1. curses that descend on us from past generations;
2. curses that come to us from some present cause.

Curses from the Past

Here we should emphasize that we can be innocent of wrong-doing, yet be the victim of a curse if we have not protected our-selves and our families through prayer. The story I shared about the Anglican missionary to Africa is a good example of this. The tragic reality is that curses can descend on us without any fault on our part. The good news is that they can be broken through God's power, once we recognize their presence.

The most memorable example I can think of is a woman who wanted prayer for a relatively ordinary problem: She had trou-ble being patient and was easily angered—a common human failing. She was a regular churchgoer; in fact, she taught Sunday school. But once we started to pray, her face changed into a snarling mask of rage. Worse yet, this ordinarily meek woman started speaking in an altered voice and insulting us. Fortu-nately someone in our group had a gift of discernment and said, "This all started in a black mass said in England hundreds of years ago, when her family was consecrated to Satan." As soon as he said this, the spirit responded indignantly, "Who told you that!"

In the first Commandment God declares,

> I, the LORD your God, am a jealous God, punishing the children for the sin of the fathers to the third and fourth generation of those who hate me, but showing love to thousands who love me and keep my commandments.
>
> Exodus 20:5–6

If someone in our ancestry did something such as consecrate the family to Satan, the disastrous results continue even beyond the fourth generation, until the curse is broken.

Three main causes of these generational curses are:

1. *If the family has been involved in the occult, especially if there have been witches or warlocks in the family tree.* When we consider that we have two parents, four grandparents, eight great-grandparents and sixteen great-great-grandparents—for a total of thirty in all—"How many of us would be in a position to guarantee that none of our thirty immediate ancestors was ever involved in any form of idolatry or the occult?"[6]
2. *If the family itself has been cursed by someone else.*
3. *If the family has been deeply involved in some kind of sinful activity.* Idolatry is specifically mentioned under the first Commandment in Exodus 20.

These generational curses can have two effects. One, God's blessings may simply be blocked. The curse forms a barrier that needs to be broken so that God's blessing can flow upon the family. Second, multiple disasters sometimes seem to target a family. (Several families prominent in the United States probably come immediately to your mind when you think of tragedy afflicting several generations.) The ancient Greeks even named a goddess, Nemesis, to represent the personal force that haunts and pursues a family to destroy it. When we use words to describe this phenomenon, words like *uncanny,* or when members of a family suffer from some foreboding or from a fear of

6. Ibid., p. 74.

death, they are recognizing intuitively that a power beyond the normal seems to govern their family's "fate."

Curses from Some Present Cause

This is the second category of curses that affect us from the outside. Earlier in this chapter I mentioned the Anglican priest in England who fell sick while he was a missionary in Africa through the hexes directed his way by a witch doctor. Much voodoo (black magic) centers around cursing people and casting spells.

Many Christian leaders are targeted by local covens and are unwittingly afflicted—at times by ordinary symptoms like heaviness or depression; at other times, more seriously, by various kinds of illness; or, worse yet, by obsessive thoughts or desires tempting them toward divisive resentment or sexual promiscuity. (I would not be surprised if the recent upsurge of pedophilia recently coming to light in a minority of Roman Catholic priests is caused, in part, by Satanist groups praying to destroy their ministry, and also the ministry of the Church itself.)

Many of the victims of these curses are, regrettably, unaware of the spiritual source of their problems; spiritual realities are discerned only spiritually. These curses may aggravate existing human problems, so experts may study the human dimension of the problem from a purely rational point of view but never identify the spiritual, supernatural component. They might not ever think to have a curse removed.[7]

Judith has had a personal experience in relation to her ancestry that has touched her profoundly. Her dad is a nearly full-blooded Cherokee, descended from those ancestors who fled to the mountains 150 years ago, escaping the tragic Trail of Tears that forced most of the Cherokees to march to Oklahoma. She is proud of that inheritance, yet had a disturbing experience twenty years ago.

At that time she was a missionary in Jerusalem lying in bed with a mysterious fever that did not respond to medical treatment. Into her room marched a missionary she scarcely knew

---

7. Dr. Scott Peck's pioneering work *People of the Lie* proposes that there is a supernatural component of evil at work in some clients who cannot be helped by purely human resources.

who was unacquainted with her Cherokee ancestry through any natural means. Nevertheless, she proceeded to ask Judith if she was of Cherokee descent, and when Judith confirmed that she was, this missionary said the Lord had told her that Judith needed to have her bloodlines cleansed of some effects of witchcraft. When Judith gave her permission to pray, this woman uttered a powerful prayer of deliverance. Immediately Judith's fever disappeared.

Then, this past summer, while our friends George and Rena Larson prayed for Judith to receive an inner healing, God balanced that powerful deliverance relating to the negative side of her inheritance. While the Larsons prayed, Judith had a vision in which Jesus appeared to her as she stood at a favorite childhood spot—a natural bridge overlooking the Red River Gorge in her native Kentucky. Stretching His arm over the beautiful forests below, Jesus said, "All this is yours." When she asked what that meant, He added, "This is your inheritance!"

Elements in Traditional Religions

These two incidents from Judith's life contain a teaching that is especially timely today when some Christians believe it makes little difference whether they are Christian, Buddhist or Hindu—"We all have our own paths up the mountain, and we'll meet at the top," that kind of leveling attitude. What needs to be affirmed is the age-old Christian belief that many traditional religions mix good elements (for example, moral teaching) along with demonic, especially if the priests of those religions are witch doctors.

With regard to traditional religions, we should avoid taking one of two extreme positions. First, some Christians tend to condemn anything unfamiliar that comes from a foreign culture—say, from India, China or Africa. They are like those Christians in Paul's time who were understandably afraid of eating food offered to idols (1 Corinthians 8); yet Paul was not afraid to eat such food, provided his eating did not offend those of a more tender conscience. (I have to admit I probably would take the safer course and refuse to eat meat offered to idols if it were sold in our supermarkets today.)

At the other extreme, we have the more common problem of those who accept anything "spiritual" that comes from another religion and automatically consider it valuable, simply because it is spiritual. Christian leaders who dismiss the existence of the demonic realm as primitive superstition disregard the dangers of demonic influence in religions that are not in the Judeo-Christian tradition—to their own peril. They seem to have lost the ability to discern the difference between the Holy Spirit and the realm of evil spirits.

There are elements of witchcraft and the demonic in most traditional religions that need to be discerned, preferably by someone who is deeply Christian but who has grown up in the culture and understands it from the inside. They are usually the ones best able to affirm the good and sift out the evil.

Let me share one remarkable example. In 1977 I met a fine priest in India, Fr. Rufus Pereira, who in two brief years had prayed to free more than four hundred individuals from demonic influence. He estimated that about a third of them were delivered from demons identifying themselves as Hindu gods. I should mention that Fr. Rufus is not a wild-eyed enthusiast but a highly educated seminary professor who studied Scripture in Rome and is highly regarded by the Indian bishops, who gave him permission to perform exorcisms.

Fr. Rufus acknowledged the noble aspects of religion in India but was also willing to face the darker, demonic side of Hindu culture. He graciously granted me an interview, in which he said:

> I love my country very much and have a great respect for Indian religion, but perhaps there is no religion that has within itself such a wide spectrum, ranging all the way from the highest form of religious endeavor to the lowest degradation of humanity—all in the name of religion. I have been led to believe that many of the gods and goddesses in Hindu mythology are nothing other than demons.

During one conference, five cases of possession surfaced while I was speaking. After my talk Rufus asked me to come and observe one young woman, a Catholic, whom they had taken to a classroom. There she was, stretched out on a table, assuming the dancing posture you see in some Hindu statues. If you tried to straighten her out, she would immediately contort her body back into its artificial posture. Later Rufus told me what this all meant:

You will remember what she looked like, this girl taking on the poses of the Hindu dancing god. (This dancing god is one aspect of the god Shiva.) What is really remarkable is that this girl knows nothing about Indian dancing, because she was brought up in a Western culture home. Yet here she was, assuming the absolutely correct dancing poses in her fingers, her wrists, her hands and feet—the exact poses of this very god. It was something fantastic to watch, as her eyes and her mouth were all changed into the features of this Hindu god. I later found that it got into her because of a spell cast by a Hindu doctor (who perhaps had lustful motives when he was treating her). Probably he called up his favorite god, the dancing god, to possess her so he could get power over her.[8]

Christians need to rediscover the fact that Jesus is primarily our Savior, the Son of God who has the power to rescue us from a very real, very personal world of evil that is present in traditional religion, whether it be Asian, African, Irish or Native American. Jesus is not a great teacher or prophet standing on a level with Buddha and Confucius. He is our Redeemer with healing in His wings, ready to free all of us from the evil that tries to drag us down.

Superstition

Then there are popular superstitions. The superstition, for instance, that Friday the thirteenth is an unlucky, cursed day seems to carry some validity, according to a study I read just last week:

This just in from scientific research: Friday the 13th is unlucky.

The risk of being admitted to the hospital because of a road accident on a Friday the 13th can go up as much as 52 percent, researchers report in the current edition of *The British Medical Journal*, which became available yesterday.

"Staying at home is recommended," said the four-member research team from Mid-Downs Health Authority, based in the town of Haywards Heath, 35 miles south of London.

The team studied traffic flow figures for the southern section of the M25 motorway that rings London, hospital admission figures and numbers of shoppers in nine southeast England stores owned by J. Sainsbury, Britain's biggest supermarket chain.

8. A transcript of my interview with Rufus Pereira appears in appendix 2.

They compared figures for five Friday the 13ths—July 1990, September and December 1991, and March and November 1992—with those for the previous Fridays in each of those months.

"There were 1.4 percent fewer vehicles on the southern section of the M25 on Friday the 13th," the report said.

"Hospital admissions due to transport accidents were significantly increased on Friday the 13th," the report said. "Our data suggest the risk of a transport accident on Friday the 13th may be increased by 52 percent."[9]

The scientists in this study ascribed the 52 percent rise in accidents, in spite of the drop in traffic, to superstitious fears leading to a lack of concentration. We know, on the other hand, that Friday the thirteenth is a day sacred to satanic covens that meet to send their curses and spells into the land. Any hospital worker, police officer or mental ward attendant will share the common experience that crime, accidents and generally crazy behavior increase around Friday the thirteenth or during the Friday closest to a full moon.

It may not be just superstition. The rise in accidents may result from covens meeting and sending out evil spirits to bedevil the land.

Nevertheless, we need not be afraid. The good news is that Jesus Christ has overcome the hosts of evil and will protect us.

What to Do

I do not want to overemphasize the power of the demonic realm, but we do need to be cautious, just as we would if we were considering a midnight stroll through Central Park in New York City.

As part of our prayer for protection, we can build upon the phrase in the Lord's Prayer *Deliver us from evil.* Most Scripture scholars say that a more accurate translation is *Deliver us from the evil one*—namely, Satan. This should be part of our own daily prayer. Consequently, every morning I pray a simple prayer:

9. *Florida Times-Union,* Dec. 18, 1993, p. A-9. (The *Times-Union* is the newspaper for Jacksonville, Florida, and this was an Associated Press report.)

Lord Jesus, I ask You to protect our family [whom I mention by name] from sickness, from all harm and from accidents. If any of us has been subjected to any curses, hexes or spells,[10] I declare these curses, hexes or spells null and void in the name of Jesus Christ. If any evil spirits have been sent against us, I decommission you in the name of Jesus Christ and I send you to Jesus to deal with as He will. Then, Lord, I ask You to send Your holy angels to guard and protect all of us.[11]

In no way do I suggest that this is *the* prayer to say. I offer it only as an example of the kind of prayer you can create if you have reason to believe you are the target of a local coven or someone who might be trying to curse or pray against you. Also, because I am in charge of a ministry, I pray in the same way for our staff, their immediate families and everyone associated with our work.

Having said this prayer at the beginning of the day, we do not keep focusing on possible dangers unless some special need for protection presents itself.

Curses that Come on Us through Our Own Fault

Now we come to those curses that people call down, sometimes unwittingly, on themselves. Here there is guilt involved, though the person usually did not intend to fall under a curse.

Derek Prince lists four primary categories of sin that he believes will ordinarily call down a curse upon us:

1. Worship of false gods
2. Disrespect for parents

10. To *curse* is to call upon divine or supernatural power to send injury upon someone; to *hex* is to affect as if by an evil spell or to practice witchcraft; to cast a *spell* is to repeat an incantation that is meant to have power to influence, to charm, to bewitch someone — such as to put someone under a spell. For example, a man might cast a spell to get a woman to fall in love with him, or vice versa.

11. By sad experience we have also learned to pray for our pets. Even while writing this chapter our daughter's horse, very strong and healthy, was suddenly struck by an unusual colic, and was dead within 16 hours of its onset, even though he had every possible veterinary attention. Again, who is to say that this was a result of a curse thrown our way by covens trying to get at us in any way they can? We simply do not know (although it did happen on the night of a full moon). Significantly, I had not included our pets in our daily prayer of protection.

3. Oppressing people, especially the weak (Derek states that, in his experience, abortion ordinarily brings a curse in its wake.)
4. Illicit or unnatural sex[12]

Relating to the first category of sin, the worship of false gods, we find in our culture that involvement in spiritualism is the most common example. Derek Prince believes that involvement with spiritualism invariably curses the descendants as well as the person directly involved.[13]

I will say more about being freed from spiritualism and the occult in chapter 16, "Spirits of the Occult," but for now I will note simply that involvement in the occult is connected to worshiping a false god, because we are either

1. *Seeking knowledge* that should come only from God, like seeking to peer into the future or learn about the fate of our dead loved ones. This is called divination.
2. *Desiring to control* other people or the circumstances of our own lives. Seeking power through supernatural means is called witchcraft.

Often people do not understand what they are getting into when they go to a fortune-teller or seek to manipulate someone through black magic by casting a spell. Without intending to worship a false god, the person is seeking knowledge (for example, knowledge of the future) or power (for example, to manipulate and influence a loved one) that comes legitimately only from God. A person turning to another source—for example, a palm-reader—is implicitly turning to the demonic realm for hidden knowledge.

The popular game "Dungeons and Dragons" is particularly dangerous in that it teaches contestants to win by casting spells on the other contestants. Some young people who have become immersed in the magical world of "Dungeons and Dragons" have ended up committing suicide.

Again, how do you prove this connection to people who do not believe in the reality of this spiritual world?

12. Prince, p. 76.
13. Ibid., p. 217.

In a thought-provoking judgment, Derek Prince equates legalism with worshiping a false god, in that legalism encourages us to rely on our human abilities to accomplish what should be accomplished only by God's power.

> Cursed is the one who trusts in man, who depends on flesh for his strength and whose heart turns away from the LORD. He will be like a bush in the wastelands; he will not see prosperity when it comes.
>
> Jeremiah 17:5–6

Prince says that legalism is particularly dangerous because it appeals to earnest, religious people and is, therefore, Satan's favorite tool to divert Christians.[14] He believes, furthermore, that most churches are under something like a curse because of this legalism, which results in a barren spiritual wasteland:

> *Theology* will be exalted above *revelation*; . . .
> *psychology* above *discernment*;
> *program* above *the leading of the Holy Spirit*; . . .
> *reasoning* above *the walk of faith*;
> *laws* above *love*.[15]

Derek is not attacking churches but speaking honestly from his own experience in helping start a community in 1970 in which the leaders relied on the Holy Spirit at the outset.

> All too soon, and without our discerning what was happening, the various features of the Galatians 3 "syndrome" began to manifest themselves. Our decisions and actions were no longer initiated by the Holy Spirit, but were based on an elaborate system of rules and concepts that had been devised. We continued to acknowledge the Holy Spirit, but as guests in a restaurant might acknowledge a waiter. If we felt we needed something, we would summon Him briefly. But for the most part we relied on methods and plans of our own devising.[16]

14. Ibid., pp. 93–94.
15. Ibid., p. 90.
16. Ibid., p. 94.

During this time their community became the center of the so-called shepherding discipleship controversy, and they became the target of severe criticism by several Christian leaders.

> It was not long before we were confronted by the outworking of the curse we had thus brought on ourselves. Its manifestations were characteristic of other similar developments throughout Church history. Personal relationships were ruptured; congregations were split and scattered; promising ministries were cut short or else diverted from God's purpose; once-enthusiastic Christians were blighted by frustration and disillusionment. Many abandoned their faith.[17]

For me it would be hard to say that this sad development was the result of a curse, and not just the kind of decline that often happens as a result of our human weakness and sin. But I have enough respect for Derek Prince's opinion to want to share it with you. Is the barrenness in our churches just the result of our human weakness, or is there something more? Does the renewal of our churches require that we pray to free them from the curse of legalism?

What to Do

Earlier I listed some sins that may bring a curse in their wake, such as:

1. worship of false gods;
2. disrespect for parents;
3. oppressing people, especially the weak;
4. illicit or unnatural sex.[18]

To remove the curse we bring on ourselves, two other elements need to be added to what I have already said about breaking curses.

First, we need to *repent* of what we have done. (Ideally we should confess it to God in someone else's presence.)

In addition, we need to *renounce* what we have done. This is different from repenting, in that repentance involves turning to God, admitting our guilt and asking Him to forgive us, while re-

17. Ibid., p. 95.
18. Prince, p. 76.

nouncing involves turning away from our wrong activity and taking a stand against the evil. Having done these two things, we can be cut free from the curse.

We can do this by ourselves, of course, since we are the only ones who can repent of our sins and take a stand against our former involvement. But it seems to help to have someone else pronounce God's forgiveness,[19] then cut us free from the curse.

Next, if you possess any objects connected with your involvement in occult activities, get rid of them. If you own a Ouija board, for instance, get rid of it. Just as God can use certain objects (like consecrated oil or water) to bring blessing, so Satan can use objects (like a ring or amulet) to bring evil on people, especially if the object has received a witch doctor's version of a blessing.

Sorcery is the use of cursed objects to influence people. I remember praying for deliverance for a man in Nigeria who had gone berserk in a prayer meeting. When we started to pray for him, one of his hands began to shake uncontrollably. When we looked more closely, we found he was wearing a strange ring. He told us a ju-ju doctor had given it to him. We asked him to take it off, and when he did, the shaking stopped.

All this grim material about curses need not depress us. Again, it is like taking out the garbage—unpleasant, but somebody has to do it. The good news is that Jesus became a curse for us by hanging on the tree, dying outside Jerusalem in order to free us from every curse, especially the curse of the Law. Jesus can transform every curse that may have touched your life, changing it into love and blessing.

> Christ has redeemed us from the curse of the Law's condemnation, by himself becoming a curse for us when he was crucified. For the scripture is plain: Cursed is everyone that hangeth on a tree. God's purpose is therefore plain: that the blessing promised to Abraham might reach the gentiles through Christ Jesus, and the promise of the Spirit might become ours by faith.
>
> Galatians 3:13–14, Phillips

In the next chapter we will look at the human (rather than demonic) variation of curses.

---

19. In churches in the Catholic-Orthodox tradition, this would be through the sacrament of reconciliation (formerly called *confession*).

8

Curselike Judgments
and Ties that Bind

W hat I will share now may help free someone who reads this to become the work of art God created him to be. "We are God's workmanship, created in Christ Jesus to do good works, which God prepared in advance for us to do" (Ephesians 2:10).

In regard to the judgments we are discussing in this chapter, I am not sure we are always dealing with the demonic. I am inclined to believe that for the most part we are dealing with natural emotional forces and false mental impressions. These are like curses but on the human rather than demonic level. (Yet some of these emotional bondages can be indwelt by demonic forces that strive to make their deadly grip permanent.)

Curses on the Human Plane

We have all experienced the effects of other people's judgments and feelings (positive and negative) toward us—their love, hate or simply their apathy.

When I face an enthusiastic audience, they lift me up and fill me with a joyful, energetic desire to share what I know with them. Their response makes me *want* to speak to them, and I speak better than I would ordinarily.

When I face a hostile group, on the other hand, something in me withers and makes me want to disappear—or face up to them and fight. I go ahead and speak, of course, in spite of how I feel, but so much energy goes into the struggle that my talk loses vitality and effectiveness.

You, too, must have experienced something similar. There is no way to avoid it. We are deeply affected by what others think and feel about us. If we were not, we would not be human. These judgments are like blessings or curses directed our way from the hearts and minds of others, especially relatives, friends and fellow workers closest to us.

Jesus was affected by the reactions of the people He tried to help, too. He wondered what happened to the other nine when only one leper out of ten healed came back to thank Him (Luke 17:17–18). And He cried over Jerusalem because the people did not recognize the time of His visitation (Matthew 23:37–39). Jesus grew frustrated when the Pharisees reproved the crowds for waving palm fronds and shouting, "Blessed is the king who comes" (Luke 19:38), and He retorted, "If they keep quiet, the stones will cry out" (verse 40).

Jesus responded at times with sorrow, at other times with anger, to the false judgments directed at Him.

Judgments that Act Like Curses

Some judgments that others make about us have the same effect in our lives as curses, even though they are on the human plane.

Judgments of Parents and Authority Figures

When we were little, our parents took on something of the authority of God, and we absorbed their judgments as if these judgments were true. (Psychologists call these judgments *parental injunctions*.) Even when children rebel against false parental judgments (judgments like "You're stupid and will never amount to anything"), something deep down in the child believes it.

These negative judgments—curses, really—may slice into the child like a knife and remain for a lifetime, until Jesus frees him and replaces the lie with a true estimate of who he truly is. These distortions can destroy the child's self-esteem. (It is significant that *shame*, a feeling of basic worthlessness, is now seen as the root of all kinds of addiction.) And this "hole in the soul" usually results from the child's belief that he has been rejected by his parents.

Take, for example, the history of transvestite Jerry Leach.[1] His mother often said, "I wish you were a girl so you could take over my beauty shop when you grow up." When Jerry started to try on dresses at age four, even his father encouraged him: "You're better-looking as a girl." His dad further confused him by accusing him of being a homosexual. (He was not; he simply wanted to dress like a woman.) Later Jerry married, but his sexual identity was confused; he longed at some deep level of his being to be a woman. His mother's statements that she would have preferred a daughter acted like a curse: He was trying to please her by becoming a girl.[2]

The good news, of course, is that Jesus can free us from bondages like this. Here is how He freed Jerry:

> Charlene (my wife) and I spent some time with Rita Bennett. When Rita prayed with me, I received a special visitation from Christ. During this prayer I was called into manhood (masculinity) as Christ approached me on the front porch of our home when I was three years of age.
>
> I saw the following. Jesus came to me as I was standing there. I had been playing with my neighborhood girlfriend Carol. She was extending her baby doll to me.
>
> I was making the decision that was to affect the rest of my life's choices.
>
> But the event took a different twist than it did some 47 years past, for Jesus was within the situation, standing beside me. I looked up into His face. Such a calmness and strength about Him! He smiled and said, "Jerry, I have something here for you. It's much better for you to play with this. It's okay to be a truck driver . . . a man. It's okay because that's what I want you to be."
>
> He then held out to me a large wood (obviously homemade) red pickup truck. It was the neatest I'd seen. I took it from His large hand and placed it on the floor to play with it. I rolled it back and forth. It was very heavy. Jesus then began to make the sounds

1. This account is taken from Rita Bennett's newsletter, *In Touch and Emotionally Free*, Fall '93; Christian Renewal Association, P.O. Box 576, Edmonds, WA 98020-0576.

2. The tragedy of such stories is that often the parents do not realize how seriously their children may take their off-the-cuff remarks. Jerry's mother and dad probably had no idea they contributed to his becoming a transvestite.

of an engine, and to my surprise sat down beside me in order to share the fun with me. He was obviously having fun with me. He rolled the truck back and forth to me, encouraging me to make the same kind of engine sounds. I did. At one point He was lying on His left side, getting more and more at eye level with me. His smile and laughter were beyond description.

Then Jesus got up and clasped my hand. We were going somewhere. Carol was still playing with her doll. Before Jesus and I stepped off the porch, He turned and took hold of me at the waist, lifting me abruptly above His head, suspending me there for what seemed a long time. I was able to view this from both within and outside of my body. At one moment I saw what appeared to be a still snapshot of the scene. And then I was looking down into the kindest face I have ever seen. His eyes were filled with joy in me. His arms were so strong. I thought, *How can He hold me in the air so long above His head?* It seemed as though His hands completely encompassed my waist. And the incredible strength! It radiated from His forearms and into His fingertips and into my arched body.

Then He set me down firmly on my feet, saying, "Come on, let's go for a walk." I bent down to pick up my red truck and took hold of His hand. I looked back and saw Carol, still in her feminine imaginary world, playing with her doll. She waved good-bye.

Ahead of us was a long sidewalk. There were large trees on either side of the walk, providing something of a tunnel-like effect. I walked with an inner confidence that I had never before known. As I looked up into the trees, I could feel the truck tucked close to my right side, while my left hand was securely fastened in Christ's firm grip. The sun was shining and I was happy. So happy! . . .

We arrived home from the conference late Saturday night. . . . Sunday afternoon I decided to go to the nearest gas station to fill up. While there, the Holy Spirit directed me to go to the antique shop on the next block, saying, "There is something I want you to see. It's a gift for you." I went and found on the counter an old, wood, red pickup truck just like the one I saw during the time of inner healing. I bought it for $10.00 (but would have taken out a loan in order to obtain it), and it now sits in a prominent place in our home, symbolizing the Lord's goodness.

I have counseled many people who have been badly wounded by similar negative or false judgments uttered by sometimes well-meaning authority figures. It is incredible how a single statement, sometimes made in jest, can be absorbed into a child's very being. Adults, too, if they are sensitive, can receive a harsh criticism and make it their own, turning it into a festering wound.

Each person's story is different. We need to be sensitive in listening and deciding how best to pray. At times people have forgotten a key incident in their lives or dismissed it as unimportant.

Judith is a good example. She always had a slight problem with her self-image, especially concerning her body. Although she was a lovely, striking-looking woman, she would turn aside compliments about her appearance, somewhat embarrassed by them. Then, when she was thirty, she attended a conference in Staten Island, New York, at which everyone was asked to forgive at least one person who had hurt him. The conference director asked the group to ask the Lord which people they especially needed to forgive.

When Judith did this, an apparently insignificant incident from grade school days popped into her mind. She was on the point of dismissing it when further instruction was given: "No matter how insignificant it may seem, pray about it."

Judith's "insignificant" incident had happened twenty years before, after she had been badly embarrassed by her teacher in the classroom. Now it was recess and she had gone to the cloakroom to cry, wrapping herself in her mother's coat for comfort. Then she decided to summon her courage, go out onto the playground and face the other kids.

Just as she got to the door, she heard some boys out in the corridor teasing the most popular boy in Judith's class, a boy Judith liked. They were kidding him and accused him of liking her, Judith. At last, fed up by their teasing, he blew up and exclaimed, "Nobody likes Judith. She's too fat and ugly."

Upon hearing that devastating remark, Judith disappeared back into the cloakroom.

At that time in her life Judith *was* chubby. But even when she grew taller, lost weight and became extremely popular, she felt vaguely ashamed about her appearance.

Now, twenty years later, this shaming experience resurfaced. So Judith asked a friend at the conference to pray with her to forgive the boy who had hurled that judgment of *ugly* at her. She thought she had forgiven him long ago, but now when she tried to say, "I forgive you," the words stuck in her throat. But at last she was able to forgive. She cried and something deep within her broke.

Ever since that prayer time fifteen years ago, she has been able to accept compliments about her appearance without turning them aside. Another fascinating side effect was that she lost five pounds that weekend without changing her diet in the slightest. And she has never regained the weight.[3]

People can pick up on all kinds of judgments: "You're a bad boy!" "You're ugly." "It's too bad you're a girl [or a boy]." "You'll never amount to anything." "Why can't you do anything like your older brother [or sister]?" "You act like a fairy!" These are among the thousands of statements that children hear, accept and proceed to live out. It is no coincidence that much of the Twelve Step program deals with shame. The power of Jesus to break these false judgments is a key to healing the deep-seated self-hatred that burdens many people in our world.

A poignant example is a priest who took a leave of absence even though he was successful as a pastor, esteemed by his bishop and beloved by his people. It was a mystery even to him why he took the sabbatical; he just knew he had to get out. When I counseled with him, it came to me to ask if there was any particular phrase he could remember his father saying. He answered immediately: "If you can't do a thing perfectly, don't do it at all!"

One thing you cannot do perfectly, of course, is be a priest or minister. His father had unintentionally burdened him with a lifetime of guilt. So we prayed to break the hold that his father's statement still had on him, that ancient perfectionistic lie. Shortly afterward he returned to his successful work as a pastor.

Self-Imposed Vows

Sometimes it is not other people's mistaken views that curse us, but our own. When painful events overtake us, we may be tempted to avoid that part of life that has caused us so much pain.

If you have been hurt by having been deserted by someone you love, you may be tempted to say, "If it hurts this much, I'm never going to love again." Or when things look dark and the joy

---

3. This is one of three experiences of immediate weight loss, through no apparent cause except prayer, that I have encountered in 25 years of ministry.

of living disappears, you may groan, "I wish I were dead." When you live through an extended time of depression, you may even feel like driving your car into a telephone pole and ending it all. (If such a desire strikes you, take it back immediately and ask Jesus to counter this self-destructive wish with a desire to live.)

Some years ago in Peru, our team prayed with a missionary, a Catholic sister, who had a common problem: She was slightly depressed and never experienced much joy about anything. When we talked with her, we could find little wrong in her life that had not been dealt with. But the next day a member of our team, Barbara Shlemon, had a vision in which she saw a girl about eleven years old holding a dog in her lap. This suggested nothing in particular to Barbara, who shared it with the sister and asked if it meant anything to her. At once the sister thought of an incident she had not remembered in years.

When she was about eleven, her best friend was her dog. But because her pet was getting old and feeble, her parents had it taken away and put to sleep. For the adults this made sense, but for the eleven-year-old girl it was devastating. Her parents, the people she most trusted, had killed her best friend. Since loving her dog had caused so much pain, she determined never, ever to trust or love again.

This vow shut down the flow of her life. It was as if she had turned the faucet halfway down so that the water of life flowed in a trickle. She asked us to pray that Jesus would break that crippling childhood vow.

The next day she sent us a joyful note: "Life breaks through! Alleluia!"

How to Pray for these Judgments and Vows

Praying to break these judgments and vows is relatively simple.

If a person has received someone else's false judgment and accepted it into his being:

1. First ask him to forgive the person who uttered it.
2. Then, like breaking a curse, say something like, "In the name of Jesus Christ and by the sword of the Spirit, I cut you free from this false judgment of _____ and declare it null and void."

3. If you sense that some demonic force is hooking into this false judgment (such as a spirit of rejection), command the spirit to leave.

If the person needs to be freed of a vow he has pronounced on himself [4]:

1. Ask him to explicitly *repent* of _____.
2. Break the vow: "In the name of Jesus Christ I break this vow of _____ and declare it null and void, no longer able to influence you. By the sword of the Spirit I cut you free from this vow and all its effects."
3. Again, if you discern the presence of any evil spirits, command them to leave.
4. Finally, and most important, ask Jesus to restore the part of the person's life that was most wounded by the judgment or vow. If he ever said, "I want to die," ask Jesus to pour His life and health into him. If he was told he was ugly, pray for God to open his eyes to the beauty of his creation, and perhaps read with him pertinent sections of Scripture, like Psalm 139. Pray to replace everything negative that has been part of his life with whatever is lifegiving, noble and beautiful in the life of Jesus.

It is amazing how often Jesus appears to a person in a vision and takes over the prayer in a most creative way (just as He appeared to Jerry, the transvestite) and does exactly those things that break the false judgment (in Jerry's case, giving him the red truck and affirming his masculinity).

Harmful Spiritual Identifications

We are all familiar with overly dependent relationships (codependence) that can harm people spiritually and psychologically.

Spiritual and Psychological Ties

Perhaps the most easily recognizable example of harmful spiritual identification is an adult man who is still overly depen-

---

4. These self-imposed vows are usually not carefully thought out or written down; they may even be simple, *unspoken* decisions that the person has made.

dent on his mother. So common is it that we even have a term for it: *Mama's boy.* What was beautiful and appropriate at the age of eight becomes distorted at the age of 38. He (and she, too) has never cut the apron strings. Part of this overly dependent relationship occurs on the human, psychological plane. The man needs to grow up and take steps to change the relationship into a more adult, mature, independent one.

It is possible for daughters to overidentify with either their fathers or their mothers; and occasionally, sons with their fathers. These are only a few of the psychological ties that need to change as a person matures.

Yet in some mysterious way, there can also be a spiritual tie that needs to be severed through prayer. My dear friend the Rev. Tommy Tyson is sometimes enabled to see, while he is praying with a person, the face or figure of another person superimposed, crowding into the person's space. When this happens, he questions the person to see if there is some spiritual or psychological bondage that needs to be cut.

A dependent relationship need not be just with one of our parents. There are many kinds of relationships, especially sexual ones, that may crowd out a person's rightful independence and they need to be cut loose through prayer.

Sexual Ties

The best example of this is the spiritual identification that seems to take place when two people engage in sex together. Something more takes place than the mere joining of two bodies; some kind of spiritual bonding happens as well.

> Do you not know that your bodies are members of Christ himself? Shall I then take the members of Christ and unite them with a prostitute? Never! Do you not know that he who unites himself with a prostitute is one with her in body? For it is said, "The two will become one flesh." But he who unites himself with the Lord is one with him in spirit.
>
> 1 Corinthians 6:15–17

Paul does not say exactly what kind of union takes place when a man becomes one flesh with a prostitute, but he seems to teach that something takes place in the spiritual realm. We know for a certainty that the union of man and wife is special since it symbolizes the union of Christ and His Church. It is not just a joining of bodies but of spirits.

Again, Tommy Tyson was the first I ever heard speak about the need to break sexual-spiritual ties. While we were speaking in Bolivia in 1970, a missionary asked how to answer teenagers regarding what is wrong with premarital sex. Tommy responded that whenever anyone engages in a full sexual relationship, a permanent bond is set up that remains until it is broken—not by the couple's breaking up, but by something like a prayer for deliverance. If a man has had a sexual relationship with six women before he marries, he brings six people besides himself into the marriage bed and spiritual confusion is brought into that marriage from the beginning. (Women usually seem to have a deeper appreciation of these relationships than men, and sense these spiritual dimensions more profoundly.) If this is true, it helps explain why so many marriages break up in an age of promiscuity.

It is an excellent idea for pastors to pray (in a private setting) for a kind of deliverance for each partner entering a marriage. Ideally confession, repentance and forgiveness precede being set free from an entangling past life.

Praying for someone to be set free from undue physical, psychological or spiritual bondage is relatively easy. Simply form a prayer under the guidance of the Holy Spirit, asking Jesus to sever each previous sexual liaison. You might pray like this for one of the partners planning to marry: "In the name of Jesus Christ, I set you free from any physical, psychological or spiritual bond that remains within you, caused by your past sexual relationships." Then pray to bless and set free those past lovers. Last of all pray that the person (or couple) receive the gift of loving faithfully, and be filled with the love of Jesus and empowered by the Holy Spirit to live out their commitment together in great joy.

9

Who Can Pray for Deliverance?

There are many reasons you may feel you cannot pray for deliverance. If you are Roman Catholic or Episcopalian, you probably have the impression that only a priest should do such a thing (a holy priest at that!). And if you belong to a conservative independent congregation or mainline Protestant denomination, your church leaders may frown on your involvement in deliverance since they may not even believe in the possibility of demonic infestation. Besides all that, if you have seen any movies like *The Exorcist*, you may be scared out of your wits by the prospect of praying for exorcism!

But in the Church it has not always been so.

In the Early Church

In the early days of Christianity, all believers were assumed capable of praying for deliverance.

Witness to this belief is the end of Mark's Gospel, where the first of the five signs to "accompany those who believe" is that "in my name they will drive out demons" (Mark 16:17). Notice that those who perform deliverance here are not necessarily apostles or elders but ordinary believers.

Then, too, after Jesus sent out the Twelve, He sent out 72 others to proclaim that "the Kingdom of God is near" (Luke 10:11). When they returned they were amazed that "even the demons submit to us in your name" (verse 17). They were rejoicing so much that Jesus had to tone down their enthusiasm by telling them to "rejoice [instead] that your names are written in heaven" (verse 20).

The ministry of exorcism continued in the early Church. After Jesus' death Philip, the deacon ordained to oversee the distribution of bread, evangelized Samaria and made a great impact: "With shrieks, evil spirits came out of many" (Acts 8:7).

After the death of the apostles, exorcisms were carried out with no mention of any special class of Christians to whom the ministry of deliverance was restricted. In fact, the Church father Origen (martyred around A.D. 253) mentioned that many Christians cast out demons "merely by prayer and simple adjurations which the plainest person can use. Because, for the most part, it is unlettered [or *illiterate*] persons who perform this work." Origen added that exorcism does "not require the power and wisdom of those who are mighty in argument."[1]

Justin Martyr (who wrote still earlier, around A.D. 150) states that "many Christian men" exorcise demons that cannot be cast out by pagans.[2] Women cast out demons, too, women like St. Eugenia in the third century.[3]

Incidentally, both Justin Martyr and Irenaeus (who wrote around A.D. 180) believed that Jews could perform exorcisms in the name of the God of Abraham, Isaac and Jacob.[4]

Tertullian (who wrote around A.D. 200) went so far as to say that the noblest Christian life is "to exorcise evil spirits—to perform cures . . . to live to God."[5] In his book *The Shows* he tried to convince pagans that there was more true enjoyment in casting out evil spirits and healing the sick than in attending the pagan plays and shows of the day. (Imagine a bishop encouraging his flock today to cast out evil spirits because it is more fun than seeing an R-rated movie!)

In all those early days we find no evidence that a Christian had to be ordained to cast out evil spirits. It was possible for *any* Christian to perform an exorcism.

1. Origen, *Against Celsus*, vii, 4 and 17.
2. Justin Martyr, *Apology II—To the Senate*, vi.
3. Evelyn Frost, *Christian Healing* (London: A. R. Mowbray & Co., 1940), p. 97.
4. Ibid., p. 58.
5. Tertullian, *De Spectaculis*, para. 29.

Nevertheless, Paul did not mention exorcism among the various manifestations (gifts) of the Holy Spirit enumerated in 1 Corinthians 12—manifestations like "gifts of healing" (verse 9). Some believe that the gift of miracles (verse 10) might refer to exorcism. It makes sense that, just as some people are specially gifted by God with gifts of healing, other people might have gifts of exorcism. Although this power is not reserved for a special class, some believers receive it to a greater degree. [6]

Some early Church writers recognized that some people were specially gifted to perform exorcism, and they compared it to the other charisms (or gifts) listed by Paul. Irenaeus writes that:

> Some drive out demons really and truly . . . some have foreknowledge of the future, visions and prophetic utterances; others, by the laying on of hands, heal the sick and restore them to health; and before now, as I said, dead men have actually been raised and have remained with us for many years.[7]

It seems, then, that even though any Christian in the early Church might be called on to cast out demons, some were recognized as more gifted by the Spirit in the ministry of exorcism. It was like today: All of us are called on at various times to pray for the sick, yet some are especially gifted as healers. When Paul asks, "Do all have gifts of healing?" (1 Corinthians 12:30), the implied answer is no. So it is reasonable to expect that some Christians will be more gifted in exorcism.

The Jesuit theologian Francisco Suarez (1548–1617) pointed out that in the early Church, the power to cast out demons was given to all the faithful, both men and women. He also believed that the ability to exorcise the demon from a truly possessed person belonged to the order of miracles and should not be attempted "without the special inspiration of the Holy Spirit."[8]

6. George Montague, *Christian Initiation and Baptism in the Holy Spirit* (Collegeville, Minn.: Liturgical Press, 1991), p. 13.

7. Frank Darling, *Biblical Healing: Hebrew and Christian Roots* (Boulder, Col.: Vista Publications, 1989), p. 181. This quote from Irenaeus' *Refutation and Overthrow of Knowledge Falsely So Called* is contained in Eusebius' *Ecclesiastical History*, Books 5 and 7 (written in the early fourth century).

8. Francisco Suarez, *Opera Omnia*, Vol. 14, p. 742.

The Narrowing of the Ministry

Over the course of centuries, several factors led to the gradual narrowing of exorcism to a specially appointed group of exorcists. We can easily see why. For one thing, it is a difficult ministry. Even the apostles were unable to exorcise the epileptic demoniac, and they were rebuked by Jesus for being insufficiently prepared through prayer and fasting (Matthew 17:20–21).

In more severe cases, insufficient spiritual protection can be dangerous to the exorcist. And if the exorcist does not know what she is doing, it can be dangerous to the person being ministered to. Victims escaping from satanic covens are aware of this and afraid of approaching just any priest or minister for help. Their latter state could be worse than their first.

The Order of Exorcist

As a result of these dangers, Cyprian wrote in the third century about a false prophetess who acted as if she were inspired by the Holy Spirit. Then an exorcist showed up, "a man approved," who discerned that she was really inspired by a wicked spirit, and not the Holy Spirit.[9] Writes Evelyn Frost:

> This shows us that in the time of Cyprian there was an order of exorcists apparently regularized and approved by the Church. It is noteworthy that none of the "very many brethren," in spite of their strong faith, attempted to exorcise this woman, nor one of the priests, but they appealed to the exorcist. This may be an indication that by the middle of the third century, the practice of exorcism in the Church had been open to abuse and required regularizing.[10]

Another fascinating factor related to the narrowing of exorcism to a specially appointed group of exorcists is that in the early days, adult baptism (usually at Easter or Pentecost) was preceded by a long preparation period, and exorcisms were always performed as part of that preparation. (It was assumed that most, if not all, pagans required freeing from demonic influence.) Sometimes these exorcisms were performed every day during the preparation period.

9. Cyprian, Epistle LXXIV, p. 10.
10. Frost, p. 60.

When exorcism was attached to baptism, the appointed offi-
cials (rather than charismatic individuals) who did the teaching
began to perform this daily exorcism, accompanied by the laying on of hands. Toward the end of the lengthy preparation, on
Holy Saturday, the bishop himself would cast out the alien
spirits.[11]

During the same period of history, those with the gift of healing did not need hands laid on them in ordination. All the evidence needed for them to be regarded as healers was whether
people actually got healed![12]

The next stage came about in the mid-third century when
Pope Cornelius mentioned *exorcist* as an order among the Roman clergy.[13] A ritual used for ordaining exorcists in Rome in the
tenth century went like this:

> When the exorcist is ordained, let him receive from the hand of
> the bishop the book in which the exorcisms are written, while the
> bishop says to him, "Receive and memorize it, and possess the
> power of laying hands on those agitated by demons, whether
> baptized or catechumens."[14]

Notice that the Church acknowledged the possibility of baptized persons needing exorcism, in contrast to the common belief held today (in Pentecostal churches and elsewhere) that no
Christian can possibly need deliverance, only pagans.

Notice, too, that services by the tenth century were becoming
increasingly formalized—"by the book," as it were. Already the
exorcists may have been losing out on the creative possibility of
working individually with each demonized person and making
up prayers tailored to that person's needs, instead of repeating
what was in the book.

One of the good things, though, was that the minor order of
exorcist was conferred before the three so-called major orders
(priesthood, diaconate and subdiaconate), so that an exorcist

11. All this is described in the *Apostolic Tradition of Hippolytus* written in Rome in
the early third century. Compare *The Rite of Exorcism* compiled by Craig Karpel (New
York: Berkley Medallion Books, 1975), pp. 144–145 (chapter on "Demon Possession" by
Henry Ansgar Kelly).
12. Ibid., p. 145.
13. Ibid.
14. Ibid., p. 146.

did not have to be a priest. The other three minor orders were acolyte, lector and porter (or keeper of the gate). Clearly these were not lofty, sacramental positions; and traditionally all these functions have been performed by laypersons.

Increasing Restrictions

Nevertheless, the exercise of deliverance ministry became more and more restricted (as things usually go in the history of the Church), until in the Middle Ages the priest became the normal minister of exorcism. Finally in our own century, in the time of Pope Pius XI, the ministry of exorcism was limited to the priest.[15]

Much of this restriction was caused by centering on possession and on the increasing rarity of exorcism in European culture. Perhaps, too, the Roman Catholic Church was embarrassed by the excesses of the Inquisition and the burning of witches. In 1614, for example, the official *Roman Ritual* of the Roman Catholic Church declared that the exorcist should not easily believe that anyone is possessed, and it gave some highly unusual symptoms to help tell whether a person was really possessed. These signs of possession included the ability to speak in an unknown tongue, the revelation of distant or unknown things, and the manifestation of other extraordinary powers (such as levitation).[16] Since these signs are so unusual, the diagnosis of possession naturally became rare, and removed exorcism from ordinary church life.

The Protestant Reformers, for the most part, deemphasized exorcism or did away with it altogether. Most Calvinists believed that exorcism was valid only in the early days of Christianity. Exorcism was connected in the Reformers' minds with Popish superstition; and although the Anglicans maintained a slim belief in a need for exorcism, their 1604 convocation passed a law "which forbids any Anglican clergyman, without the express consent of his bishop obtained beforehand, to use exorcism in any fashion under any pretext, on pain of being counted an impostor and deposed from the ministry."

15. Ibid., pp. 149–150.
16. Ibid., p. 151.

136

In that restrictive atmosphere, the question of who should perform an exorcism would hardly come up. The question, rather, would be: Is there ever a need for exorcism?

Yet a slim belief did remain. In the Catholic Church, for instance, there persisted a recognition that Christians who were not possessed might still need to be freed from oppression;[17] and theologians distinguished between *solemn exorcism*, a formal liturgical rite that was

1. Only for a *possessed* person
2. Performed only by a *priest*
3. Performed with the permission of the *bishop*

and *private exorcism*, in which a minister (including a layperson) could pray in his own name for someone oppressed by evil spirits.

St. Alphonsus Liguori, the most prestigious moral theologian of the seventeenth century, wrote that "private exorcism is permissible to all Christians."[18] Most Catholic moral theologians up to our own day recommend that priests occasionally pray quietly, even silently, for private exorcism (what we would call deliverance), especially in the confessional.[19] Writes the Rev. James McManus:

> St. Alphonsus stated the Catholic tradition when he said that everyone may exorcise privately, but only the priest, with permission of the bishop, may exorcise solemnly. Since this is the Catholic tradition we have to ask ourselves how we lost sight of it and why it is that exorcism has become such a bone of contention in the modern Church. We lost sight of our own tradition, it seems to me, because we lost sight of the basic distinctions that the moralists of the past made. We reduced all exorcism to solemn exorcism, for which the permission of the bishop is required, and as the bishop appoints only holy and prudent priests for such an exorcism, most high priests simply presumed that they would never have to perform an exorcism.[20]

17. Ibid., p. 150.
18. St. Alphonsus Liguori, *Theologia Moralis*, III, p. 492, as quoted in *Deliverance Prayer* by Matthew and Dennis Linn (New York: Paulist Press, 1981), p. 244.
19. Appendix A, "Exorcism in Catholic Moral Theology" by James McManus, C.S.R., in *Deliverance Prayer*, pp. 242-251.
20. Ibid., p. 246.

Yet some reputable theologians continued to state that no special permission of the bishop was needed to perform a private exorcism. This left the door cracked open a little bit, a door that has opened wider in recent times as the deliverance ministry has been revived.

Still, the deliverance ministry has, over the centuries, been gradually shut down. In Protestant churches it has been almost abolished since, for the most part, few believe in its necessity. In the Catholic tradition—Roman, Orthodox and Anglican—belief has remained in Satan and the need for exorcism, but in the last three centuries the ministry has been severely restricted. In 1709, for instance, in a reaction against the excesses and abuses of the Inquisition, the Vatican banned five manuals of exorcism, and in 1725 it instituted extensive controls.[21]

In 1972 Pope Paul VI dropped the four minor orders, including exorcist, as steps on the way to priestly ordination, with the assumption that *exorcist* was now obsolete as an order.[22]

Part of the reason for this dropoff of belief in the need for exorcism was that experts in the field, like Fr. De Tonquedec, the official exorcist in Paris for nearly half a century, claimed he was never convinced he had run up against a real case of possession. Instead, he said he thought that psychotics produced the symptoms of possession through their subconscious and through all the ceremonies surrounding exorcism. "Call the devil and you'll see him; or rather not him, but a portrait made up of the sick man's ideas of him" was De Tonquedec's evaluation of his own work as official exorcist.[23]

Still, in 1972 Pope Paul VI stoutly upheld the traditional belief in Satan's existence:

Evil is not merely a lack of something, but an effective agent, a living, spiritual being, perverted and perverting. A terrible reality. . . . It is contrary to the teaching of the Bible and the Church to refuse to recognize the existence of such a reality.[24]

21. *A Manual of Exorcism* (Transl. from a Spanish manuscript of about 1720), (Hispanic Soc. of Amer.; distributed by Interbook Inc., New York, 1975), p. 7.
22. *The Rite of Exorcism, Op.Cit.*, p. 147.
23. Ibid., p. 160.
24. "Deliver Us From Evil": General Audience of Pope Paul VI, Nov. 15, 1972. Reported in *L'Osservatore Romano*, Nov. 23, 1972.

Reawakening

Counter to the dying out of exorcism in the mainline churches, Catholic and Protestant, came the reawakening by Pentecostals of the supernatural gifts at the beginning of the twentieth century, including the power to cast out evil spirits. The baptism of the Spirit, praying in tongues, prophecy, healing and deliverance were all awakened in a powerful way—not without problems, but certainly awakened.

Emphasizing the priesthood of all believers, they did not separate the duties of clergy and laity in praying for deliverance.[25] As we still see in groups like Full Gospel Business Men's Fellowship, laypersons pray regularly for deliverance. But as time went on, Pentecostal churches began to exercise more authority, with only evangelists, pastors and missionaries actually performing most of the exorcisms.

The rediscovery of the need for many people to be freed from demonic influence culminated in mass exorcisms—whole congregations of people under the ministry of nondenominational leaders like Derek Prince and Don Basham who taught extensively on the subject of spiritual warfare.[26] Their mass exorcism ministry in the 1960s and '70s attracted a large measure of criticism in charismatic circles, and David DuPlessis refused at times to appear on the same platform with them as a protest to their group exorcisms. Their position, though, was that exorcism had been neglected so long, and so many people needed it, that they had to do something, regardless of criticism, to help the many victims of demonic oppression. We were, as they saw it, in a crisis situation.

Just as the baptism of the Spirit and a lively understanding of the ministry of laypersons spilled out into the mainline churches through the influence of pioneers like the Episcopalian Rev. Dennis Bennett, so the gifts of healing and deliverance were introduced to mainline churches through leaders like Mrs. Agnes Sanford and the Rev. Alfred Price (one of the founders of the Order of St. Luke).

25. *Dictionary of Pentecostal and Charismatic Movements*, article on "Exorcism" by L.G. McClung, Jr. (Grand Rapids: Zondervan, 1988) p. 291.
26. An excellent book still in print is Don Basham's *Deliver Us From Evil* (Grand Rapids: Chosen Books, 1972).

Nevertheless, the deliverance ministry has been received by mainline denominations with more caution and criticism than the baptism in the Spirit, healing and even praying in tongues. Deliverance is feared because of the disgraceful memories of the witch hunts of medieval Europe and the Salem witchcraft trials, coupled with recent horror stories of failed exorcisms. In Germany twenty years ago, for example, two priests failed in their exorcism of a young woman, who ended up starving herself to death. The two priests and their imprudent exorcism were blamed for her death.

In any case, caution rules in all the traditional churches. In some we even see a basic disbelief in the existence of the demonic realm.

So What Is the Answer?

The best solution, I believe, to the problem of who should perform deliverance is that we not be tied down to a particular order of exorcist in the Church. The reason for the Church's caution is real: Not every headstrong zealot should exercise the ministry of deliverance. Some supervision and authority are needed.

But since deliverance is a ministry that usually needs to be exercised without delay, Christians with a gift for it and who often pray for deliverance should have general permission from their church authorities, whom they should keep informed about what they are doing.[27]

Unfortunately, in most places we cannot turn to religious authorities. Most have no experience themselves, either practical or theoretical, in praying for deliverance. Nor do they understand it, because spiritual warfare (much less exorcism) is simply not taught in most mainline seminaries. Furthermore, Satan is regarded in many seminaries as merely a poetic symbol of evil rather than a real, personal entity. So you have a classical example of the blind leading the blind.

Yet the Church authorities are right: There are in the deliverance ministry practical difficulties and abuses. Often the people with experience are unlettered theologically and may not be able to explain what they do to the satisfaction of church leaders. And—what is really dangerous—some embrace simplistic

27. Michael Harper, *Spiritual Warfare* (London: Hodder & Stoughton, 1970), p. 62. These suggestions are, in fact, carried out by the Church of England.

solutions ("All depression is caused by demons") and do great harm to suffering people.

In the present deteriorated situation, there is no perfect solution to our dilemma. But we can lay out a few guidelines: Everyone *can* pray for deliverance, but not everyone *should!*

Our Involvement on Three Levels of Spiritual Warfare

To solve this practical problem, we need to be keenly aware of three levels of spiritual warfare, with varying degrees of involvement by Christians:

Protection

First, we *all* need to know how to protect ourselves and our families against the attacks of evil spirits coming from outside ourselves and how to drive off their attacks.

Simple Deliverance

Second, *most* Christians may be called on to pray for people who are lightly oppressed or infested by evil spirits, and *some* will be called on to pray frequently for those who are not possessed or severely demonized. Most Christian counselors should be able to pray for their clients when they find evidence of demonic infestation.

There are, however, a number of Christians who should *not* pray for this kind of simple deliverance:

1. Those who are unusually sensitive and are themselves subject to spiritual attack
2. Those who cannot discriminate between the need for deliverance and the need for inner healing
3. Those who enjoy power trips and whose zeal to fight Satan comes across as anger at the victim asking for help
4. Those with insufficient experience and knowledge

There are many other indications that, except in emergency situations, a particular person may not be equipped to pray for deliverance. The problem is, we tend to be blind to our own faults and may think we are called to pray for deliverance when we are blind to the damage we can cause. We tend to remember the successes we have had and conveniently disregard our failures.

For this reason, we all need to be accountable to someone who can freely call us to task and tell us when we are unbalanced, erratic or even harming people who have already been chewed up and hurt.

Heavy Deliverance

The third level of spiritual warfare involves cases in which the person is severely demonized—usually when there has been involvement in the occult. A *few* Christians with a ministry of deliverance can pray for these cases of major demonic infestation.

Here Church tradition has wisely exercised caution and described the exorcist as someone who is

1. *Holy,* because the evil spirits often know our unknown sins and can reveal them in public (unless they have been confessed and forgiven)
2. *Wise and experienced in deliverance*
3. *Endowed with the charism of deliverance*
4. *Empowered by the Spirit,* because when we are dealing with powerful demons, we need special spiritual power inaugurated by the baptism of the Spirit to minister without fear of being invaded by the demons ourselves

The Need for Empowerment

There is, indeed, always a danger that the exorcist will be hurt in a heavy exorcism. But some people take this danger too far. The title of Malachi Martin's book *Hostage to the Devil* indicates his personal belief that the exorcist becomes a hostage by getting involved in this warfare:

Every exorcist must engage in a one-to-one confrontation, personal and bitter, with pure evil. Once engaged, the exorcism cannot be called off. There will and must always be a victor and a vanquished. And no matter what the outcome, the contact is in part fatal for the exorcist. He must consent to a dreadful and irreparable pillage of his deepest self. Something dies in him. Some part of his humanness will wither from such close contact with the opposite of all humanness—the essence of evil; and it is rarely if ever revitalized. No return will be made to him for his loss.[28]

28. Malachi Martin, *Hostage to the Devil* (New York: Reader's Digest Press, 1976), p. 10.

I personally view this as too grim a picture of exorcism, one that surrenders to Satan's desire to intimidate us. If it is true that the exorcist loses life every time he gets into combat, or that, as in the case of *The Exorcist*, two priests lose their lives freeing one girl from Satan (in chess terms, losing two pieces in return for one), who would want to get into such a ministry? Beyond that, what does such a view say about the power of God? Who is stronger—Jesus Christ, who has shackled all the principalities and powers in His triumphal procession, or Satan?

The people I know in the deliverance ministry have to face various spiritual attacks. Naturally we would expect that. Usually these are annoying attacks from outside, as it were, like your car mysteriously stalling on the way to an exorcism.

A more authentic Christian tradition is represented by the Church father Origen, who was certain that

> Christians have nothing to fear, even if demons should not be well-disposed to them; for Christians are protected by the supreme God . . . Who sets his divine angels to watch over those who are worthy of such guardianship, so that they can suffer nothing from demons.[29]

Origen argued against the heretic Celsus, who

> cannot believe in the ability of God . . . to give to those who serve him a power by which they may be defended from the assaults directed by demons against the righteous. For he has never beheld the efficacy of those words, "In the Name of Jesus," when uttered by the truly faithful, to deliver not a few from demons and demoniac possessions and other plagues.[30]

There *are* real dangers to the exorcist when dealing with severely demonized or possessed people. These can be avoided, however, if the exorcist prays for protection, utilizing the Spirit's power that Origen spoke about. I believe that Malachi Martin spoke the truth about some exorcists being chewed up by demonic attack, but I think much of their pain could have been avoided if they had been further empowered through the baptism of the Spirit (which we will talk about in chapter 23). It is

29. Origen, *Against Celsus*, viii. 27, in Frost's *Christian Healing*, p. 60.
30. Ibid.

not that they were not effective ministers or that the Spirit was not in large measure with them. But clearly it was not enough.

Just as the apostles, who were believing, baptized Christians and who were "ordained" at the Last Supper, were not fully empowered for ministry until Pentecost, so many ministers need more of a filling with the Holy Spirit to carry on the more difficult parts of their ministry successfully.

You may disagree with my analysis of why some exorcists "die," in part, every time they perform an exorcism, and why they sometimes need to pound on the demons for unremitting weeks to accomplish their task. If so, I challenge you to come up with a better solution. But one thing I believe: The exorcist who has taken all the necessary precautions and who ministers in the power of the Holy Spirit should feel safe and protected when called upon to perform an exorcism.

Part 4

Getting Ready

10

How to Prepare

Many times I have had to pray to free a person from evil spirits when the need surfaced unexpectedly during a healing service. There you are praying for a person when suddenly it erupts. The person's eyes roll back and he starts to scream or show some other unusual manifestation.

This is hardly an ideal situation. (Real life is seldom tidy and ideal.) But you pray and ask God for wisdom as to whether you should complete the deliverance or postpone it. Sometimes it seems best to try to finish the deliverance then and there. But ideally you should choose the best time and place in order to prepare yourself, your team and the person who needs the deliverance.

Long-Term Preparation

To truly prepare, you should be free of any serious sin. Notice I said *serious*. All of us are sinners: "If we claim to be without sin, we deceive ourselves and the truth is not in us" (1 John 1:8). But if you have serious, unconfessed sin, the major evil spirits who know your past are quite capable of embarrassing you in public by exposing your sins. (This is different from the spirits' taunts and intimidation: "You're too tired to cast us out. You don't have enough strength." That kind of gamesmanship happens all the time.) Thank God I have never been present when private sins have been revealed publicly, but I know it happens.

Because of the possibility of the exposure of the exorcist's sins, the Roman Catholic *Rite of Exorcism* requires that the exorcist be "properly distinguished for his piety, prudence and integrity of life. He ought to be of mature years, and revered not alone for his office but for his moral qualities."[1]

Yet fear of the shock of public disclosure of sin is not the most important reason for personal preparation. The exorcist needs to be mature and sensitive to bless and not harm the person suffering from demonic oppression. Ideally we need a lifetime of preparation to equip us with prudence and compassion. But those drawn to praying for deliverance are often impetuous, snap-judgment personalities—precisely the kinds of people who should not be praying for deliverance. The tragedy is, they do not know their weakness.

Thoughtful persons who *are* aware of their weaknesses and who understand the difficulties involved may hesitate to pray at all. As a result, the people who should not pray for deliverance—who have no self-doubts and call that faith—are often the very ones who rush in. As Paul Tournier, the astute Swiss psychiatrist, wrote:

> People who have the sort of mind that sees only one side to every question tend towards vigorous action. They succeed in everything they do because they do not stop to split hairs and have abounding confidence in their own abilities. Your successful journalist, for instance, is inclined to simplify every problem and condense it into an arresting phrase. On the other hand, those with subtle and cultivated minds tend to get lost in a maze of fine distinctions. They always see how complicated things really are, so that their powers of persuasion are nil. That is why the world is led by those who are least suited to raising its cultural and moral standards. It is only a few who manage to combine both tendencies; and in my view a lively Christian faith is the best precondition for the accomplishment of this miracle, because it gives both profound understanding and simplicity of heart.[2]

1. C. Karpel, comp., and the Rev. Philip Weller, trans., *The Rite of Exorcism* (New York: Berkley Medallion, 1975), p. 15. As I said before, the Roman Catholic Church restricts the Rite of Exorcism to 1) priests; 2) praying for people who are possessed; and 3) in a ministry that has the permission of the bishop.

2. Paul Tournier, *The Person Reborn* (New York: Harper & Row, 1966), pp. 20–21.

Here Tournier is talking about journalism and politics, but exactly the same thing happens in the deliverance ministry. Uneducated people with simple faith who see things in terms of black (the devil) and white jump in to pray for deliverance at a Pentecostal meeting in a restaurant, while few theologians are out there in the field casting out evil spirits. They tend to see the deliverance ministry as filled with problems, including the biggest problem of all: Do demons really exist?

The exorcist should be the rare kind of person Tournier describes who combines simple faith with an awareness of difficulties; someone who can join a knowledge of psychology and human frailty with the exercise of the gifts of the Holy Spirit (like discernment). Such a mature person is always prepared to pray for deliverance.

Immediate Preparation

There are a number of questions to answer as you consider prayer for deliverance.

Who Should Pray?

The first question to ask is, "Am I the one to pray for this person?"

Just because the person is in great need does not necessarily mean I am the one to pray. For one thing, the case may be beyond my ability. Certainly God's grace can supply, and many times I have been called to minister in what seemed well beyond my own capabilities. Still, our human knowledge and experience (which are God's gifts) enter into the question of whether I should minister. If a victim of Satanic Ritual Abuse who has multiple personalities comes to me for help, ordinarily I refer him to a member of our staff who has had experience working in this area. I would be derelict in my desire to help him if I tried to do all this myself. In fact, it would be spiritual pride.

But when we cannot pray for a person in need, we do not want to discourage him, so we can at least pray for a blessing. Sometimes when I am not sure whether to pray for deliverance, I put my hands on the person's head, turn the prayer over to the Holy Spirit and simply pray in tongues. If Jesus wants a deliverance to develop, it does; otherwise the prayer remains a simple blessing.

Time is another factor in who should pray. There are so many people who need prayer that you will burn out quickly if you try to minister to all of them. Even Jesus with just three years of public ministry needed to go off alone with His disciples to get some rest.[3]

Early in my healing ministry I learned a healthy lesson at the first healing seminar I ever attended, a small, select one for about fifty clergy and medical professionals. There I met and secretly admired a minister others referred to as "the miracle-worker of Michigan." I thought to myself, *Wouldn't it be wonderful to be known as the wonder-worker of Missouri?* After the last meal, where I felt privileged to sit at the same table with him, he said to me, "Oh, how I wish I were in your place!" I was surprised and asked him why. Then I learned he had suffered a nervous breakdown and was on sabbatical, worn out by his visits to the sick who had called on him for help. That taught me an unforgettable lesson.

We need to share our ministry, teach others to minister and ask the Lord, "Do you want me to pray with this person just now?"

Time and Place

If we do decide to pray for deliverance, we also need to decide on the best time and place. People who sense they need deliverance usually seem to wait until the end of a healing service, perhaps around midnight. They come up after the crowd has thinned out and you are drained, and then ask for help. You cannot blame them for wanting privacy and time to talk, but deliverance prayer does not always go quickly; and midnight, when you are exhausted, is usually the worst time to begin praying.

Whatever the circumstance of confronting the need, you need to make a decision: Should you pray a short prayer; set another time when you will be rested and spiritually prepared, and when you can gather a team; or refer the person to someone else who can help him over a prolonged period of time? Never let Sa-

---

3. I wrote a chapter on "Having to Say No" in my book *Power to Heal* (Notre Dame: Ave Maria, 1977), pp. 111–124, based on my own difficulties in seeing people in need, yet having to balance my desire to help with the need to survive by taking time off.

tan choose, if you can help it, the time or place of combat. You choose it under the guidance of the Spirit.

In setting another time, you need to decide whether to try to accomplish the deliverance in one session, or whether to see the person over a period of time in regular sessions (for example, two hours a week for three months). I think the best plan is usually to see the demonized person over a period of time for a combination of counseling and prayer.

That ideal is not always attainable. In my travels I meet many sufferers desperately seeking deliverance who will be able to attend only one or two meetings. I wish I knew of mature exorcists in every city to whom I could refer them; sometimes I know of none. That is part of the tragedy and one of the reasons I am writing this book.

Prayer and Fasting

It goes without saying that *prayer* and *fasting* are part of the preparation mandated by Jesus Himself. I have already mentioned the time the disciples were unsuccessful in healing a boy afflicted by an evil spirit, and whom Jesus told that they had failed because "this kind can come out only by prayer [some of the early manuscripts add *and fasting*]" (Mark 9:29).

The Gospel says nothing about how long the disciples needed to pray (and fast) in preparation, or how they were to pray. Clearly there are degrees of difficulty in deliverance. Some of the weakest spirits depart during a period of praise and worship. The more powerful spirits (especially the occult ones) are far harder to dislodge and require more preparation. So when people ask how long they need to pray and fast before praying for deliverance, I think the best answer is simply to seek the guidance of the Spirit.

A Team

The last thing to consider in preparing, aside from choosing a time and place, is whether you are going to need a team. We will discuss this in the next chapter.

11

Selecting a Team

Here again we are talking about an ideal, for it is ideal to pray for deliverance with a team you know and trust.

My own experience has seldom matched this ideal. Often when I am on the road, I do not really know the people who have invited me to speak, and it is hard to form a team on the spot. Happily, now that I am married, I usually pray at healing services with my wife, Judith, who has a true gift of discerning spirits. That is a natural start for a team right there. Yet even then the time and place are usually not ideal—when, for example, we are trying to pray for three hundred people at a healing service two thousand miles from home.

Nevertheless, we need to talk about the ideal of forming a team because praying for deliverance with a team is the best way to pray.[1] There are four main reasons:

Preventing the Possibility of Scandal

If a man is ministering alone to a woman, or vice-versa, there is always the possibility of sexual temptation. Certainly if you have another person or an entire team ministering with you, you will not be tempted as you might be if you were working alone. One reason Billy Graham has maintained his reputation

1. In this context I recommend chapter 5, "The Power of Community," from the Rev. Leo Thomas' *Healing as a Parish Ministry* (Notre Dame: Ave Maria Press, 1992).

for integrity is that he has always made sure he is never alone in a room with a woman other than his wife. Spirits of lust in particular can easily work through a demonized person to increase any dangers that may already be present.

A priest on our team was ministering to a woman in Japan. She knew no English and he was working through an interpreter, praying to free her from a spirit of lust. Suddenly the woman asked in perfect English, "How would you like to sleep with me?"

On another occasion I was praying to free a woman in Chile from a number of spirits. She was on the floor on her back when she began to wiggle her hips and assume a number of seductive poses. This was a major distraction, naturally. A female member of our team was angered by the provocative display and immediately took over the prayer to cast out the spirit of lust that had surfaced.

Giving One Another Rest

A mundane but very real reason to work with a team is that deliverance is tiring (not to say exhausting). Some deliverances go fairly quickly, but you never know beforehand how long it is going to last. If you have been leading prayer for deliverance for several hours, it helps if you can turn the prayer over to someone else who has spiritual authority, retire to the next room and rest for a while—or take a walk. If you do not rest, your concentration may grow weak and you will not be nearly as effective.

Restraining the Demonized Person

Usually there is no violence in deliverance prayer, especially if we take the precaution of commanding the spirits to be quiet and not to resist. But some of the more powerful occult spirits may prove difficult to control. One nearly possessed woman to whom our staff was ministering took a chair and smashed a window. Several times I have been threatened by personal injury, although I was actually injured only once, and that was before we started praying. I was being introduced to the person (who had made a pact with Satan and was suffering extreme demonization) when she leaped up out of her chair, scratched my face and tore the cross from around my neck.

If there is any danger of this happening, you may want several strong assistants to restrain the demonized person (much as happens in a mental hospital). But this degree of violent demonization is rare.

Utilizing a Variety of Gifts

The main reason for having a team is simply that most of us do not manifest all the spiritual gifts to the same degree. As Paul says, different Christians manifest a variety of spiritual gifts to build up the Body of Christ (1 Corinthians 12). In short, we need each other. I need people on the deliverance team whom God is more likely to use in those areas in which I am weak; while I, too, have certain strengths to offer in a successful deliverance.

Here are some of the areas in which it is helpful to have tested gifts:

Spiritual Authority

In chapter 9 we said that the person who can best pray for deliverance is a person endowed with maturity and spiritual authority. Some authority is given directly by God (I have seen some unordained laypersons pray with great effect), while for others the authority seems to come with their ordained office. Experience in casting out spirits is certainly a help here, but I have seen people pray successfully with little experience but real spiritual authority. (There is a first exorcism for all of us, and we would never start if experience were an absolutely necessary requirement!)

How good it is when two or more members of the team have this spiritual authority, so that they can trade places and rest from time to time. While all Christians have the basic authority needed to cast out evil spirits, some people exercise more of it than others. In dealing with the stronger spirits in the hierarchy of spirits, this can prove a key factor.

Some Jews who went around driving out evil spirits tried to invoke the name of the Lord Jesus over those who were demon-possessed. They would say, "In the name of Jesus, whom Paul preaches, I command you to come out." Seven sons of Sceva, a

Jewish chief priest, were doing this. The evil spirit answered them, "Jesus I know and Paul I know about, but who are you?" Then the man who had the evil spirit jumped on them and over-powered them all.

Acts 19:13–16

These particular exorcists apparently had some success be-cause they had already been driving out evil spirits by invoking the name of Jesus. But here they were out of their league, pre-sumably because they were not yet Christians or empowered by the Holy Spirit.

The Gift of Discernment

While you can work by ordinary discernment—figuring out which spirits are present by talking to the demonized person or by commanding the spirits to name themselves—the ideal way (if you do not have the gift yourself) is to have someone on the team discern

1. whether a spirit is present;
2. the identity of the spirit.

We dealt with these questions in chapters 5 and 6.

The Gift of the Word of Knowledge

The word of knowledge that Paul speaks about in 1 Corinthians 12 has been defined in different ways by Scripture scholars; but Pentecostals have come to use the term for a gift enabling some-one in the healing ministry to identify the root experience that has caused the sickness or demonization, even when the person has forgotten or cannot identify it.

This gift is especially helpful when the root cause of the de-monic activity—such as Satanic Ritual Abuse—is so painful that the victim has had to block it out in order to survive without a disintegration of her personality. (Frequently a person with dis-cernment also manifests the word of knowledge, with both gifts coexisting in the same person.)

Intercessors

How much easier it goes when one or more persons are present who are content just to praise God in the background or quietly pray for the success of the deliverance. We also have several friends who are able to come up with an appropriate Scripture text for the part of the deliverance we are working on, and who come forward and share it.

Certain Scriptures seem to have a great power to bother and even drive out spirits whose nature runs directly counter to that text. One passage that particularly seems to torment the spirits is in Paul's letter to the Philippians:

> Your attitude should be the same as that of Christ Jesus: Who, being in very nature God, did not consider equality with God something to be grasped, but made himself nothing, taking the very nature of a servant, being made in human likeness. And being found in appearance as a man, he humbled himself and became obedient to death—even death on a cross! Therefore God exalted him to the highest place and gave him the name that is above every name, that at the name of Jesus every knee should bow, in heaven and on earth and under the earth, and every tongue confess that Jesus Christ is Lord, to the glory of God the Father.
>
> Philippians 2:5–11

Forming a Team

The ideal deliverance team is probably made up of five or six people. Yet hardly ever do we find this perfectly gifted team in real life.

One last thing. In forming a team you need to find people you can work with. You may know some people who are clearly gifted, but somehow you are uncomfortable working with them. Perhaps they say too much. Perhaps they have a bit of competition in their makeup and want to take charge at the wrong time. None of us is perfectly matched, yet some defects are such distractions that the combination on the team divides our attention, rather than helping us focus on the wounded person we are praying for.

We should look for people who work easily together—who love and trust one another. We do not want to have to keep glancing out of the corner of our eye to see what some member of the team will come up with next. The great and genuine love of the members of a team for one another is in itself a tremendous force for healing.

12

How the Demonized Person Prepares for Deliverance

Ordinarily it is best to hold a separate interview with the person who is a candidate for deliverance, although this is not always possible. (In a large healing service, for instance, deliverance may erupt spontaneously, although even here the prayer for deliverance can often be postponed until a better time.)

The Interview

The most important element in the interview is the candidate's openness and honesty. The interview need not be structured, provided the person feels free to share what he knows and can remember. What we seek to discover is the reason the evil spirit has come into the person's being. It is not always the person's fault, but there is always a reason. Only when we know the area of weakness are we able to pry the spirit loose and strengthen that area so the spirit cannot return.

Is there anything the person has done that has contributed to this situation? Has there been sin on his part? He may, for example, remember playing the Ouija board. If this demonic infestation has come about in any way through his own fault, he needs to confess this sin and ask God's forgiveness—either at the time of the interview or at the beginning of the actual deliverance session. Ideally the confession should be out loud in the presence of a mature Christian, as in James 5:15–16:

> The prayer offered in faith will make the sick person well; the Lord will raise him up. If he has sinned, he will be forgiven.

Therefore confess your sins to each other and pray for each other
so that you may be healed.

In the Catholic tradition this ordinarily takes place with a priest
in the sacrament of reconciliation.

Satan is a vicious legalist, and if any unconfessed sin is connected to the demonic infestation, the invading spirit will probably
not leave when you pray, or else it may leave for a short time but
will come right back and invade the area of the victim's weakness.

*Is the victimized person infested because of another person's
sin?* A woman may be afflicted by a spirit of fear or lust caused
by her having been raped as a child. Naturally she does not need
to repent of a sin she did not commit, even though she often
feels dirty and guilty. What she *does* need to do is forgive the person who sinned against her. This can be very difficult if the emotional damage has been severe.

I have come to realize that forgiving an enemy who has hurt
us deeply is, humanly speaking, almost impossible. What we
need is grace—the gift of Jesus. I must pray that the love and forgiving power that Jesus has for this person will enter me so that
I can be filled with the forgiveness He won on the cross when He
cried out, "Father, forgive them, for they do not know what they
are doing" (Luke 23:34). On my own I may not be able to forgive,
but with God's help I can. This does not mean, of course, that we
condone the sin committed against us; only that, as St. Augustine said, we fiercely hate sin but love the sinner.

Because of the emotions attached to the wounding, deep forgiveness usually takes time, and we must not force people to pretend. If they say they do not want to forgive, I ask if they can *will*
to forgive without necessarily feeling like doing it. Sometimes the
best we can do is ask, "Are you willing to be willing to forgive?"

At the very least, though, we need to be able to relinquish any
desire for vengeance—an eye for an eye or a tooth for a tooth:
"Never take vengeance into your own hands, my dear friends:
stand back and let God punish if he will" (Romans 12:19, Phillips).

After the person has repented, confessed his sin and forgiven
his enemies (if needed), there are two key questions to ask:

1. "Do you have any idea *when* this problem first started?"
2. "Do you have any idea *why* it started?"

You will often find that just by getting the person to talk, you may learn not only when the problem started and why, but perhaps even what spirits are present. Roberta, for instance (whom I mentioned in chapter 1), was able to identify the King of Terrors, whose name was pinned to her dress when she was consecrated as a child by a satanic high priest many years before.

Some people are shy and have a hard time talking. At other times the demons surface and actively block you from talking to the person. If this blocking occurs, command the spirits to stop interfering: "I command you, spirit of mockery, in the name of Jesus Christ, to stop interfering, so I can talk to _____!"

Interviews can be short when the person is ready for deliverance and when we know what we are dealing with. They can be even shorter when the demonized person is innocent of occult involvement.

Preparation can take time, on the other hand, if the demonized person blows hot and cold or has too shaky a foundation to maintain his deliverance. I have friends who require that some of their counselees prepare (as well as show sincerity of purpose) by spending six months before deliverance by praying and reading Scripture regularly, becoming part of a fellowship group and attending church regularly. They have found that people who have led an unstable life need to build a solid foundation. And even if you do manage to cast the evil spirits out, they will simply return. (For those of you who are fearful, I want to emphasize that someone leading a solid Christian life need not fear that the spirits will return.)

Identifying the Spirits

We must try to identify the spirits in a general way, because our approach to deliverance will be very different depending on the kind of spirit we are dealing with.

There are (as I said earlier) four basic categories of spirits, so you will need to sort out whether you are confronting

wounding spirits;
sinful spirits;
occult spirits;
ancestral spirits.

Wounding Spirits

These are the spirits that have hooked into the wounds of the victim's past. The sin that causes this demonic infestation is not primarily the person's own sin, but another person's sins that have left deep wounds.

A good example of this kind of spirit is *rejection*. A little girl may have been rejected by her mother or father, making it hard for the woman later in life, on a purely natural level, to believe that anyone could ever really love her; and she will find it hard to trust anyone. A spirit of rejection moving into that wound will intensify the human rejection and make it even harder for the woman to trust.

She may need to repent for hating the perpetrator, but basically she is more sinned against than sinning, more a victim than a perpetrator.

Sinful Spirits

Here your interview may reveal that the demonic infestation has been caused by the person's own sinful actions. If the sin has been intense and willful, or if it has been indulged in over a long time, then the evil spirits have, in a sense, been invited in.

A man may have learned to handle his personal problems with violence, then enlisted in the Marines and found a rationale for justifying his violence in war. He may be discharged from the service with medals on his uniform but have marital difficulties because of the habitual patterns of violence in which he has indulged. Also, his ungovernable temper may be intensified by various spirits that have entered him over the years.

Some of these spirits of sin (such as *murder*) are fierce and difficult to dislodge. Others (such as *vanity*) come out whining and simpering.

Occult Spirits

Your interview may reveal that the person has engaged in occult activities. It is important to learn this because the occult spirits are the most tenacious and difficult to drive out. (The next chapter will show how this is done.)

Discovering if occult spirits are present is especially important because they will try to block any prayers for healing you may attempt.

Ancestral Spirits

A number of other spirits do not fit into these three categories. The most important among them are the ancestral or familiar spirits that identify themselves as the restless spirits of the departed. There is a variety of other spirits, like the spirit of false religion and the spirit of legalism, that are not easily categorized. We will discuss some of these assorted spirits later in chapter 18.

A Questionnaire

To help pinpoint some of the problems in the initial interview, you may want to make up a series of questions to ask, similar to the questionnaire the nurse gives you when you go to a physician for the first time. Do not feel bound to use a questionnaire every time you interview someone to decide if he needs deliverance; only if you have time to pray over an extended period of sessions. But an orderly questionnaire can help you not to miss anything significant.

Here is my synopsis of a questionnaire that several members of our staff have developed.[1] We do not propose it as *the* ideal, just a model to encourage you to develop your own.

Deliverance Questionnaire

Have you ever, just for fun, out of curiosity or in earnest:

1. Had your fortune told by tea leaves, palm-reading, a crystal ball, etc.?
2. Read or followed horoscopes or had a chart made for yourself?
3. Practiced yoga or Transcendental Meditation?
4. Attended a séance or spiritualist meeting?
5. Had a reincarnation reading about who you were in some previous existence?
6. Played with a Ouija board, tarot cards or "Dungeons & Dragons"?
7. Played games of an occult nature using ESP, telepathy, etc.?

1. Notably Mrs. Norma Dearing, who learned it from her father-in-law, Father Frank Dearing, a respected and revered pioneer in the healing ministry in the Episcopal Church in north Florida.

8. Consulted a medium, acted as a medium or practiced channeling?
9. Sought psychic healing or had psychic surgery?
10. Practiced table-lifting, lifting bodies, automatic writing or soul travel?
11. Used any kind of charm for protection?
12. Practiced water-witching to find out where to dig a well?
13. Read or possessed books on witchcraft, fortune-telling, ESP, psychic phenomena or possession?[2] Had anything in your home that was given to you by someone in the occult?
14. Been fascinated by demonic topics in movies? Had a fascination with the occult?
15. Accepted the writings of Edgar Cayce or any other New Age author?
16. Practiced mind control over anyone, cast a magic spell or sought a psychic experience? Contacted a psychic in person or through a psychic hotline?
17. Made a pact with Satan or been involved in Satan worship?
18. Attended witchcraft or voodoo ceremonies?
19. Known of any relatives or ancestors who have been involved in witchcraft, pagan religions, fortune-telling or who have used magic spells?
20. Visited a shrine or temple of a non-Judeo-Christian religion?
21. Been involved in Freemasonry? Had anyone in your family involved?
22. Embraced the fallacy that we are self-sufficient and do not need God?
23. Used LSD, marijuana, cocaine or any "mind-expanding" drugs?
24. Had a problem with alcohol? How about other family members?
25. Exposed yourself to pornography in magazines, TV or stage shows, books, topless bars or X-rated movies?
26. Had a problem with habitual masturbation?
27. Been involved in sexually deviant practices?
28. Been involved with a number of people sexually?
29. Had an abortion or fathered a child who was aborted?

2. There can be a good reason to read such books. The difference is when people read them to direct their lives.

30. Wished yourself dead?
31. Wished somebody else dead?
32. Attempted to take your own life?
33. Attempted to take (or taken) someone else's life?

In utilizing such a questionnaire, we must realize that some activities (such as playing the Ouija board) are clearly forbidden, while others may involve extenuating circumstances. You may have a sufficient reason for studying the works of Edgar Cayce (preparing a lecture on the subject, for example, or learning more in order to answer the serious questions of a counselee who has been an Edgar Cayce follower) and not be harmed.

Furthermore, it is quite possible to attend a séance, play the Ouija board or engage in some other occult activity and not be affected afterward. After two people play the Ouija board, both need to repent, but one may be bothered afterward by an occult spirit while another is not troubled at all. One or both or neither may need deliverance. Nevertheless, these questions are good to ask, for they may help reveal the reason some people are troubled by evil spirits, and they may bring to our attention areas of our past lives in which we need to repent.

Be aware, too, that there are some activities that are not clearly forbidden and about which there are reasonable doubts. Among these are *hypnotism* and *yoga exercises.*

There are dangers in being hypnotized, when your will is unprotected and you can be exposed to something invading your soul. But some people believe hypnosis can be justified with two precautions. First, that you have a sufficient reason for doing it. A person's memory may be blocked to anything earlier than age ten, for instance, and represent a barrier through which hypnosis may break. The second precaution is that the person conducting the session is reputable and protects the client. Putting people into trances as a parlor game is clearly dangerous, for spiritual as well as psychological reasons.[3]

Similarly with the practice of yoga exercises we find dispute. Some Christians say it is beneficial to practice such exercises

3. Psychotherapists use hypnosis for good reasons, such as recovering a client's past when his memory is blocked because of severe emotional wounding. But the Holy Spirit through the word of knowledge can reveal what we need to know about the client's past. Often, too, when we pray with clients, their past opens up to them and they can remember those painful events.

without getting into yoga philosophy. Others say you cannot do it because the exercises are intimately connected with the philosophy underlying them.

Personally, when I am not sure, I prefer to take the safer course. At the same time we need to avoid coming to snap judgments and condemning practices with which we are unfamiliar, just because we have heard someone else condemn them.

Steps to Take

Once you discover in the interview what needs healing and what needs deliverance, try to help the person

1. *repent* and ask God's forgiveness for any sins he has committed;
2. *forgive* those who have injured him;
3. *renounce* any occult activities he may have practiced.

There is a difference, as I pointed out earlier, between repenting and renouncing. *Repenting* means that we acknowledge a sin, confess it as sin, ask God's forgiveness and turn from it. *Renouncing* adds a deeper dimension. In addition to being sorry for what we have done in the past and resolving to change our life, we repudiate, cast off and take back our previous commitment by making an explicit declaration of abandonment. By renouncing our occult activities, we are taking back what we have previously surrendered to the realm of evil.

After finding out (with or without a questionnaire) the areas to pray about in the deliverance session, you may also want to make some suggestions to the person about how best he can pray in the coming days and what he should read in the particular area where he needs the most help.[4]

---

4. Mrs. Joy Lamb, the Director of Intercessors at Christian Healing Ministries, has written a prayer manual, *The Sword of the Spirit . . . the Word of God,* published by Lamb's Books, Inc., P.O. Box 9520, Jacksonville, FL 32208. This little book contains a number of Scripture quotes for various areas of need, like protection, deliverance and inner healing.

Part 5

How to Pray
for Deliverance

13

How to Pray for Deliverance

The Basic Form

We now arrive at the most practical section of our book: What is the basic form of deliverance prayer? (The three chapters following this one will describe its three main variations, depending on the kind of spirit we are dealing with.)

The first thing to realize when we are performing a deliverance is that deliverance prayer is different from prayer for healing. In fact, it is not prayer at all; it is a *command*. And it is directed not to God, as prayer is, but to an evil spirit, ordering it to get out. This command is backed up by God's authority, in the name of Jesus Christ. Paul, for instance, cast out the soothsaying spirit from the slave girl who kept pestering him:

> She kept this up for many days. Finally Paul became so troubled that he turned around and said to the spirit, "In the name of Jesus Christ I command you to come out of her!" At that moment the spirit left her.
>
> Acts 16:18

Healing prayer, on the other hand, is directed to God. We certainly do not command God to do anything; we only ask Him—in this case to heal.[1] We are the creatures; God is the Creator.

---

1. Some prayer for healing can be a form of command, directed at unruly nature, restoring nature to its original created order, with the authority of God behind the command (e.g., Jesus rebuking the fever oppressing Peter's mother-in-law; Luke 4:39). This kind of prayer is something like exorcism, commanding the evil of sickness to depart.

Then the Lᴏʀᴅ answered Job out of the storm. He said:
"Who is this that darkens my counsel with words without knowledge? Brace yourself like a man; I will question you, and you shall answer me.
"Where were you when I laid the earth's foundation? . . . Have you ever given orders to the morning, or shown the dawn its place. . . ?"

Job 38:1–4, 12

When we pray for healing, our basic attitude is that of entreaty; I am a servant (or, better yet, a friend) asking a favor. Based on a promise, but still a favor.

Preparations

I hope you will already have had the chance to form a team and interview the person seeking deliverance. Certainly it helps if you know the counselee's history and how the spirits gained entrance. It especially helps if you know the identity of the main spirits. If not, the first part of the deliverance session will involve talking with the counselee and learning as much as you can about how and why the spirits gained entry and who they are.

The session begins, of course, with prayer. First we call on Jesus Christ to give us wisdom and guide us in our prayer. We call on His authority to cast out the spirits. We ask the Holy Spirit to anoint us with power and the love of God to heal as well as free the person. We ask God to fill the room with His power and love to overflowing. Nothing evil can survive in such an atmosphere.

We call on the holy angels (especially the archangel Michael) to minister to us, surround us with their protection and do battle for us, while the "communion of saints" who are in heaven, the "great cloud of witnesses" of Hebrews 12:1, intercede for us.

Lastly we forbid, in the name of Jesus Christ, any communication in the realm of evil spirits, as it might affect the spirits that are troubling the counselee; and we forbid these spirits to draw power from any spirits outside the person.

Having finished praying for protection, we are now ready to proceed with the deliverance itself.

Helpful Suggestions

Exercise Compassion

Remember again that you are not angry at the counselee, for whom you need to feel compassion. Do not further wound her by increasing the shame and self-loathing she probably already feels.

Speak in a Calm Voice

It is like dealing with children: If you really have authority and know who is in charge, you can command quietly. If the demons sense that you are calm and in charge, they will, like children, obey your commands.

They will also sense if you are insecure, and it will take longer to drive them out. (In the beginning most of us are a little unsteady; that is to be expected.) Shouting and blustering at the demons simply demonstrates our own insecurity. Or we may get loud because we are angry at the demons. The danger is, how does the victim sort out that anger from anger directed personally at her? So it is better to remain calm.

Look the Person in the Eye

This is not absolutely necessary, but it does seem to help. In chapter 5 I mentioned that when you look into the eyes of a person who harbors a demon, you seem to be looking at something else in there. You can often identify the evil spirit (whether hate or mockery or pride or something else) simply by that gaze.

In an account of the massacres in Rwanda, *Time* magazine quoted a missionary on its cover saying, "There are no devils left in Hell; they are all in Rwanda." The accompanying article quoted a U.N. official describing the young men who were killers: "If you look in their eyes, there is something there that is not in the eyes of normal people."[2]

Looking into the person's eyes seems to confront the evil spirits directly and helps in casting them out. I have found that the spirits, even if they seem defiant, are afraid to look us in the eye and will do whatever they can to avoid it. Sometimes (as I already mentioned) the eyeballs will roll upward, leaving you looking at nothing but the whites of the eyes. Usually I ask the

2. Nancy Gibbs, "Why? The Killing Fields of Rwanda," *Time*, May 16, 1994, p. 59.

person to look at me. Ordinarily, if she still has command of her body, she will do it. But if the spirits are strong, they will force her to turn away. If this happens you can say to the spirit, "In the name of Jesus Christ I command you to look at me"—and keep doing it (calmly) until it releases its grip and the person does.

Or when you are praying for people as they come forward, some may drop to the floor before they reach you. Usually this is because the power of God is so strong that they cannot stand up, but sometimes an evil spirit will do the same thing. The person wants to come forward, but the spirits are fighting desperately to keep you away.

Decide How to Handle Temporary Possession

Sometimes in a deliverance session, spirits that have never demonstrated their presence but have influenced the person's life in more subtle ways feel threatened enough to come to the surface and take over the victim's personality as they fight to keep her in their power. Afterward the person expresses surprise at what happened. At one moment you are talking to an apparently normal person; the next moment that personality is no longer there and you are face to face with a demonic presence.

If this happens you will need to make a decision: Is now the time to confront the spirits that have risen to the surface and drive them out? If they surface while you are still trying to interview the person before the actual exorcism, you can command them to let go and say, "I want to speak now to _____, not to you. I command you to let go of her voice and allow her to speak."

This temporary possession often occurs when you are leading the person to commitment to Jesus Christ. She may get as far as the name *Jesus*, then be able to stammer only, "Jee, Jee, Jee," and not be able to finish.

One of the unusual aspects of temporary possession is that later the person usually cannot remember anything that occurred during this time. If the real person was submerged for two hours during the deliverance prayer, she probably will remember nothing she said or did during that time. She may have been shouting curses at you, or thrashing around and screaming, but afterward, mercifully, she will have no memory of it at all. In the end she will probably feel refreshed and ready for a celebration, while you and your team will feel exhausted and ready to go to sleep on the spot!

The phenomenon of temporary possession makes highly problematic the question of proving to church authorities, in order to get permission to do a formal exorcism, that a person is possessed. All you can say is that the person ordinarily acts normally, but occasionally seems to be possessed.

Temporary possession also explains why some serial murderers say they are surprised the next morning when they read in the paper about the horrible crimes they committed. They are telling the truth: Something else at the time took over. Truly the devil made them do it.

Ultimately, of course, they are responsible for whatever led them to fall under Satan's control (for example, heavy involvement in Satanism). But the tragedy is, their true selves would probably not have committed those monstrous crimes. Moreover, if they repent and turn their lives over to the Lord of the universe, they are salvageable human beings, not monsters.

Decide Whether to Touch the Person

Here we find two contrary opinions. Some hold that you should not touch the person if you do not have to; that it is contaminating and possibly dangerous. My own experience, on the other hand, is that the power of the Holy Spirit flows out from us to the afflicted person. If the evil spirit seems lodged in the person's throat, I will place my hand lightly on the throat. The evil spirits cannot stand being close to us, and the laying on of hands increases the pressure on them to get out. By touching their victim, you increase the spirits' discomfort and hasten their departure.

The laying on of hands is not essential, of course, and I respect the opinion that you need not (or should not) touch the person.

The touch should not be harsh. On the contrary, it can be a sign of love, which evil spirits cannot abide. (Several times I have even encountered a spirit characterized by a fear of touch. "Do not touch me," it shouted.)

I remember praying with a woman who had never known her mother's love. I asked Judith to hold her and rock her in her arms as a mother would. This was before our marriage, and the spirit in this woman taunted Judith, "You've never been a mother. You don't know how to do it!" The woman, who had been a patient in a mental hospital, was set free that night.

The Actual Prayer for Deliverance

By the time you start praying you should know (through a preparatory session or at the beginning of this deliverance session) the identity of the evil spirit you are going to cast out first. Ideally this knowledge comes through someone on your team who has the gift of discernment (as we have discussed) or through your interview and the discernment you have gained through ordinary counseling.

With the team around you, you will probably want to sit facing the afflicted person, who is also seated. If the person has not yet committed her life to Jesus Christ, she can do so now. She also needs to repent of any sins connected with her need for deliverance and renounce any activities connected with the occult. Because it is good to make sure the person is committed to Jesus and as repentant as she can be, considering that evil spirits are trying to prevent her from doing this, you might want to spend an entire preliminary session on these two areas.

After these preliminaries are taken care of, ask the person to look you in the eye. Pray silently, asking the Holy Spirit to guide you in deciding which spirit to cast out first. Sometimes you start with what seems to be the main spirit, the strongest. If you get that one out, the other, weaker ones will follow with less resistance. At other times you start with the lesser spirits, especially if the main spirit is unusually powerful. It is like digging out a big tree stump: If you cut off the lesser roots spreading out into the ground, the main stump will finally be cut off from its supporting tentacles and be loosened enough for you to pull it out.

There may also be blocking spirits that get in your way, like skirmishers in the army that try to protect the major spirit. (Among these spirits we find *mockery, lying, confusion, sleepiness* and *game-playing.*) You need to either bind these up or cast them out.

I remember praying with a woman for deliverance (a missionary, no less) when a spirit of mockery surfaced. The woman held up an imaginary wineglass and toasted the prayer team. She also made some witty remarks to try to distract us with laughter. And she really was funny! When we realized what was going on, however, we commanded the spirit of mockery to stop the foolery that was distracting us from the task at hand.

The heart of the deliverance is, of course, the deliverance prayer itself, which has several very definite components. The ordinary deliverance prayer contains the following elements:

1. *The authority* that forces the evil spirit to go: the name of Jesus Christ
2. *The command,* which is the form of deliverance prayer
3. The one *to whom* the command is directed: the evil spirit (Ideally the spirit is commanded by name.)
4. *What* you command the spirit to do: "Depart! Go! Now!"
5. *How* the spirit is to go: "quietly, without hurting anybody"
6. *Where* the spirit is to go: "to Jesus Christ" (or else "to hell")[3]

1. "In the name of Jesus Christ..."

We cast these spirits out not by our own authority, but by the power of the name of Jesus Christ. (The "name" really means the "Person" of Jesus Christ.)

> The seventy-two returned with joy and said, "Lord, even the demons submit to us in your name."
>
> Luke 10:17

2. "...I command you..."

It is no polite request we make of the evil spirits; we use authority. If there is doubt or hesitation in your voice, the spirits will pick up on your fear and try to further intimidate you ("We are stronger than you are"; "You will never get us out"; etc.). Believe fully in the authority of Christ to drive the spirits out. True it is that you cannot do it, but Jesus Christ within you will free the captive.

---

3. Those with a journalistic background will recognize four of the five Ws you look for in journalistic writing. *Who* is "you evil spirit of _____." *What* is "Go!" *When* is now. *Where* is to Jesus Christ. *Why* is not included because you do not have to explain that to the demon.

3. "... you spirit of_____ ..."

When possible, identify the spirit by name (for example, spirit of hate, spirit of lust, etc.).

4. "... to depart ..."

This part of the command is self-explanatory.

5. "... without doing harm to _____ [name the person by first name or entire name] or anyone else in this house, or in her family, and without making any noise or disturbance ..."

There have been times other people have been attacked (or even entered) by the spirits as they leave. Sometimes, too, pets in the house have been invaded and behave strangely afterwards. You can avoid all this by praying for protection before and during the deliverance.

Evil spirits like to create uproar and frighten you off by ugly and sickening performances, so command them to be quiet and not to create any disturbance. This will lead to a peaceful deliverance or, at the very least, cut down on any violent or noisy displays.

6. "... and I command you to go straight to Jesus Christ to dispose of you as He will. Furthermore, I command you never again to return."

Some exorcists command the demons to go to hell or "return to the abyss," but I prefer to send them to Jesus and let Him do that, if He wishes. A human failing is for us to become infected by what we fight, and it is an occupational hazard for an exorcist to become harsh and judgmental.

Even the archangel Michael, when he was disputing with the devil about the body of Moses, did not dare to bring a slanderous accusation against him, but said, "The Lord rebuke you!"

Jude 1:9

Occasionally you do not have to name the evil spirit, but simply, as you look into the person's eyes, command the spirit at whom you are looking to leave. You are already in contact with it and you can tell it to go.

So here you have the basic form of a prayer for deliverance. Fashion it as you will, developing it in your own way. Sometimes just a simple *Go!* is enough to force an evil spirit to flee.

How to Tell When the Spirits Have Left

Sometimes the spirits go instantly. Other times it takes hours or even days for the more powerful spirits to let go. Obviously we do not want to keep hammering away if a spirit has already left. Sometimes the spirits pretend to go, however, and then go underground, biding time, hoping you will be the one to get tired and leave them alone.

How can we tell when the spirits have left? There are three ways.

The Team's Discernment

The easiest way to know whether a spirit has left is (as we described in chapter 5) through the gift of discerning spirits. If you yourself do not have this gift, it is wonderful to have someone on your team to whom you can turn and ask, "Has that one gone?"

Once the first spirit has gone, you can ask, "What's surfacing now?" And the team member with discernment can identify the next evil spirit that needs to be cast out.

The Victim's Discernment

It amazes me that most people for whom I have prayed seem to know if a given demon has departed. Even when you cannot see a difference, the person will look up and say, "It's gone. I feel so much lighter now."

When there are a number of evil spirits present (as there usually are), the person can usually tell if there are any more left. She also knows when the last one has gone. It is as if the person being delivered has the gift of discernment during the time of prayer.

If I were to estimate how often this happens, I would say about ninety percent of the time. Obviously this is a wonderful gift that helps us free God's people from bondage.

Human Observation

Even without the supernatural gift of discernment, we have a number of ways to tell when a spirit has left, just by human observation. Looking into the client's eyes you can often see a change. An expression of alien hate may suddenly change as the eyes soften and clear, and once more you are looking into the eyes of a human being.

Frequently the spirits come out with a struggle. Often people cry out; sometimes they are thrown to the ground. Distressing as these manifestations are, they can be a help, for the screams will change to silence and the body struggling will be transformed into a body at peace as the deliverance comes to an end. (The prayers commanding the spirits to come out peacefully help in diminishing all these violent demonstrations.)

Sometimes the spirits seem to be lodged in a particular part of the body, which they torment with pain. The person may bend over, for example, with stomach pain. The usual course is for the pain to rise to chest level while we are praying, then to the throat and finally through the mouth. If the spirit comes out through the mouth, it is usually accompanied by retching or coughing. If the person retches, material often comes up. It is not vomit; it is more like phlegm. We just let the person cough while we continue to pray. After a while it ceases; then you can ask, "Is it gone?" The person will say, "Yes," or, "Not quite; there's still something left." So you continue to pray. To make this transition easier, we try to have a plastic-lined wastebasket or pail present.

I know this must sound weird to those who have never seen it, but it is a common phenomenon in the deliverance ministry. I would guess that this coughing phenomenon occurs at least half the time we pray for deliverance.

Other bizarre, violent phenomena occur during deliverance prayers. We read about these ugly displays in the ministry of Jesus:

> "Be quiet!" said Jesus sternly. "Come out of him!" The evil spirit shook the man violently and came out of him with a shriek.
>
> Mark 1:25–26

Sometimes we see people convulse; other times we hear them scream. In our church culture we are embarrassed by such unseemly displays, but the Gospel writers were matter-of-fact about it. When these manifestations occur, and when the convulsions give way to peace and the shrieks give way to silence, you can judge that the spirit has probably gone. Note that the man screamed and was convulsed even after Jesus had told the spirit to be quiet. Apparently Jesus wanted to prevent the spirit from engaging in a lengthy argument and postponing its exit.

One Session or Many?

After each spirit departs, you must decide whether to go after the remaining spirits that are present. At times you can finish it all in one session, which may last for ten minutes or for hours—or days. Sometimes it is more merciful to finish the deliverance in one session. If you want to attempt to pray for the entire deliverance this way, be sure you have the time and strength.

At other times it is wiser to take more time and schedule a number of one-hour sessions a week apart, perhaps over months. For spirits that have entered through human weakness (for example, *depression*) or sin (for example, *murder*), the person needs time to change long-established patterns of thought or action, and may be overwhelmed if you try to do the deliverance all at once. It may be like the time following surgery when you need to convalesce and learn once again to walk.

Praying and listening to the Holy Spirit are the most important things you can do. It is not technique or the loudness of our voices; it is the power of God working through us as we listen and follow the Spirit's guidance.

Filling In the Emptiness

After the spirits have left, there remains a spiritual vacuum in the counselee. So we finish our prayer by asking God to fill in any empty space with those characteristics of Jesus that are the opposite of the evils that have left.

It is remarkable that there is, for every one of our sins and frailties, some aspect in the life of Jesus that serves as its antidote. "All I have is yours," said Jesus at the Last Supper (John 17:10). In place of anxiety and fear, Jesus said, "Peace I leave with you; my peace I give you. I do not give to you as the world gives. Do not let your hearts be troubled and do not be afraid" (John 14:27). In place of lies and confusion, Jesus is "the light of the world" (John 8:12) and "the way and the truth and the life" (John 14:6). In place of hate, the Spirit pours the love of Jesus into our hearts (Romans 5:5). In place of lust we receive the pure love of God in Jesus (1 John 4:10).

So end every deliverance on a positive, God-centered note by praying for an infilling of every strength and virtue that characterized the life of Jesus.

> The secret is simply this: Christ *in you!* Yes, Christ *in you* bringing with him the hope of all the glorious things to come.
>
> Colossians 1:27, Phillips

Other Helps

Anything that brings us into the presence of God will make the evil spirits uncomfortable and help us deliver the afflicted person. Having team members pray in the background, or playing prayerful music on your cassette or CD player, will torment the evil spirits and encourage them to come out sooner. You might also ask someone to read pertinent Scripture passages, especially any sayings of Jesus that run counter to the nature of the spirit that is resisting you.

Mentioning the precious blood of Jesus, which He shed on the cross to free us from evil, also has a profound effect in freeing people of demonic influence. There is a wonderful old Pentecostal tradition of singing "There is Power in the Blood" before, during or after an exorcism, and this has a rejuvenating effect on me whenever I grow weary in the middle of a difficult session.

One passage that especially distresses the demonic world is the hymn in Philippians 2:6–11, which ends with

> Therefore God exalted him to the highest place and gave him the name that is above every name, that at the name of Jesus every knee should bow, in heaven and on earth and under the earth,

and every tongue confess that Jesus Christ is Lord, to the glory of God the Father.

verses 9–11

Other helps, used in particular by those in the Catholic tradition, include oil, water and salt, all previously prepared by a blessing that asks God to use these elements in healing and casting out demons. The ancient prayer to bless water says, in part: "May you be a purified water, empowered to drive afar all power of the enemy, in fact, to root out and banish the enemy himself, along with his Fallen Angels."[4]

The water is used to sprinkle the room (or the person). The salt is sprinkled in the room before the prayer begins, or else the person can eat a bit of it. And the oil is used for anointing the afflicted person.

At times I have seen an amazing reaction when I anointed the afflicted person with oil that had been blessed. Even though it was room temperature, the person jumped as if touched with a red-hot iron. It is not the person who reacts in this way, of course, but the spirits working through the person and trying to avoid coming in contact with a channel of God's power—like putting a finger into an electric outlet and being shocked by its power.[5] (You can read more about this in chapter 19, "Deliverance through 'Blessed Objects.'")

Other of my friends have their counselees hold or look on a crucifix. Still others place the Bible in the person's hands. All these reminders of the life of Jesus and the power of the Spirit have some effect in hastening the exit of evil spirits.[6]

I realize that, according to your Christian background and tradition, you may find some of these aids acceptable and others not. If they are not acceptable to you, just leave them aside; none is essential.

4. From *Prayers and Blessings from the Roman Ritual,* compiled by Michael Scanlan, T.O.R. (Steubenville, Oh.: Steubenville University, 1978), p. 4.

5. For more information on the blessings of oil and water, consult the booklet recommended in the previous footnote or Appendix 2 in my book *The Power to Heal* (Notre Dame: Ave Maria Press, 1977).

6. We have an upside-down discernment process here: We can discover what is holy and what serves as a channel of God's power by gauging how much the kingdom of Satan reacts against it!

After the deliverance session is finished, give your counselee some follow-up suggestions (see chapter 20) and end the session by praising God.

Finally, after the person has left, do not forget to pray for all the members of the team to be cleansed of anything harmful they may have picked up from contact with the evil spirits.

Following is a cleansing prayer that I made up to say after a deliverance session. Use *I* or *we* as appropriate:

Lord Jesus, thank You for sharing with me (us) Your wonderful ministry of healing and deliverance. Thank You for the healings I (we) have seen and experienced today. But I realize that the sickness and evil I encounter is more than my humanity can bear. So cleanse me of any sadness, negativity or despair that I may have picked up.

If my ministry has tempted me to anger, impatience or lust, cleanse me of those temptations and replace them with love, joy and peace. If any evil spirits have attached themselves to me or oppress me in any way, I command you, spirits of earth, air, fire or water, of the netherworld or of nature, to depart now and go straight to Jesus Christ, for Him to deal with as He will.

Come, Holy Spirit, renew me, fill me anew with Your power, life and joy. Strengthen me where I have felt weak and clothe me with Your light. Fill me with life.

And Lord Jesus, please send Your holy angels to minister to me and my family, and to guard and protect us from all sickness, harm and accidents (and guard me on a safe trip home).

I praise you now and forever, Father, Son and Holy Spirit!

Final Suggestions

If you can get the afflicted person to take part in her own deliverance, it will assist you greatly and make the session go more quickly. Often the spirits will not allow the person to cooperate with you, but you should try to get her to become involved as personally as possible.

First, ask her to repeat the sinner's prayer or the baptismal vows, concentrating especially on two key elements:

"I accept Jesus Christ as my Lord, as my Savior and as my Deliverer."

"I renounce Satan with all his works and pomps."

Second, ask the person to repeat after you the parts of the actual deliverance prayer:

"In the name of Jesus Christ
I command you
Spirit of _____
To leave me now
And go to Jesus Christ
For Him to deal with
And I command you never again to return!"

I also ask the person to help me by interrupting at any given point during the deliverance to let me know from her point of view what is going on. This can be very helpful. She may say, for instance, "I feel something moving around inside my stomach." Or she may say, "I hear a voice in my head telling me to kill myself." This identifies a spirit of self-hatred or suicide. All this helps direct us in how best we can pray.

Remember, too, my earlier recommendation to have one person (or a couple) clearly in charge. And remember, if you get tired, don't be afraid to take a rest or appoint someone to spell you and take over for a time.

I hope all this does not sound overwhelming. Deliverance is exhausting but very rewarding. And it is not all that complicated.

The delight and celebration of seeing a person freed of demonic shackles and emerging from prison is just glorious! What the French must have felt two hundred years ago on Bastille Day is like the joy we feel when one of God's children bursts out of prison and emerges into the light.

14

Freeing a Person from Spirits of Trauma

Having described deliverance prayer in general, we now concentrate on different kinds of deliverance prayer, beginning with spirits of trauma.

Spirits of trauma are the most common category of evil spirits that afflict people, yet the literature on deliverance pays them the least attention.[1] Earlier I mentioned that the people I know who are most experienced in a balanced ministry of healing and deliverance estimate that about three out of four sufferers from demonic infestation fall into this group.

When these spirits identify themselves, they give names like *grief, rejection* or *fear.* These are not sins, of course, but represent our most common emotions. Emotions are one of God's gifts to humanity and help move us to action. Fear is not in itself a problem, but *fear* as a spirit can invade the emotion of excessive fear, which *is* a problem, and make it more of a problem. Demonic fear blocks its victim's free will so that he behaves irrationally and is tempted to commit desperate acts.

Spirits of trauma move in when a person

1. suffers a severe emotional trauma; and
2. is unprotected spiritually.

1. A noteworthy exception is a book by John and Mark Sandford, *A Comprehensive Guide to Deliverance and Inner Healing* (Grand Rapids: Chosen Books, 1992).

We have found that even before birth a baby can recognize if he is wanted;[2] and if he is not, a spirit of rejection can hook in. From then on the person will be prone to rejection, which may be intensified by the spirit of rejection. We can compare this to stepping on a rusty nail (the natural wound), which is then invaded by a tetanus infection. The spirit makes the rejection worse and tries to block anything that might heal it, like affirmation or love later on in life. People affected by these spirits may or may not sense that a spirit is present; but they will definitely sense that they are not free in this area and that their fear or anxiety (or whatever other emotion is agitated) is beyond their ability to control.

A loving, sensitive woman I'll call Pat came to us for prayer some years ago. Her presenting problem was a deep depression that kept her trapped in fearful insecurity. Pat had been abused verbally and physically by her mother and had never known a father's protection. Spirits had moved into these areas and helped make her depressed, suicidal and unwilling to risk marriage.

When Pat went to see Judith, she heard a voice saying to her, "You're a fool for coming. Nothing's going to happen." Such voices are often the spirits' attempts to block healing. In her case, spirits of despair or hopelessness intensified her natural feelings (based on a sad lifetime of rejection), telling her that nothing good had ever happened or ever would happen to her. These spirits, along with many others, had been with her even before birth.

We prayed for Pat an hour or two each day for five days, mostly for inner healing but accompanied by some deliverance. It turned out that a few years before, Pat had had a prophetic dream in which she saw a tiny embryo firmly encased in cement. During the dream a bolt of lightning hit the casing and broke it loose, exposing the tiny prisoner.

When Judith prayed for me, this dream came to mind, and I saw the infant lying *outside* the casing. A light came into the scene and shone on the infant. The baby turned pink and then red. I

---

2. You can read the amazing research about infants picking up on whether or not they are loved in a book Judith and I wrote, *Praying for Your Unborn Child* (New York: Image/Doubleday, 1989).

watched the baby receiving new life. A voice came to me and said, "I sent you as a gift to your parents." At this point I realized how rejected I had felt, and that I wished I had never been born.

Since Judith's prayer I have been slowly coming to life and realizing how good it is to live, to have been created, to be human, to be flesh and to have the Incarnate Word become flesh of my flesh.[3]

At the end of the week, Pat was freed from depression. And the happy outcome was that she married soon afterward.

How Are Spirits of Trauma Different?

Pat's healing is an example of the difference between deliverance from spirits of trauma and deliverance from other kinds of spirits.

How They Enter

The first way spirits of trauma are different is that they enter a person not through the victim's sin, but through someone else's. The victim has been wounded. In Pat's case, the sin was that of her mother, who had not wanted Pat. Thus was Pat traumatized even when she was in the womb, long before she was capable of making any conscious decision to sin or not to sin, to give in to despair or to fight it. In her dream she saw herself as an embryo encased and immobilized by cement.

This scenario seems unfair—an innocent child hurt through no fault of her own. But we know from experience that this is what often happens in life. A lovely forty-year-old woman may come to us for counsel because she cannot relate physically to her husband, nor can she fully trust him. We find that she was the victim of her father's incest from the time she was eight years old until she was fifteen. We can exhort her to trust her husband, forget the past and all the rest, but she cannot. All this is beyond the reach of her willpower.

This is what we all experience in our fallen human condition, some in one way, some in another. This is the tragic human situation Paul described. Something inside him drove him to do the wrong thing, something over which he was powerless:

3. From a letter reprinted in *Praying for Your Unborn Child*, p. 125.

I have the desire to do what is good, but I cannot carry it out. For what I do is not the good I want to do; no, the evil I do not want to do—this I keep on doing. Now if I do what I do not want to do, it is no longer I who do it, but it is sin living in me that does it.

Romans 7:18–20

Oppression is beyond our control, but it is for this reason that we need a Savior: We cannot do it on our own.

Just today in our local newspaper I read a typical example of an overpowering emotion that could not be silenced by reason or will.[4] A man was finally convicted of rape after his victim came forward to accuse him 22 years later. He was convicted only because six other women, encouraged by the first woman's example, came forward to corroborate her accusation.

And what was the woman's motive for breaking her silence and bringing her past into the light? First, she decided to accuse the man, a friend of her father's, because she wanted to silence the shame she had felt all those years. Second, she found herself tormented by an unfounded fear that her three-year-old daughter would also be molested. These emotions of shame and fear lay beyond the reach of her will, and 22 years had not been enough to silence them.

This testifies to the wisdom of the traditional Christian practice of praying for the protection of infants. The idea behind infant baptism is not only to fill the baby with God's life from the very beginning, but also to protect him from evil. The Roman Catholic ceremony for baptism has traditionally included a prayer for exorcism, just in case the baby has already picked up some demonic influence from the outside world. I used to think this exorcism prayer was a harsh and needless part of the beautiful baptismal ceremony. But I have since changed my mind, and recognize the wisdom of praying for the child to be freed of anything evil he may already have picked up from his family or environment. At the very least, this baptismal exorcism illustrates a traditional belief in the Church that an innocent person can be invaded by an evil spirit.

4. *Florida Times-Union*, August 25, 1994, pp. 1, 8.

How They Leave

The good news is that a person who has been afflicted for years can be freed from these burdens of the past. Furthermore, since he was guiltless in becoming contaminated, deliverance is relatively easy compared to the struggle that often takes place when we pray to free a person from spirits of sin or the occult.

The most significant difference from other forms of deliverance is significant indeed: This is one deliverance in which you do not necessarily have to deal directly with the evil spirit. Since the spirit of trauma entered through an open spiritual or emotional wound, and since the victim is usually innocent of sin, the spirit usually leaves once that wound has been healed. It has no more place to dwell, as it were, and has to leave on its own. If it does not leave automatically after the healing prayer, it can be confronted afterward and cast out easily.

The important thing to remember is that when you discover you are dealing with a spirit of trauma, your primary focus is not on deliverance but inner healing. After healing takes place, the spirit has to depart.

What Is Inner Healing?

Simply put, inner healing (in contrast to physical healing) is the form of God's healing that cures our emotional and spiritual wounds. These wounds usually result from hurtful episodes or broken relationships in our past that prevent us from acting freely or relating freely to other people in the present. Willpower ("the Law") and discipline, necessary as they are in many areas of our spiritual growth, are insufficient in themselves to heal us in these areas of deep wounding.

If a girl has never known her father's love, or, worse yet, has been abused verbally, physically or sexually by her father, she may find it hard to believe in or accept God's love, especially the love of God the Father. By willpower she can decide to believe—in her head, as it were—that God loves her; but she will find it difficult, if not impossible, to feel in her heart that God really loves her.

One morning recently at one of our conferences, a priest shared a beautiful experience he had had during the healing service the night before. He was in his seventies and had suffered, he told us, from an excessive fear of dying—especially of how he might die. He was afraid of losing his mind and all his faculties, as he had often seen happen with elderly people. By conscious faith and willpower, he had told God for years that he not only accepted death, but any manner of death God might choose for him. Still, he was afraid—and all his human energy could not get at this fear.

Sitting at the breakfast table with us, his eyes glistening with tears, the priest said he had rested in the Spirit[5] for about an hour at the healing service. During that time Jesus had accomplished what only God could do: free him from his fear.

This is only one of thousands of stories I could share about how God frees people from the emotional wounding that affects all of us in one way or the other, some more deeply than others.

Many excellent books have been written on this subject, and since this book concerns deliverance rather than inner healing, I will simply add a few important points about inner healing.

The most important distinction to make is between the need to repent and the need for inner healing. *When you have sinned, you need to repent. But when others have sinned against you and permanently influenced or even damaged you (though they may not be aware of it), you need to receive inner healing in order to once again become free.*

At other times our wounding does not come from anyone's sin in particular, but just because we are surrounded by a fallen, destructive world. If your mother died in an auto accident before your very eyes when you were three years old, you might well need healing, not only for the terrible shock of seeing her die, but because for years you were deprived of her presence and love, which has affected the entire course of your life.

A moving example of the simple tragedy of life is the well-known story of how C. S. Lewis reacted after his wife, Joy, died of cancer. He had written philosophically for years about pain and death, but when she died all his religious thoughts failed to console him and he shrieked out, as it were:

An overdose of sleeping pills would do it. I am more afraid that we are really rats in a trap. Or, worse yet, rats in a laboratory.

5. This phenomenon is described and discussed in my book *Overcome by the Spirit* (Grand Rapids: Chosen Books, 1990).

Sooner or later I must face the question in plain language. What reason have we, except our own desperate wishes, to believe that God is, by any standard we can conceive, "good"? Doesn't all the *prima facie* evidence suggest exactly the opposite?[6]

The next morning Lewis spoke of this outburst as a "yell." Eventually he worked his way through his pain, through prayer and writing, to achieve a certain peace. But a child who suffers the death of a loved one is often left with a permanent wound from which only Jesus Christ can free him (perhaps later in life) through prayer.

Most traumas do not result in a demonic infestation, but some of them do. A spirit of fear might enter the child who saw his mother die in the car accident. There is also a spirit called death that can attach itself to this kind of memory.

You need not repent if you have been wounded severely by the sins and attitudes of others, or by the harsh realities of life in an imperfect world. There is nothing for you to feel guilty about. But the one important thing you need to do is forgive those who have hurt you.

How can you tell when you are just dealing with an ordinary human wounding, needing inner healing, and when there is also a spirit of trauma attached to it? At our last conference, when we were praying with the people coming forward, one man burst out with deep sobbing, then curled up on the floor, shaking. Did he need only healing, or was there also a spirit present?

The only way of telling is through the gift of discernment. The man sobbing exhibited such extreme facial expressions that I thought he was probably tormented by a spirit of grief. But the person with me, who I know has excellent discernment, said he was simply suffering extreme human grief.

In the practical order this is important. If a spirit is present, you might hold the person at arm's length, look him in the eye and tell the spirit to calm down and depart. If it is simply a profound outburst of emotion, a more appropriate response would be to encourage him to cry, to bring him close and perhaps even to hold him while you pray, until the sobbing has been transformed into peace.

This is precisely what happened.

6. C. S. Lewis, *A Grief Observed* (New York: Seabury Press, 1961), p. 26.

How to Pray for Freedom from a Spirit of Trauma

Since prayer for inner healing may be enough to free a person from spirits of trauma, you will want to get to the inner healing prayer as soon as possible. The spirits will try to block the prayer if they can. So you may want to formulate the prayer in the following steps:

1. Protection

First, pray for protection in the way I described earlier.

2. Binding

Bind off the spirit(s) from impeding the healing by a prayer that goes something like this:

In the name of Jesus Christ I command you not to interfere with this prayer. I bind you off from influencing _____'s will, from his mind, from his imagination or emotions, from his memories and from his body. I cut you off by the sword of the Spirit from stirring up _____'s grief [or fear or any other primary emotional problems]. I command you to be quiet and to leave when we finish our prayer for healing.[7]

3. Extending Forgiveness

If the person has not already forgiven the people who have injured him, help him to do this.

4. Inner Healing

Now lead him in a prayer for inner healing. There are many ways of doing this, but all inner healing involves asking Jesus to go back to that moment in time, or to that broken relationship, that continues to influence the person. The prayer does not obliterate the memory; it is nothing like some forms of psychotherapy (like electric shock) that block out the memory. What Jesus does is take the poison out of the memory, so it can no longer harm the person in the present, and transform it—sometimes in an extraordinary way.

---

7. This is just a suggested way of praying, of course; I do not want anyone slavishly copying a rigid form. Make up your own prayer, if you wish.

The simplest prayer for inner healing begins in a quiet location where your prayer will not be disturbed. Then ask Jesus to return to the memory of the event or to the broken relationship where the wounding took place. Remain in silence and see what Jesus may do. For an expanded explanation of how best to pray, consult any of the reputable books on inner healing that are available.[8]

After we finish the prayer for inner healing, the spirit(s) of trauma should leave quietly, since they no longer have any foothold: The wound they were infecting has been healed.

At times, however, the spirit hangs on and you need to confront it and cast it out. But once the healing has taken place and it has lost its hold on the person's past, it should be relatively easy to cast out. At other times you may find it best to cast out the spirit of fear or incest (or whatever) first, to help make the prayer for inner healing go more easily.

The difficulty with beginning with deliverance, rather than inner healing, is that since we are ministering to a wounded person and not to an evil spirit, and since the person has already been wounded by broken relationships and a shattered life, we may further wound the person in the process of trying to help.[9] The feeling of life being against me, and of my being a rotten person, can be worsened by someone deciding that something evil resides in me and starting to command it to go. It is usually more helpful to represent Jesus as He heals and comforts, rather

8. A few of the available resources on inner healing: chapter 13 of my book *Healing* (Altamonte Springs, Fla.: Creation House, 1988); *How to Pray for Inner Healing for Yourself and Others* by Rita Bennett (Grand Rapids: Fleming H. Revell, 1984); *Inner Healing* by Mike Flynn and Doug Gregg (Downers Grove, Ill.: InterVarsity Press, 1993); *Healing Life's Hurts* by Matthew and Dennis Linn (Mahwah, N.J.: Paulist Press, revised edition 1993); *Healing the Wounded Spirit* by John and Paula Sandford (Tulsa: Victory House, 1985); *The Healing Gifts of the Spirit* by Agnes Sanford (San Francisco: Harper & Row, 1966); *Healing of Memories* by David Seamands (Wheaton, Ill.: Victor Books, 1985); *Healing the Hidden Self* by Barbara Shlemon (Notre Dame: Ave Maria Press, 1982); *Inner Healing through Healing of Memories* by Betty Tapscott (Kingwood, Tex.: Hunter Books, 1987). Two "cassette books" on inner healing are available from Christian Healing Ministries (P.O. Box 9520, Jacksonville, FL 32208): "Love and Healing," three tapes by Judith MacNutt, $15; and "Inner Healing: A Multi-Faceted Approach to Wholeness," featuring five speakers, including Judith and myself, $50.

9. The woman I mentioned earlier who broke her silence after 22 years said that ever since being molested sexually, she had battled feelings of depression, low self-esteem and an inability to trust people. This is typical.

than in His authority and anger as He confronts and commands evil to depart.

For this reason, if you do start by commanding the spirit to depart, make sure the way you do it—the look in your eyes and the tone of your voice—does not give the impression that you despise the victim of evil, rather than the evil spirits themselves. In praying against evil, it is easy to make the victim feel that he himself is evil, and it is hard to maintain the balance between hating the sin and loving the sinner.

If you do need to confront and cast out an evil spirit, before or after praying for inner healing, do it in the way I suggested in the last chapter.

On occasion I have prayed from the platform at a large, public healing service to free people from the spirits of trauma whose names came to me in prayer. I have done this calmly, and usually there is little audible response. Afterward anywhere between ten and twenty people out of a congregation of, say, two hundred will tell me they felt something quietly leave. The following is from a letter I received from a woman recently:

When you prayed on Saturday night for the spirits of grief and rejection to leave in the name of Jesus, I felt something moving through my body each time and out both arms, which were raised in prayer. It was awesome. At the same time I became aware of great peace all through my body.

On Sunday morning I woke up with the worst pain from colitis I have had in a long time. You told a story about a woman troubled by the spirit of *hatred of men*. I have experienced that for a long time; and, just as my mother suffers from colitis, I believe I got the feeling of hatred for men generationally through her. I also have a feeling she was sexually abused as I was, but she has never talked about it. When you rebuked the spirit of *hatred of men*, I felt that leave me, too.

Right before the session, still in pain from the colitis, even though I'd taken a lot more medicine than normal, I asked a friend to pray for me and the pain went totally away. I felt a deeper peace in that part of my body than I've ever felt. Praise God in Jesus Christ!

Further Insights

Ask Jesus to Fill the Wounded Nature

Because the spirit has come into the person because of his weakness (not necessarily sin), it is important that, following upon the healing and deliverance, we ask that Jesus' life come into that person's life to fill up whatever was missing. Most woundedness goes back to a lack of love in one way or another, and what is most needed is to fill the person with an experience of God's love. Often Jesus appears to the person, or speaks to him, at such a depth that he can no longer doubt he is loved. He may see Jesus' face, or see Jesus looking at him with such tenderness and affection that the shame that previously bound him will simply disappear. Or Jesus may say something like, "You are my beloved child. I created you and have loved you from the beginning."

In countless ways Jesus fills our wounded nature with His love, His forgiveness, His joy, His peace, His affirmation, in order to replace with His life and health everything in our lives that has been torn and broken.

Spirits of Trauma Come in Clusters

Spirits of trauma, like most evil spirits, usually come in clusters, all similar in nature, feeding off the same wound, as it were. If the main problem is rejection, you may find other related spirits like loneliness, self-hatred and self-pity.

The Person May Need to Repent

Wounds of trauma can eventually lead the person into sin for which he needs to repent. If he has suffered rejection and dwelt on it in an unhealthy way, he may willingly have indulged in self-pity or begun to contemplate suicide as a way out. In this case he also needs to repent.

Build Up Strengths to Counteract Weaknesses

As a follow-up to inner healing and deliverance, the person should take steps to build up strengths that will counteract his weaknesses. For years he has gotten used to feeling and thinking in certain destructive ways, and he needs to change those habitual patterns, or else the same problems and spirits will return. I have seen a spirit of rejection return only two hours after it was cast out because the woman felt slighted at the dinner table by someone ignoring her.

Another help is choosing spiritual reading that counteracts the person's predominant weakness. He should concentrate on passages in the Bible that build up virtues he needs. For those who suffer from self-hatred, I often suggest *A Stranger to Self-Hatred—A Glimpse of Jesus* by my friend Brennan Manning.[10] If the person's life has been filled with sadness, he might read passages like Psalm 23 and the last chapter of Isaiah, rather than the Lamentations of Jeremiah. He should read books that represent the joyful aspects of Christianity rather than books that go heavily into the sins of our society and what is wrong with the Church. I realize that many Christians avoid the harder parts of Christ's teaching; and denial of the cross is not what I favor at all. It is just that some people need to balance their lives for a time.

We need direction to help us in those areas in which we need encouragement; and, ideally speaking, we need a wise spiritual director (although in these days it is difficult to find one) to point out the faults we are blind to. Our prayers and even our recreational activities should be directed somehow to our healing.

I have always tended, for instance, to take life seriously and be overly responsible. I find it hard to take time off to play when ministry or work is at hand. In one way this results in much good; but without balance it harms family relationships and leads to weariness. So I have taken steps to change it—going out once a week, for example; spending more time with our children; reading the lives of optimistic saints like Dame Julian of Norwich. I still have a distance to go in all this, but I know the direction I need to take.

What does this have to do with casting out spirits of trauma? A great deal. Most of us tend to be blind to our greatest weakness, even though our friends see it clearly; and most Christians need to take steps to balance out their weaknesses and make a plan to change their lives over a prolonged period of time. The steps we need to take in attempting to change long-established habit patterns are roughly the same whether we suffer from or-

10. Brennan Manning, *A Stranger to Self-Hatred, A Glimpse of Jesus* (Denville, N.J.: Dimension Books, 1982).

dinary human weakness or a weakness intensified by demonic aggravation. If the problem is serious, however, the measures we take to counteract the destructive tendency must be decisive and exacting.

All Deliverance Requires Inner Healing

Sometimes the inner healing comes first. Some people have such fragile personalities—take, for example, those victims of severe abuse who have multiple personalities—that they may need to be built up with inner healing for a long time before receiving deliverance. At other times, the prayer for inner healing comes only after we pray for deliverance, when a spirit of trauma stands in the way and blocks healing.

In any case, even when there has been sin, there is also weakness in the past that contributes to our repeating the sin again and again. So all those who need deliverance also need inner healing, at some point, to shore up the weakness that inclined them to sin.

The opposite is not true: All candidates for inner healing do not also require deliverance.

Balance Law and Grace

Some Christians have a hard time seeing that many people who sin or suffer various weaknesses are victims. To them it seems that if we encourage inner healing, we are being soft on sin. "It's sin," they say. "Get them to repent."

Repentance itself, of course, is a gift (see 2 Timothy 2:25). And the Gospel teaches that none of us can live up to the Law, especially the Law of the Gospel. We need a Savior. We must become disciplined and take action for what we are responsible for. But in part we are helpless and need to turn to God for healing or deliverance.

Alcoholics Anonymous has understood that message: You cannot stop drinking on your own. If you are an alcoholic you must admit you cannot quit drinking simply by your own will-power; you need to turn to a power higher than yourself. The step over which the alcoholic has some control is to admit he is *out* of control, helpless in the area of his addiction. Where he is free to act and must act is to connect with AA or a sponsor. In part, then, he is free; in part he is in bondage. But as long as the alcoholic thinks he is free—"I'm not an alcoholic; I can take a drink or not take a drink"—he cannot be helped.

So there is a balance between our need to discipline ourselves to the extent that we can and our need for grace, God's gift of healing. Deliverance ("The devil made me do it!") and healing do not enable us to avoid responsibility. Some people's area of freedom is very small, perhaps five percent, while their bondage is extreme, perhaps 95 percent. Others are almost totally free (with God's grace, of course) to act or not to act, to sin or not to sin. Yet I have found that even those who think they are most free are often blind to the sins that hold them captive, in ways that most of their friends see only too clearly.

To say that all human problems can be solved by repentance tends to make us judgmental and leads to our becoming harsh Pharisees: "It's always the sinner's fault and he requires punishment. Build more jails; mete out harsher punishments!" Jesus understood that we are all under the dominion of evil and that we need compassion, healing and deliverance as well as repentance and conversion.

In Romans and Galatians Paul lashed out against those who relied on the Law to make them holy, religious people who thought willpower enabled them to live according to God's ideal. It used to be the Old Law; now it becomes the New Law, which can be just as harsh. We hear it in sermons all the time. The Gospel, by contrast, teaches that we cannot make it on our own. We need grace, salvation, healing, deliverance.

These are all part of Jesus' central message: We do not have a new Lawgiver; we have a Savior. Hear the resolution of Paul's agonized cry over the fallen human condition:

What a wretched man I am! Who will rescue me from this body of death? Thanks be to God—through Jesus Christ our Lord!
Romans 7:24–25

15

Spirits of Sin

Spirits of sin, as the name suggests, are spirits that lodge themselves in their victims because of sins they have committed.

Spirits do not enter us simply because we have sinned. At times we all sin. But spirits of sin enter some people, mysteriously, for one of two reasons:

1. because these people have sinned *habitually* over a prolonged period of time; or
2. because they have committed a particularly *intense* sin (a violent act of murder, for example) that has opened the gate to let the spirits come in.

When we sin over a long period of time, we are disregarding God's will and moving away from the protection of His Kingdom. We are building a home for sin and eventually a spirit of sin may move in.

Unforgiveness is one of the most common spirits of sin that we encounter. We all have a hard time fulfilling Christ's law of forgiving our enemies, but if we dwell on our injuries and let bitterness and a desire for revenge build up, at some point a spirit of unforgiveness may enter.

We can usually recognize a spirit of sin by the name it gives when we ask it to identify itself. Some of the more common ones are *lust, unforgiveness* and *despair,* but there are countless others. Some are identified by general names like *hatred,* while others are specific in the vices they specialize in, like *hatred of men* or *hatred of women.* The simplest rule of thumb is that for every variety of sin, you can find an evil spirit that torments people in that area. So the names are almost too numerous to list.

It is worth mentioning that when a woman has an abortion, a spirit called *abortion* sometimes enters the woman or the doctor. Derek Prince, who has had an extensive ministry in deliverance, believes this almost always happens. At the very least we should pray with women for the healing of their post-abortion trauma.[1]

Deliverance from a Spirit of Sin

The special aspect of freeing a person from this kind of spirit is that the person must repent and ask God's forgiveness for the sin, as well as for hurting anyone who has been harmed by the sin.

Since sin unrepented served as the entrance for the evil spirit, that door has to be shut. Because the person sinned willingly, chances are they will find it hard to shut that door firmly. If a person harbors a spirit of pornography that entered through his frequent reading of pornographic magazines and viewing of porno videos, he will probably not have a strong desire to quit. But until he is ready to repent of his participation in pornography, the spirit has a right to stay where it is. Either you will be unable to cast it out or, if you do, it will come back as soon as it can.[2]

In a celebrated passage of his *Confessions,* St. Augustine describes the struggle against the habit of sin that everyone experiences in one way or another:

> The enemy held my will; and of it he made a chain and bound me. Because my will was perverse, it changed to lust, and lust yielded—to become habit, and habit not resisted became necessity. These were like links hanging one on another—which is why

1. An excellent book on this subject is *Will I Cry Tomorrow?* by Dr. Susan Stanford-Rue (Grand Rapids: Fleming H. Revell, 1990).

2. All the suggestions in this chapter should prove helpful for Christians belonging to churches that provide confession for sins (the sacrament of reconciliation).

I have called it a chain—and their hard bondage held me bound hand and foot.[3]

I in my great worthlessness . . . had begged you for chastity, saying: "Grant me chastity and continence, but not yet." For I was afraid that you would hear my prayer too soon, and too soon would heal me from the disease of lust which I wanted satisfied rather than extinguished.[4]

How well St. Augustine describes the weakness in our own wills that makes it so hard to repent! We do not know whether evil spirits were within him blocking his repentance. Certainly he believed that Satan was making it harder for him to change his lifestyle. He was already a believer by this time but could not change without more of God's grace.

What spirits of sin do is add a driven, compulsive aspect to sin. If a person is already addicted to any sin, a spirit will cause that sin to be still more addictive or compulsive. And if the person repents and the spirit is cast out, but then the person falls once again, the spirit can easily return.

One of my friends, a counselor, once worked with a man addicted to pornography. He also harbored a spirit of pornography. After a number of sessions he realized that pornography was harming his marriage and he made up his mind to quit. He repented and the counselor cast out the spirit helping to drive his lustful compulsion. For several months he was much changed. Then, in a moment of boredom, he picked up a pornographic magazine someone had left in his car and gave in to temptation once again. Instantly the spirit came back. The man was no longer free but driven by the spirit working on his previous habit of addiction.

"When an evil spirit comes out of a man, it goes through arid places seeking rest and does not find it. Then it says, 'I will return to the house I left.' When it arrives, it finds the house unoccupied, swept clean and put in order. Then it goes and takes with it seven

---

3. St. Augustine, *The Confessions,* translated by Frank Sheed (New York: Sheed & Ward, 1943). Book Eight, V, p. 164.

4. Ibid., p. 170.

other spirits more wicked than itself, and they go in and live there. And the final condition of that man is worse than the first."

Matthew 12:43–45

Many times when the person is not sure she really wants to give up her sin, you can ask whether she is willing to receive prayer for a willingness to relinquish the sin—if she is willing to be willing. One of the most common examples of this is being willing to forgive. Forgiving enemies goes so contrary to our human desire for vengeance, as well as our sense of justice, that we find it very hard to forgive. "The other person is wrong," we reason. "He injured me. Why should I forgive him until he changes and asks for forgiveness?" Yet forgiving *enemies*, not penitent friends or relatives, is one of the most striking requirements Jesus made for living according to God's commandments (Matthew 5:38–45).

Forgiving those who have injured us is a requirement for healing to take place, and *unforgiveness, bitterness* and *resentment* are among the evil spirits that dwell in us when we stubbornly refuse to forgive over a long period of time. If you were to pray with people from Northern Ireland or Israel or the West Bank, you would find that the cycles of murder and vengeance in those parts of our world lead to a natural desire for vengeance, which is compounded by evil spirits that drive the victims of violence to take revenge and murder their oppressors.

Frequently when we ask people to forgive those who have injured them, they cannot bring themselves to do it. Then we ask them if they are willing to ask God to help them be willing to forgive. If they say yes, we can pray something like this:

Lord Jesus, by the power of forgiveness that is beyond our power, and which You won on the cross when You said, "Father, forgive them, for they know not what they do," pour out Your own forgiving love into _____'s heart, so that she may be able to forgive this person who has hurt her so deeply.

You can add to this prayer any particulars about the person (such as, "Help her to forgive her father") or about the incident (such as, "When she was molested").

We really do need Jesus' power to forgive since it is so far beyond our human ability, especially if the wound is deep and has permanently impaired our lives. We need to pray with people for the willingness to repent because changing from the old creation to the new is beyond our human abilities:

> If anyone is in Christ, he is a new creation; the old has gone, the new has come! All this is from God. . . .
>
> 2 Corinthians 5:17–18

Then, after the person has repented, we can pray in the ordinary way for deliverance from any spirits of sin.

The Need for Compassion

As you can see, when you are dealing with spirits of sin, you have a two-step process:

1. helping the person truly repent;
2. praying with the person for deliverance.

Repentance is seldom easy because even the most hideous sin usually results from the person's brokenness. The sinner is probably not fully free, even when there are no evil spirits present to make the problem worse. Jesus treated sinners with compassion, especially those who sinned out of weakness, and with more respect than He did the pious, self-righteous, hard-hearted Pharisees. He knew that sinners are often seeking something good in their sin, even if they are seeking happiness in the wrong way. The alcoholic may be trying to deaden the pain of a failed dream. The liar may be trying to protect her reputation in order to be loved and respected. Like Jesus, we need to be gentle with sinners, as we trust God will be forgiving toward us in the midst of our own weakness and sin.

For this reason, inner healing is usually needed, just as it is in freeing people from spirits of trauma. Often the person is unable to repent until after inner healing has taken place. In this case you may have not two but three different processes to help with:

1. helping the person truly repent;
2. praying with the person for inner healing;
3. Praying with the person for deliverance.

And you need to make a wise decision, with the Holy Spirit's guidance, as to the best order in which to proceed.

Suppose a spirit of lust has invaded a woman because she indulges in a promiscuous lifestyle. She entertains a new boyfriend every week and they tumble into bed almost as soon as they meet. She tells you that she knows her behavior is wrong, she is afraid of contracting AIDS and she is consumed with shame. She also tells you "it just feels so good to be held for a few minutes," so she does not know if she even wants to stop. Furthermore, she may be honest enough to tell you that she cannot promise to change.

It is clear, I think, that we need to find out where she was deprived of the true love every child needs growing up. Where did such a devouring hunger for affection come from? We may need to pray for Jesus to fill this in before she is able to repent, and before deliverance can ever take place. Otherwise this emptiness will remain; and even if you cast out a spirit of lust, the weakness will return.

Almost every sin has a hold on us because of an emotional weakness. Fear of failure in school inclines a young man to compromise his Christian standards and cheat. Fear of her boyfriend's ridicule leads a young woman to drink too much at a party or give in to his pressure to spend the night with him. Then, if she gets pregnant, fear may influence her into making a hasty decision to abort the baby.

> To you, who were spiritually dead all the time that you drifted along on the stream of this world's ideas of living, and obeyed its unseen ruler (who is still operating in those who do not respond to the truth of God), to you Christ has given life! We all lived like that in the past, and followed the impulses and imaginations of our evil nature.
>
> Ephesians 2:1–3, Phillips

Paul admitted that sin had made a home in him and that he could do nothing about it (Romans 7:18). Only through Jesus Christ can we be set free:

> It was God's gift of grace which saved you. No one can pride himself upon earning the love of God. The fact is that what we are we owe to the hand of God upon us. For we are his workmanship,

created in Christ Jesus to do those good deeds which God
planned for us to do.

Ephesians 2:8–10, Phillips

Consequently, if the person has a hard time repenting, her re-
luctance is only natural. We need to pray for God to help the sinner become truly sorry and want to change. Repentance is the
key—not as a formula of words but as a turning point in our
lives. We will struggle until we are transformed into that new
creation Jesus calls us to be when He replaces our emptiness
and shame with His own life and love.

Only when our emptiness is filled with His love, and our guilt
and shame are replaced by His forgiveness and light, will there
be no more room for unclean spirits. At last the death of sin will
be swallowed up in life:

"Where, O death, is your victory?
Where, O death, is your sting?"
The sting of death is sin, and the power of sin is the law. But
thanks be to God! He gives us the victory through our Lord Jesus
Christ.

1 Corinthians 15:55–57

16

Spirits of the Occult

More and more attention is being paid these days to Satanism and witchcraft. Even a certain degree of respectability is being given to witches. They are regularly granted Halloween interviews on radio and television; and I know of at least one witch who was appointed to the faculty of a Christian institution. In a day when many question the reality of the demonic realm, movies often feature witches and satanic horrors, and there is an increasing fascination with the occult. Young people make pacts to kill themselves or their parents or teachers. Many police departments train officers to detect and deal with satanic crime. Stories keep surfacing of how a few daycare centers and schools have become nests of child abuse controlled by satanic cults.

Yet by and large Christian churches ignore these aspects of the decline of our society and civilization, as if they were outside the domain of the Church and best ignored. Just last year our daughter, who goes to a Christian high school, went to two slumber parties in which the girls brought out Ouija boards that had been given them by their mothers. At one party the hostess mother told the girls not to worry, her daughter's Ouija board was just a harmless game.

On the other hand, I have listened to the anguish of many victims of just such occult practices who are trying to break loose. The spirits of the occult are the most tenacious and vicious of all spirits. In contrast to spirits of trauma and sin, which often leave on their own when their victims repent or receive healing prayer, spirits of the occult need to be confronted directly and cast out.

What Is the Occult?

The occult (the word comes from the Latin for "hidden" or "secret") represents the spiritual realm where people seek either

1. Knowledge or
2. Power

from any source other than God, when the kind of knowledge or power sought can come only from God. When we seek such power or knowledge, we are opening ourselves, even when we do not realize what we are doing, to the realm of evil spirits. The vast majority of people who get involved in the occult do not realize they are doing anything wrong.

Unwitting Involvement

Some people seek *knowledge* and are often hooked by curiosity. The Ouija board, for instance, spells out answers to our questions about our future (the kind of knowledge that can come only from God) or about the fate of dead loved ones (again, known only by God). Parents may want to know if their son who committed suicide is happy in the afterlife—a very human question. Their desire is not to connect with Satan; it is to connect with their son. But in seeking this forbidden knowledge, they open themselves to demonic influence. Evil spirits take over the Ouija board and mix fascinating bits of truth with one or two major falsehoods.

Other people seek *power.* They may go to a devotee of voodoo, for example, to put a spell on someone they want to influence to fall in love; or to put a curse on someone they hate.

Most people seeking illicit knowledge or power do not know they are entering Satan's kingdom where they can become permanently oppressed, even though both Scripture and Christian tradition have always forbidden these activities. Many Christian pastors regard these practices as silly and superstitious and refuse to preach about them. Most of the spirits of the occult that I have encountered were contracted when the sufferer unwittingly entered Satan's territory and, as John Wimber picturesquely describes it, was "slimed."

Many years ago a friend of mine, a respected minister we will call Al, lost his wife, who died unexpectedly in her thirties. The loss was tragic and Al was left to care for their two young children. Unsure what his next move should be, he decided to consult a trance medium (who was also a minister) to whom the controversial Episcopal bishop Alfred Pike had turned when his son committed suicide. A trance medium is one who gets in touch with a "spirit guide," who takes over the medium's voice and "channels" information from the "other side" to the seeker.

When Al went for his appointment, the minister went into a trance state and his spirit guide, "Fletcher," took over. Even though Al and the trance medium had never met, the spirit guide knew some things about Al's past that the trance medium could not have known in the natural order. The spirit guide came up with the university Al had attended and the branch of knowledge he had specialized in. Moreover, it knew two hidden things about Al's family that Al himself did not know, and which he had to check out when he got home. Al was amazed to find out they were both true.

The spirit guide, using the medium's voice, assured Al that his wife was happy over on the other side. But the guide also told Al that his wife loved him so much she did not want him to marry again, yet she encouraged him to satisfy his sexual needs by taking a mistress.

Al played all this to me on a cassette tape he had made of his interview. He had been hoping to remarry and find a mother for his two children, but now he was confused because the knowledge was supernatural, and he wondered if he should follow the advice.

Al was right: The knowledge *was* supernatural—or, more correctly, preternatural—but it was not from God.

This is the kind of occult involvement we often find. Notice, too, the surprising thing: A Christian minister seeks occult knowledge by going to another Christian minister, a trance medium who is deeply involved in the occult and who has been recommended by yet another minister—in this case, a bishop who had also sought occult knowledge. Whether Al unwittingly took on a spirit of the occult at that time, I do not know. It was the last thing he intended. But this kind of involvement is what often results in a person's becoming oppressed.

Deliberate Involvement

Going deeper into the occult realm, we find serious involvement when a person contacts the realm of Satan directly and knowingly in order to gain power or knowledge. The celebrated model of this is Faust, who sold his soul to the devil to achieve money, fame and the adulation of women. When he was dying he tried to take it all back, but the devil held him to his contract and hauled him off to hell. Christopher Marlowe wrote the powerful Elizabethan play *Dr. Faustus* and, since he himself was involved in Satanism, served as a consultant to Shakespeare when he wrote about the three witches in *Macbeth*.

In those involved directly in the occult, we find levels of serious infestation.

Some teenagers who get involved as individuals or small groups simply read about Satanism, decide it is exciting and find out how to hold meetings and cast spells by reading manuals in a do-it-yourself form of Satanism.

Higher up in their seriousness and involvement are organized covens under the leadership of witches and warlocks. Here, too, there are levels.

Lower down are groups involved in the messy details of animal sacrifice, groups that perpetrate some of the grosser crimes we read about. They leave behind all kinds of evidence pointing to their activity, like the statues that are desecrated in churches after Satan worshipers have broken in and conducted their rites.

More serious are the higher realms of Satan worship that are kept secret, in which professional people seek power in their careers and in government circles. Far from wanting attention, they try to live without attracting the notice of anyone outside their own inner circle. Few know who they are. Furthermore, they despise the crudity of the lower forms of Satanism. Often they are descendants of families that have long been given over to Satan worship.

In these explicit forms of Satanism, the victims are eventually led to make a written or blood contract with Satan. It is difficult for people who go this far to break out.

Here above all, churches need trained exorcists who can help free the victims who do decide to try to escape Satan's grip. The following is taken from a letter sent me by a priest who wanted to help a woman who had signed a blood contract and who had stolen a Communion wafer in order to desecrate it. (I have changed their names to protect their identities.)

I made a special effort to speak privately with Bishop A. He told me, in a roundabout way, that he had washed his hands of the case and didn't seem to know how to handle it.[1] This didn't aid my own frustrations.

. . . On this day all hell seemed to break loose (pardon the expression). I saw Y. that morning and she was tripping, to say the least, after taking five 10 mg Valiums.[2] Naturally she was very despondent and was obviously suicidal, but she did tell me that she would like me to destroy her contract and to keep the Eucharist that she had in her possession. . . . The decision was made to admit her to the mental health center, if there was a bed available. She agreed to this. She then asked to see me privately to fulfill the promise she had made.

We went into a small room and she asked me to say the binding prayer, which I did, and this enabled her to give me the following items: tarot cards, the Eucharist and the contract. Handing over the tarot cards was no problem. However, when she reached into her pocketbook to take out the Eucharist, she began to shake and have difficulty speaking. In order to make her more responsive, I repeated the binding prayer and prayed to the Holy Spirit. Her eyes began to roll around and her face became distorted as she ripped the Eucharist out of the envelope. With superhuman strength she would not allow me to take it out of her hand. She started to make inhuman groans; in voices not her own she proceeded to say that she was a pig for Satan. Then she desecrated the Eucharist by crushing it with her right hand and throwing it all over the room. (At this point I began to feel ill at ease, to say the least.)

She seemed to quiet down for a few moments, during which time I prayed to the Holy Spirit to give me the strength I needed to confront Lucifer. With great anguish and shaking, she removed

1. Previous unsuccessful efforts had been made to help her; you can understand the bishop's frustration. Yet churches need better understanding and ability to help these victims.
2. Members of satanic groups are often hooked purposely on drugs, which compounds the problem of deliverance.

the contract from her pocketbook and proceeded to rip it up. After doing so, she took her right hand and scratched the back of
her left hand until the blood flowed freely. The contract fell to the
floor and I was able to retrieve it. She instructed me to anoint her
right hand and to prepare myself for any violent reaction on the
part of Satan.[3] When I did anoint her right hand, some external
force ripped her hand from mine and threw her arm against the
wall. I was able to anoint her left hand, however, and finally her
right. At this point she seemed to experience some relief, and the
blood stopped flowing from her hands. I helped her profess her
faith in Jesus Christ, which she did with some difficulty.

I went home that evening and proceeded to burn the desecrated Eucharist and the contract. When I lit the fire, the stench
accompanying the burning was not of burnt paper but smelled
like burning hair.

Avoiding Involvement

This letter gives some idea of the difficulty in getting rid of
spirits of the occult, which come from hell itself—the "netherworld," a higher (or lower) realm than most spirits come from.
These spirits, called demons[4] by the witches, are stronger than
ordinary evil or unclean spirits (the more generic terms). The
ministry to Y. has gone on for some time and illustrates the
length of time and complexity of trying to help someone who, at
one point, gave her will over to Satan, but now has the desire to
serve Jesus Christ and escape the torments of the demonic
world.

It is important to teach people, non-Christians as well as
Christians, to protect themselves from becoming demonized by
getting involved "innocently" in spiritualism or the occult. We
need to delineate as clearly as we can the areas of activity that
are gateways to oppression.

In chapter 12 I offered some questions we can ask people to
see if they have been involved in anything that opened them
up to oppression. Some of these activities are clearly occult
and we must steer clear of them—activities like having our for-

3. When people make a contract with Satan they use blood drawn from a cut made
near the thumb of the right hand. One of the signs that a person is a member of a coven
is a scar in this place.
4. *Demons* in the satanic understanding are sent from the netherworld or hell. The
other evil spirits roam and influence the five areas of earth, air, fire, water and nature.
These five categories constitute *unclean* or *evil spirits.*

tunes read, playing the Ouija board or attending séances. Other activities fall into gray areas over which knowledgeable Christians disagree. Is hypnotism allowable in some instances? Are yoga exercises, without accepting yoga philosophy, acceptable?

Paul was faced with the same kinds of questions when he was asked if it was all right to eat meat sacrificed to idols. He acknowledged that although the sacrifice was demonic, he himself felt free to eat the meat. Yet he admitted that other Christians could not in good conscience eat what had been offered to idols. For the sake of preserving peace, though, he abstained from eating such meat in the presence of Christians who had a more tender conscience.

I have to admit, had I been living in Paul's time, I would probably not have felt safe eating the meat of an animal that had been offered to a false god. But the main thing to point out here is that some activities are clearly forbidden because they are dangerous, while in other areas good and knowledgeable Christians can disagree.

Important Considerations

Here are some important things to remember before ministering:

Minister in Love

When we minister to people under the influence of spirits of the occult, we need to be especially aware that we are ministering to human beings and not demons. This is easy to forget when the spirits take over, submerge the human personality and you are faced with an ugly face spitting insults at you. You may also be tempted to think, *What kind of wretched human being would get himself involved in a coven where they torture children?* In the midst of all this, your ministry *must* be characterized by love:

As, therefore, God's picked representatives of the new humanity, purified and beloved of God himself, be merciful in action, kindly in heart, humble in mind. Accept life, and be most patient and tolerant with one another, always ready to forgive if you have a difference with anyone. Forgive as freely as the Lord has forgiven you. And, above everything else, be truly loving, for love is the golden chain of all the virtues.

Colossians 3:12–14, Phillips

Be firm in relation to the spirits but loving in relation to the person who lives underneath all this confusion. Realize that even for those who have been involved in the worst crimes of Satanism, crimes like child sacrifice, the person was probably lured into the coven by the promise of a group that cared. (Many members of covens are basically lonely, lost personalities.) Then the person was probably drugged and coerced into performing horrible acts like murder or sexual degradation with the threat that worse would happen to him if he did not.

Be Sensitive to God's Timing

Never react just to a demon, and above all do not let Satan dictate your schedule. We have talked in some detail about timing. At the end of a long healing service, when someone erupts with demonic manifestations, you may want to pray at that time, but you do not have to. We respond to God, not Satan.

Pray and ask for our Lord's guidance. Ordinarily it is better to arrange another time when you have more time and energy, and when you can talk with the person and find out how the problem got started.

For Whom Do We Pray?

Since prayer for deliverance from the occult can last a long time, and since as a human being you have limits of time and energy, you are not called to pray for everyone who asks for help. In fact, some people are specifically sent by covens to destroy our ministries by wearing us out or making false accusations later on. Seek guidance in prayer before taking anyone on.

It is a tragic situation when so many people seek help and but so few are equipped to minister adequately. We need to be taught how to minister. Would that there were seminaries to train ministers in praying for deliverance! We also need to surround ourselves with people we trust to minister deliverance wisely.

And we must be prepared to experience some failures. Do not let this discourage you, any more than a medical doctor would give way to gloom or abandon his practice if some of his patients did not get well. Just be sure to act as wisely as you can, taking counsel from others with more experience, acting under authority (if possible) and working with a team whenever you can.

Furthermore, when you minister to people who have been involved heavily in Satanism, you may not have the spiritual gifts you need to cast out demons higher up in the echelons of Satan's kingdom. Eventually you may grow to that level; we all start out as inexperienced novices. But we need to be realistically aware of our limitations as well as our spiritual gifts. Be humble enough to refer the oppressed to someone with more spiritual authority. Do this not out of fear but out of wisdom, and after seeking the Spirit's guidance in prayer.

On the other hand, the first time you pray (if you ever do) for someone who is really possessed, or close to it, you will feel out of your depth. It is true, of course, that in your own humanity you are overmatched. But if the Lord has inspired you to pray, He will supply you with His power to free the sufferer. Try to surround yourself with fellow Christians you know who can help you minister deliverance.

Consider the Degree of Occult Involvement

Finally, just as there are levels of fierceness and strength in the hierarchy of evil spirits, there are levels of spiritual power required to cast out spirits of the occult. Most Christians in the healing ministry can probably pray for people who have gotten involved in spiritualist practices without realizing the danger. But not everyone should try to pray for deliverance from more serious types of occult involvement; there is danger in getting in over your head. For example, the spirit indwelling a person consecrated to Satan by a satanic high priest needs to be cast out by someone with real spiritual authority.[5]

Furthermore, the exorcist should exhibit a life of spiritual strength and integrity. Stronger spirits have attributes of knowledge enabling them to know your sins and weaknesses, and, unless those sins have been confessed and forgiven, they will humiliate you by announcing them to the onlookers. The stronger spirits may even try to attack and enter you, or someone else on

5. Some of my friends believe that only an ordained priest or minister should attempt this.

your team, or in your family, even at a distance. I have already stated that all of us are guilty of sin, but that serious, unconfessed sin is not something I want to bring into a deliverance situation. The exorcist needs the protection of a pure, honest Christian lifestyle.

To sum up, there are degrees of occult involvement that our deliverance ministry must take into account:

1. *The unwitting entrance into Satan's kingdom* by engagement in spiritualism or other occult practices (e.g., playing the Ouija board) without intending to contact Satan
2. *Knowingly seeking spiritual power to harm or dominate someone* by such practices as casting spells (e.g., going to a voodoo practitioner or witch because you seek success in love or want to curse an enemy)
3. *Becoming a channel or witch*, allowing a spirit to take over part of your life (e.g., automatic writing)
4. *Commencing a knowing, direct relationship with Satan* by making a pact with Satan
5. *Becoming part of a coven engaged in Satan worship*, with the most severe levels of evil involving sexual orgies, torture, blood sacrifices (animal or human) and parodies of Christian worship

The names of the occult spirits that identify themselves at these different levels change as they go up the scale. At lower levels you find *spiritualism* or *spirit of the Ouija board*, on up through spirits like *witchcraft* and *divination*, on through *Antichrist*, until you reach the top with personal names like *Beelzebub*.

These highest levels of spirits are especially hard to cast out, for at least four reasons:

1. They rule over entire families and clusters of spirits they have brought with them.
2. They have supernatural attributes (the demonic reverse of the gifts of the Holy Spirit)—attributes like knowledge, enabling them to read into your past or your imagination; and communication, enabling them to influence another spirit inhabiting someone else to erupt in another part of

the room or church, thereby distracting you from your prayer and frightening bystanders.

3. They can draw power from other spirits higher than they are in the hierarchy of spirits.

4. They are protected by a number of blocking spirits, which surround them with a rebellious, lying defense system.

Work with the Person

If someone needs deliverance from a spirit of the occult because he attended a séance in high school, he may not need any lengthy preparation. But if he has gotten deeply involved in Satanism, he has built a structure of sin that will make it very hard for him to receive or maintain deliverance. The demons have enough of a stronghold in him to fight back tenaciously or return quickly if they are cast out.

For this reason, you may want to ask the person requesting deliverance to prepare for weeks or months ahead of time. He needs to pray regularly, become part of a Christian support group, read Scripture daily and attend regular church services. Even though seventy percent of his personality, let's say, is not free, the thirty percent that is free needs to be purified and strengthened to stand against evil. He needs spiritual direction to change habit patterns that have long formed strongholds of weakness and sin, where the evil spirits have settled in to work their compulsions.

Do not take it as an inflexible rule, however, that you should always wait. Sometimes you are called to pray on the spot.

Do not let the demonized person expect you to do all the work. He must help to the extent that he can, even though that may not be much. Some people are so tormented by demons that when they try to pray, obscene thoughts flow compulsively through their imaginations. When they try to read the Bible, their eyes go out of focus. And when they attend church services, they are in such torment that they are forced to get up and leave. So be patient and understanding.

One man, nearly possessed, phoned me long distance to ask for me to pray for his deliverance. Instead I put him in touch with a reputable Christian community in his own city that had experience in praying for deliverance. I also phoned them to expect his call for help. Imagine my surprise when he phoned me back the next day to say that they had come to visit that very day but had left hurriedly when he hurled a Bible at them. They figured he was not really looking for help. "Didn't they know the demons forced me to throw the Bible at them?" he complained to me. "I *did* want help."

Work with the person to free him gradually, if you cannot do it all at once. It may take months, perhaps even years. Listen in love to whatever the person tells you, but listen especially to the nudgings of the Holy Spirit as to how and when you are to pray. There is no specific technique, no specific order that you can rely on; the only sure guide in deliverance is the Holy Spirit.

The person you minister to must desire to be whole and follow Jesus. It is not enough to simply want to be free from demonic torment, although the person may begin with that as a motive. You need to show him the larger picture. We need to seek the Healer, not just the healing; the Savior, not just freedom.

Steps for the Counselee to Take

From all we have said so far, you can see that praying for freedom from spirits of the occult requires more thorough preparation than any other kind of deliverance prayer.

Here are steps the counselee should take prior to deliverance prayer:

Commit Your Life to Jesus Christ

A person who seeks healing of any kind should be committed to the Healer, Jesus Christ. But with this kind of heavy deliverance, it is particularly important to make sure the person you are praying for has made a commitment to Jesus, since he has wandered, directly or indirectly, into Satan's dominion. In order to get out he needs to voice an explicit agreement to serve God and no one else—to transfer his allegiance to the Kingdom of God.

So talk to the person about this and help him commit his life to Jesus Christ as his Lord and Savior (or recommit it, if he is already a Christian). I usually ask the person to pray to accept Jesus in his own words, but often the person is not sure what to say. In this case, encourage him to repeat the sinner's prayer after you.[6]

When a person has been heavily involved in the occult, however, we often find that he becomes blocked when he tries to speak out, especially when he comes to the key phrase *Jesus Christ.* He just cannot get it out; or he seems to black out while his eyes roll upward, until all you can see are the whites of his eyes.

When this happens, command the spirits to stop their interference and loose the person's voice and tongue: "I want _____ to speak, not you. Now set _____ free, in the name of Jesus Christ." After he is finally able to make his commitment, I ask him to repeat it several times. Each time it comes more easily, and you can see that the hold of the spirits on the person is weakening, until finally he can speak freely.

Repent

Next (just as with spirits of sin) comes repentance. Ask the person to repent of every act he has committed that has led him into an involvement with the occult.

If he let a friend read his palm, or some such activity, he might have been acting from a certain innocence. But even though it did not in his mind constitute a serious sin, he still needs to seek God's forgiveness and turn from the sin. Let his confession be honest: "Lord, I didn't know what I was doing, but now I realize I shouldn't have done it. I'm sorry that I did, and I ask for Your forgiveness."

If the person was involved more deeply in the occult, he probably realized it was wrong. And because the spirits have a "right" to oppress him, they may make it hard for him to speak words of repentance. You will have to bind the blocking spirits and free him from their influence so he can ask for forgiveness.

Renounce

Here is an element we do not find in freeing people from spirits of trauma and sin: The person involved in the occult must

---

6. Here is an example of the sinner's prayer or a prayer of commitment: "Lord Jesus, I confess that I have sinned against You, and I ask that You forgive me for all my sins. I believe that Jesus Christ is the Son of God, who shed His blood on the cross for the remission of my sins. I give my life to You and ask that You come into my heart, that I may live with You eternally. In Jesus' name. Amen."

not only repent of but renounce his occult activity. In repenting he told God he was sorry, that he was turning away from the sin and that he was making a firm decision, with God's help, to stay on the right path from now on. In renouncing he goes a step further by not only turning away from sin and the occult, but by actively turning *against* it.

In repentance he might say, "I'm sorry, Lord, that I used to go to fortune-tellers, and I ask for Your forgiveness." In renouncing he makes a more explicit stand against his previous involvement in the occult: "In the name of Jesus Christ, I renounce fortune-telling and any involvement in the occult that I have ever had."

Simply ask the person to renounce his occult activities in his own words, but if he has difficulty, ask him to repeat after you an appropriate prayer of renunciation. If the deliverance is one of the more serious ones, it is good to ask him to make the promises contained in the baptismal rite:

Q: Do you renounce Satan and all the spiritual forces of wickedness that rebel against God?
A: I renounce them.
Q: Do you renounce the evil powers of this world which corrupt and destroy the creatures of God?
A: I renounce them.
Q: Do you renounce all sinful desires that draw you from the love of God?
A: I renounce them.
Q: Do you turn to Jesus Christ and accept Him as your Savior?
A: I do.
Q: Do you put your whole trust in His grace and love?
A: I do.
Q: Do you promise to follow and obey Him as your Lord?
A: I do.[7]

An important element in renunciation is the willingness to get rid of any books or objects connected with occult involvement. Destroy them. This means getting rid of Ouija boards, tarot cards or jewelry with satanic emblems on it. It may sound extreme, but as long as these objects remain in our homes or of-

7. *The Book of Common Prayer* (New York: Oxford University Press, 1979), pp. 302–303.

fices, evil spirits seem able to draw power from them and are harder to dislodge.

Bookburning these days has a bad name, deservedly, and stands for all that we abhor by way of religious bigotry. Yet burning is the classic way of destroying objects connected with Satanism:

> A number who had practiced sorcery brought their scrolls together and burned them publicly. When they calculated the value of the scrolls, the total came to fifty thousand drachmas.
>
> Acts 19:19

Of special importance: If the person has made an agreement with Satan in writing, and provided he can get the document back, he should give it up to you to be burned. Often there are several written covenants, and one or more remain in the possession of the coven, so it may be difficult or impossible to get them all. Just do what you can. It is very hard for the demonized person to destroy the pacts, so it is better for him to give them to you. Also, when a person has been that heavily involved, you need to guard against his lying about having gotten rid of the contracts.

The Actual Deliverance

We have already covered the general outline of praying for deliverance, but in praying for deliverance from occult spirits we find several complicating factors.

First, this kind of deliverance is usually much more difficult, and we must confront the evil spirits (demons, in this case) directly in order to cast them out.

Second, this kind of deliverance is more dangerous, especially as you move upward (or downward, so to speak) in confronting more powerful demons. If the person has made a direct commitment of some kind to Satan, there is danger to the exorcist, but even more to the person who wants to be freed. At this level you really need to know what you are doing. Not everyone should be involved in deliverance ministry at this level, and the traditional cautions of Church authority hold especially true here.

At the more superficial levels of involvement (e.g., playing the Ouija board), you may not need a team to help, although it is certainly advisable. But at the deeper levels of involvement you will want the help of a team. You may even want one or two physically powerful individuals ("bouncers") present in case the person needs to be restrained, although usually the binding prayer of command is enough to stop any violence.

You can also expect to find several spirits that will act as blockers and try to prevent you from getting at the main spirits. Among the more common blocking spirits (as we saw in chapter 13) are *mockery, deceit* and *game-playing.* When you find yourself stymied in the beginning of a deliverance, you may find that one of these spirits is causing the problem. A spirit of sleep, for example, causes the person to nod off when you are trying to talk to him. When these spirits (or aspects) emerge, the human personality seems to be submerged and replaced by the demonic personality, which is talking to you (or leering at you).

Your response should be a binding prayer, such as: "We will have no more game-playing. I bind you, spirit of games, in the name of Jesus Christ, and I command you right now to stop."

After you get past any demonic defenses, you can begin to discover how the spirit entered and how it plays on the person's weakness. How did it get started and hook into the person? You can find out about this either by talking to the person or by finding out the names or aspects of the spirits. (Do this either by the gift of discernment or by forcing them to name themselves.) In many ways this is the most important part of the deliverance process, because your ultimate goal is not just to cast out demons but to build up the wounded human being whom Jesus wants to fashion into a new creation, coming into the fullness of his potential as a child of God.

Pray for healing as much as possible, and enlist the victim's own purpose of amendment and every good, creative quality God has already implanted in him. When you are praying for deliverance and the human being is submerged, you may want to reestablish contact with the person underlying the demonic manifestation by saying something like this: "I don't want to talk to you now. I want to talk to Bill, and I command you in Jesus' name to let him surface so I can speak to him."

Because the spirits have their own hierarchy and are ranked according to their power, the more powerful spirits hold lesser spirits under their control. The more powerful spirits also exhibit attributes like intelligence, knowledge and power—all of a preternatural magnitude—that make them hard to dislodge.

Their purpose is always to destroy, and they will do all they can to prevent you from freeing the person who has been so long in their grip. "You will never get us out." "He belongs to us." "She's my pig!" These are statements you often hear.

These spirits come in groups or clusters. Like removing that tree stump, with many intertwining roots going deep into the victim's personality, you will probably have to spend a long time praying them out. You must decide (as we have discussed) whether you plan to spend hours or even days in prayer (with time off to sleep and rest, of course), or whether you plan to approach the deliverance process in time segments of, say, two hours a week, and uproot a certain segment of spirits each week. Or you may simply give spiritual direction and encouragement, joined to healing, for some of those sessions.

Deliverance from spirits of the occult is like major surgery, and the human personality needs time to make changes in long-established thought and emotional patterns. In deliverance from occult spirits it is usually better, if possible, to work with the person over a long period of time. If a member of a coven is trying to leave and has thirty multiple personalities, it may harm the fragile human being underneath to try to sort it out in one long session: Which personalities are fragments of the human being that need to be reintegrated into the person, and which are demonic entities that need to be discarded? These are not easy questions and require the utmost experience and prudence in the exorcist.

The process really does resemble pulling out a tree stump: An exorcist can do violence to the person in trying to pull it all out, as it were, with a tractor. Better to do it one root at a time, so a cavernous hole in the ground does not result. The candidate for deliverance often recognizes the problem even if the exorcist does not. "Who will I be if these spirits leave? I won't even know who I am without them. I'm afraid." I have heard this many times and it is a reasonable fear. We must be ready to help build the person into the person God meant him to be.

Because the spirits of the occult can enter a person through ancestry, and because a spirit of witchcraft can come down through the generations (like the curses we discussed in chapter 7), it will continue to be passed down until that particular ancestral connection is broken and any spirit of the occult is cast out. At times we pray for an entire family—grandparents, parents, children—asking Jesus to cleanse the bloodlines and free the family from any spirits that have been passed down. This is usually done peacefully and easily when the family in this generation is doing their best to live Christian lives and have not themselves been involved in the occult.[8]

Seals

Most people, even those in deliverance ministry, have not heard of seals; yet they are a major reason we get stuck in difficult cases.[9] Like many satanic elements, it is a parody of our being sealed by the Holy Spirit in holy baptism.

In ancient times an imprint of the owner's seal was put onto belongings so they could not be broken into. I still have my great-uncle's seal that he stamped into wax to seal his important letters. Christian tradition holds that, just as a letter or package was sealed in ancient days, baptism impresses on you a spiritual seal that symbolizes

- *Dedication* to God (you belong to Him)
- *Protection* by God from evil (an intruder cannot break the package open)

Similarly a person can be sealed for Satan signifying that

- He is dedicated and belongs in some way to Satan
- He is protected and cannot be freed until the seal is broken

It may sound strange, but this seal is a spiritual reality, like a spiritual shield, that covers and protects any evil spirits in a person until it is broken.

8. If you want to learn more about the more difficult, complicated aspects connected with deliverance from the more powerful demonic spirits, I recommend the sixteen tapes of the 1988 Deliverance Conference, especially those by Fr. Richard McAlear and Mrs. Betty Brennan (available through Christian Healing Ministries, P.O. Box 9520, Jacksonville, FL 32208-0520; $60.00 for the audio tapes, $149.00 for the video).

9. For this teaching I am indebted to the knowledge, wisdom and experience of Mrs. Betty Brennan and Fr. Richard McAlear.

Only a few people you pray with have been sealed by Satan, but it does happen, so you need to know that it happens in at least three ways:

By Contract

The first way is by a contract, which can be

In blood
In words
(Occasionally) by desire

To break free from any contract the person has made, he needs to renew his baptismal promises or their equivalent *three times*. (We reviewed these vows earlier in this chapter.) These promises contain two main elements:

1. Renouncing Satan and all his works (turning away from evil)
2. Giving your life to Jesus Christ (turning toward goodness and life)

After renewing his promises, the person needs to break and take back the contract. He should do it as specifically as it was made. Have him renounce it three times. (According to some experts you need authority to break the contract; in the Roman Catholic or Episcopal Churches that would be the priesthood.) With the authority of Jesus Christ the exorcist *breaks the seal*, then proceeds with the deliverance.

In confirming the value of this mysterious process, I would like to share with you that I have seen this take place several times. I was getting nowhere with the deliverance, then prayed to break the seal. The first two times nothing happened, but the third time there was a visible reaction as the spirits loosened their hold and started to go.

By Dedication

The second way a person is bound by a demonic seal is through dedication. Unlike a contract (in which the person himself contracts the seal), a dedication represents something done to the person. Namely, he is dedicated to Satan.

This is what happens to children who are dedicated in satanic rituals. Satanic dedication corresponds to infant baptism or dedication among Christians. Once a person becomes an adult, he must himself make the contract (the mirror image of an adult committing his life to Christ). When people get involved in occult practices, such as taking their child to a local witch for healing, they may end up dedicating him unwittingly. They may realize later that something is wrong with their child, but they cannot figure out why the child has behavior problems. People who have been dedicated to Satan may live in tension, even though they are attending church, and not know why.

To free a person from a dedication,

1. break the dedication, then rededicate the person to Jesus. If he is an adult, he must do this himself, too.
2. *break the seal.*
3. perform the deliverance.

Before Birth

Spirits of the occult can enter into a baby *in utero*, before birth; and when they do, they are protected by a seal. But this does not happen unless the parents, or persons in authority over the child, allow this in some way to happen. (The current breakdown in family life contributes to this.)

The method of breaking this seal is the same as breaking a dedication. The prayer to break a seal is simple. You can say something like this:

In the name of Jesus Christ,[10] I break every seal of Satan and I set you free by the sword of the Holy Spirit.

This *in utero* seal is the most common cause of a satanic seal, since many spirits that we encounter have entered before birth. An example of an *in utero* seal is an adult with a spirit of rejection that became lodged in him when he was in his mother's womb and she did not want the baby but contemplated aborting it.

10. Or, "In the name of the Father, and of the Son, and of the Holy Spirit."

17

Satanic Ritual Abuse (SRA)

In dealing with spirits of the occult, we must discuss the relevant topic of satanic ritual abuse (SRA), the awful programming that covens use to purposely invest their victims with occult spirits.

Recently I received a disturbing letter:

> I am writing to you in hopes that you may be able to shed some light on the past. I remember you as a priest; my family really put you up on a pedestal.
>
> I know my sister spoke with you several years ago about her ritual abuse. I, too, have been recovering memories of how our neighbor A_____ abused me in horrendous ways. Other adults were involved, too. Their abuse does appear to have been satanic. I remember being forced to take part in many rituals, and I was forced to watch horrible things. I was physically, sexually, emotionally and spiritually abused. It began when I was about three years old and lasted until I was ten, when we moved out of state.
>
> My parents now know what happened to us. (Several of my sisters also suffered in this way.)
>
> Since then I have been through a lot of therapy trying to heal those wounds. My life has been a long, difficult journey, but I am finally in the light of Jesus. I feel that, because of the abuse I endured, I have been gifted by God. I can walk in the light and yet know about the evil in the world. When I take Communion I remember the horror of the Satanists' meetings in which they

mocked our rite, so good, so Christ, and it brings me to tears every time. What the Satanists did to me now makes me appreciate God even more.

You knew my parents fairly well. Did you ever sense evil around A_____? What blows me away is that we were surrounded by the Catholic Church; priests and nuns came to our home as a regular occurrence. Our house was blessed numerous times. We went to church regularly. But nobody noticed! I exemplified an abused child and nobody ever noticed!

She wondered why I did not know. But no, I did not suspect anything. I never had the chance to really talk to the children, and only saw them several times seated at the family dinner table. Theirs was a large family, quiet and well-behaved.

Nor did I suspect the perpetrator. I did not know him well, only as a friend of their family, and I played tennis with him maybe ten times. But I never sat down at the table with him, nor did we ever have a conversation except briefly before or after tennis. I suspected nothing. This perpetrator was a successful businessman—friendly, too.

Furthermore, I had never heard of such a thing as satanic ritual abuse in the 1960s. If the children *had* confided in me, I am not sure where I would have turned to find out what to do.

This revealing letter, coming 25 years after the fact, brings out several important points.

First, that the mainline churches are ignorant (as I was then) about the realities of spiritual warfare. Seminarians are, by and large, not prepared to help people who are trying to escape covens and who are in danger of their lives, physically as well as spiritually. Some police departments have specialists better versed in satanic abuse than the local clergy. Yet the clergy above all should be the experts to whom SRA victims can turn to help them escape the nightmare of their past (and present) lives.

The letter also intimates that good people are often unwilling to believe that something as awful as ritual torture exists. It is like the Christian peasants living in the vicinity of Auschwitz who ignored what was belching out of the nearby smokestacks. They did not want to know the awful reality.

Another crucial point: The perpetrators are not all creepy, beastly kinds of people. Many of them (like the businessman) seem to be, hard as it is to believe, normal, cheerful people.

The strange phenomenon of SRA is much more common than we would like to believe. I asked a therapist who deals with SRA victims in our area of Florida how many people might be victims. Although it is impossible to get exact figures, she estimates that in our own locality there are probably hundreds.

Satanic ritual abuse is a real problem, and if you are working in the area of deliverance, read some of the literature on the subject. I summarize in this chapter what I believe every Christian should know.

It Is Real

Although it is true that some parents are accused wrongly of victimizing children years later (false memory syndrome), there is convincing evidence that Satanist groups do victimize people, especially children.[1] Evidence of these cases is of necessity piecemeal since the survivors are fearful of speaking openly.

Just last month I met an intelligent woman who had been forced to leave the city where she had once lived after she found that her husband, from whom she was separated, was a warlock. He had been taking her two young children to satanic rituals on the weekends when he had visitation rights. There the children (whom I met) had been raped and forced to kill animals in sacrifice. In fact, the children admitted they had helped to kill human victims. The mother was not paranoid and believed enough of what her children had told her to uproot her career and home and begin life all over again in a strange city.

This kind of crime, with child witnesses, can hardly be proven in court. The mother had simply taken the safest course of action and fled.

Many critics, I know, counter, "Where is the evidence?" I suggest that these critics have never talked to a survivor of this kind of abuse. Nor will they find most such victims (children, for the most part) eager or even able to tell their stories. Nor can they give you corroborating witnesses, for the only other persons who saw these crimes are members of the coven.

1. You will notice that at least four of the examples I give in this book are victims of SRA, examples like Roberta in chapter 1 and the woman whose letter you read at the beginning of this chapter. These are people I know; they have nothing to gain by lying, and I believe them because I know them. Nor are these forgotten memories dredged up by a psychotherapist's suggestions.

One study of survivors of ritual abuse showed that for 65 percent of those surveyed, the abuse began when the person was three years old or younger.[2] Because these survivors have been threatened with death if they ever tell anyone what they have suffered, we should not be surprised to find them fearful and hesitant to talk.

If a survivor does open up to you, listen with compassion. We are trained to be skeptical when someone comes to us with a wild story, but I think you can see that this initial skepticism is, from the victim's point of view, exactly the wrong response. She is already afraid to talk. In the coven they are taught to trust no one and programmed to believe that even if they tell the truth, no one will believe them. Margaret Smith, who has written a fine book on ritual abuse,[3] had to go through *six* therapists until she found one who understood what she was saying.

If you ever meet with an SRA survivor, be patient; the survivor will probably not remember everything that happened and may seem confused. She will also find it difficult to believe that you care about her, because she has been programmed not to believe in love either.

For victims of ritual abuse, love means betrayal. As part of their training in the cult, they may have been forced to kill a favorite pet whom they loved as their best friend. No matter how often they are told that you care, that you really love them, they will find it hard to believe. In addition, "love" in the coven is all bound up with sex—and perverted sex at that. Yet true love is what the survivor needs desperately, far more than a lecture.

The survivor may also seem hostile to you, since some survivors have been programmed through hypnosis to want to hurt any Christian counselor they may open up to. They may also have been programmed, on the other hand, to kill *themselves* if they ever talk to an outsider about life in the coven.

So if an SRA victim comes to you for help, you are dealing with a delicate life-and-death situation. Since SRA is a complex, difficult subject, it is important for you to know or find someone in your area with experience in dealing with SRA to whom you can refer the survivor for help.

2. Margaret Smith, *Ritual Abuse* (San Francisco: HarperCollins, 1993), p. 117.

3. Smith's book *Ritual Abuse* is not about satanic ritual abuse only, but is an excellent resource on ritual abuse in general.

Since this is a book on prayer for deliverance, my caution is that you *not* begin by praying with such a survivor for deliverance. Eventually the person may need some deliverance; but most of all she needs safety, love and time to heal:

1. a safe person, first of all (ideally, a community), in whom she can trust;
2. a safe place to be, where she will feel protected from pursuit;
3. and more than anything, love; someone to teach her the meaning of love and trust—not just in word but in reality.

All this takes much time; we are talking months and years. Then, too, the survivor needs a long period of counseling and inner healing to change the deep habit patterns of fear, shame and distrust.

Somewhere down the line she may need deliverance, but premature deliverance may end up destroying her, especially if she has multiple personalities, since most of them need to be integrated, not cast out.

What Is Satanic Ritual Abuse?

SRA consists of all the emotionally, physically and sexually abusive acts that take place during satanic rituals. Not all covens are violent in this way, only some, since (as we saw in the last chapter) there is a wide variety of satanic groups, ranging from adolescent, do-it-yourself groups that dabble in witchcraft all the way up to secret groups that have been deeply involved in Satan worship for generations.

As for the rituals themselves, the covens have their own feasts that mock the main Christian feasts. These rituals concentrate on two areas:

1. *Fertility feasts* rising out of ancient pagan rites. These rites occur at such times as the vernal equinox (the first day of spring, March 21) and May Day. These fertility feasts are celebrated with sexual orgies.
2. *Sacrifice rituals,* ceremonies that mock the death of Jesus on the cross. The covens ritualize, when possible, a black

mass in mockery of Catholic worship. The nude body of a woman is used as the altar, fecal matter takes the place of bread, and blood (ideally, human blood) and urine take the place of wine and water. During these liturgies the satanic high priests and priestesses deck themselves out in priestly robes.

Other special times for satanic celebrations include Halloween; the monthly times of the full moon; Beltane (April 30), a matriarchal holiday; the marriage of the Beast (September 7); and periods around Christmas and Easter. The abuse often occurs during these feasts.

What is its purpose? Aside from honoring Satan by mocking God, degrading human beings and turning what should be loving relationships into hateful, distrustful ones, its main purpose is to gain control. The cult wants total control over its members' lives so that they will be afraid ever to leave.

The way cults achieve control, significantly, is through the two evil trends that are destroying our society: violence and perverted sex. In satanic rites, violence and sex are elevated (or lowered) to an almost unbelievable level of evil.

Violence

Satan's purpose is to mock the suffering and crucifixion of Jesus by killing innocent humans, especially babies or children. Since it is dangerous and impractical most of the time to have human sacrifice, animal sacrifices are usually substituted. At some point each member of the cult is forced to participate in such a ritual murder.

Usually the training begins with the children of the coven's members. For instance, an adult, preferably the child's father, takes a knife, puts it into the child's little hands, clasps his hands over the child's hands and guides the knife to do the cutting and letting of blood.

Requiring a new member to participate in ritual murder forces that person, much like a member of the Mafia, to share in a major crime. As a result she is afraid of being charged with murder if she ever tries to escape from the coven. She will also see firsthand that the coven is not afraid to murder, and will be terrified of being killed if she ever tries to break loose. And finally, by being forced to commit horrible acts, she is led to believe she is truly evil, different from ordinary people. No wonder she hesitates to open up and talk to a stranger!

After seeing herself debased as evil, she receives some compensation within the coven by being lifted up as a member of a powerful, secret group. Children growing up in the coven may be given special roles of honor later (for example, high priesthood), which gives them one more reason never to leave.

Torture is another weapon used to instill fear and shame in victims—the kind of torture so cruel that most people have difficulty believing anyone would even think of such things. Parents are forced to torture their own children. (In one study 67 percent of the survivors remembered their fathers as their abusers.[4]) One three-year-old boy told his grandmother his mother had bitten into his penis, drawing blood.[5] Since children are not "court-worthy" and their testimony in court will not hold up, it is open season on children if their parents are not there to (or will not) protect them.

Usually the torture perpetrated, like that of the secret police of dictatorial governments (and sometimes our own, like anti-Vietcong squads in the Vietnam War), leaves no marks. Perpetrators may administer electric shocks to the most sensitive areas of the body or insert needles into the genitals. Some doctors belong to covens and make sure the torture leaves no marks and is expertly done. Other psychiatrist and psychologist members plan post-hypnotic sessions of programming and brainwashing.

Again, aside from the pain that supposedly honors Satan, the purpose of the torture is to ensure the permanent control of the group. The children learn to trust no one; they are taught that they will almost certainly be betrayed by those closest to them—especially when their parents are the ones who perform the torture. When victims are murdered, the body is destroyed and the place thoroughly cleaned up. One coven has a funeral director as a member who takes efficient care of disposing of the bodies.

The answer to skeptics who question the reality of SRA by asking "Where is the evidence?" is that there isn't any! Nor are there witnesses to come forth and talk about what they have

4. Smith, p. 138.
5. Ibid., p. 6.

seen, because they too shared in the crimes (though they may have been forced into it).

Perverted Sexuality

While sacrifice is at the center of the great satanic feasts, just as the cross is at the center of Christianity, other feasts celebrate fertility with orgies, carrying on an ancient pagan tradition. Children do not wear clothes at these meetings and are frequently molested. They are taught that the only way to be intimate with another person is through sex—but sex without love, because love is seen as a weakness to be despised. Sexual ritual abuse is specially designed to glorify lust and desecrate the human body and Jesus' commandment to love. Also, by connecting the black mass with a naked woman's body, thereby connecting religion with sexual images, Satanists pervert the memories of their victims so that real religious ceremonies will inevitably bring back lustful imaginings.

Satanism, as you can see, is Christianity turned on its head. The love proclaimed by Jesus is mocked by Satan's hatred, and faith is transformed into distrust.

Multiple Personalities

Faced with such experiences, people have to survive psychologically; and splitting off into other personalities is actually a God-given gift enabling children to survive an intolerable emotional experience. Treating these "alters" (the technical term for multiple personalities) as if they were spirits to be cast out by exorcism is an awful mistake. The alters are, for the most part, not the problem. They are the solution, in that they are the only way the victim (especially a child) can survive. If you are a child forced to help kill someone, for example, it is too painful to believe you are the kind of person who can commit murder. So the "murderer" part of you might split off as an alter, a personality cruel enough to perform such a vicious action.

For most people with no firsthand experience of these horrors, hearing about someone who manifests several dozen alters simply sounds weird. So some simplistic Christians who practice deliverance decide that these alters must be demonic (especially since the alters have names, as demons do) and proceed to try to cast them all out.

Instead, the alters are parts of the person's real personality that need to be put back together. The destruction wrought by some well-meaning exorcists has so harmed people with dissociative identity disorder (multiple personality disorder), known as DID (MPD), that some states (like Virginia) will revoke the license of any psychotherapist who attempts exorcism on a patient.

I want to emphasize that multiple personalities are not the problem; they are part of the solution—a creative, God-given gift to help a victim survive an impossible emotional situation. These splits are not truly separate entities but are all parts of the entire person that need to be integrated. Sometimes people contain several hundred of these personalities. Obviously bringing these splits back together takes time.

I prayed a short prayer once for a woman who had thirty alters, after which one of those alters was integrated (remarkable considering it was such a short prayer). But it might have taken a year or more before all thirty would be integrated. Writes Margaret Smith:

> If you do find someone with these alters, it is important that you learn about MPD and treat them gently. Do not cast them all out.
> Survivors are not only victimized by the attitude our society has towards people who were abused, but they are also victimized by clergy and psychiatrists. One survivor recalls:
> "I was given an exorcism by the Catholic Church. I don't have evil entities inside of me—I have multiple personalities!"
> This caused further splitting.[6]

The ideal person to help an SRA victim is a Christian psychotherapist who believes in prayer for inner healing and deliverance. Nevertheless, a reputable non-Christian psychologist is more likely to help than a simplistic Christian prayer warrior whose only solution is to try to cast out the alters—an impossible task since these alters are mostly fragments of the person's personality. Such rough treatment will only fragment the person into more multiples and destroy the good name of the much-needed but much-maligned ministry of deliverance.

6. Ibid., p. 174.

Evil Spirits

Although alters are not evil spirits, cults do often send evil spirits into their members when they are hypnotized or drugged. These spirits are programmed to act on post-hypnotic cues that serve as triggers to force the victim to act in a set way and prevent them from leaving the coven.

The person may be programmed, for instance, through post-hypnotic suggestion to forget during daily life the horrors that take place during the coven's meetings. She simply cannot remember what has happened. But in the middle of the night (when the meetings are usually held) the phone rings, a trigger word is spoken that means *Come*, and the person puts on her clothes and goes to the meeting. When she returns home at 4 A.M. she forgets everything that happened when she was with the coven.

Since the victims may have demonic spirits of the occult residing within them, these spirits eventually have to be cast out; but this is not the place to start. There are probably also spirits of trauma that have attached themselves to the awful violence the victim has experienced, but these should depart when the victim receives inner healing for her deeply painful past.

Usually "guardian" spirits are sent into the members of the coven to prevent exorcists from getting past them and into the secrets of the victims' programming. These programs usually contain a self-destructing curse placed on the person in case she ever tries to become a Christian and turn traitor to Satan. I assisted a therapist recently who is working with a woman programmed to commit suicide by starving herself to death because she has become a Christian and is trying to escape the coven.[7] Other coven members are programmed to kill themselves through crashing their cars on the highway. Each alter, as it surfaces, is gently, patiently led to commit itself to Christ,

7. About thirty years ago the ministry of exorcism in Europe was widely discredited when two priests in Germany got permission from their bishop to perform a formal exorcism on a woman they regarded as possessed. She starved herself to death and the priests were blamed. This case scared off the Catholic Church from allowing any more exorcisms. I suspect the priests had the right diagnosis but not the skill and experience to get to the bottom of the woman's self-destructive programming; so they hammered away with the formula of exorcism as written in the book. Tragically the coven was successful in killing not only the woman but, for a number of years, the ministry of exorcism.

while the demons that try to prevent this are either bound or cast out. But it takes time.

What to Do

I want to offer eight specific points with regard to the healing of SRA victims.

1. Remember that the healing of these victims (barring a miracle) takes time. The reintegration of the personality may take years. We are not talking about healing someone at the altar railing with a brief prayer after Communion, although a certain amount of blessing and healing will take place there.

2. Ordinarily the person who does the counseling and prayer needs to know a great deal about SRA and DID (MPD).[8] Preferably this person is a professional Christian counselor.

3. The victim is terribly lonely, desperately afraid and has been deprived of love. What she needs most is the love of Jesus. Even if you do not feel you are equipped to pray with the person, you can at least show her this love. But be aware she is bound to doubt any love or concern because she has been programmed to fear and distrust you. And she will probably sexualize any mention of love.

4. The victim needs a safe place and safe people to be with. Get a list of reputable organizations and therapists who can help with her legitimate fears that she will be murdered or that the coven will kill her loved ones. (Sometimes her husband or children still belong to the coven.) Just seeing a person once a week is probably not enough. You may need someone else to help support her during the week.

5. If you are the person trying to help the victim, listen carefully to all she is able to tell you, knowing that many of the alters will not surface until much later. Eventually you should be able to draw up a kind of map of the alters. You will probably also find that certain evil spirits are serving as guards to prevent you from discovering what you need to know to set the person free. Eventually you hope to get the alters to communicate with each other and merge back into the total personality.

8. Again I recommend an excellent book on DID (MPD), *Uncovering the Mystery of MPD, Case Studies* by James Friesen (San Bernardino: Here's Life Publishers, 1991).

6. At the beginning of any counseling or prayer session, bind up any evil spirits to prevent them from deceiving you or blocking the session. If you pray for inner healing for the victim's traumatic experiences, any wounding spirits hooked into those memories should depart.

7. The victim will harbor some personalities loyal to the coven, personalities you may not find out about right away. These loyal alters are programmed to respond to triggers like phone cues. It is also possible that the person you are counseling still goes to coven meetings at night (unless she is in a safe place and cannot be reached by telephone) and honestly remembers nothing about them. Remember, she is not lying!

8. You may also need to pray for deliverance for some of the occult evil spirits that have been instilled into the victim directly by the coven. When these are injected into the victim, the coven can also specify what aspects they want to attach to the demonic presence—aspects like *murder, hate* and *rage*. Clearly you will need great spiritual discernment and wisdom to know when to pray for deliverance and how to go about it.

Further Observations

All this is complicated enough, but there is a further complicating factor. Some Satanists who are professionally equipped to do so (like psychotherapists, sociologists and ministers) are assigned to write articles for professional and religious magazines and journals that cast doubt on two things:

1. The reality of victims' memories. After all, it does sound strange to most of us that a person would forget something as traumatic as torture or sexual abuse, remembering it only many years later. (Post-hypnotic suggestion can account for some of this blotting out, as can the natural, self-protective ability of the human psyche to consign to oblivion any trauma that is too painful to face.)
2. The reality of the demonic component of the activities of the coven. For example: "It is unscientific, superstitious and ridiculous to attribute these psychotic imaginings to evil spirits, as if they were real."

In addition, some writers and novelists in no way involved in Satanism write about covens and recognize the horrors of what they do, but only on the level of the evil human proclivity to seek power and control over people's lives. Evil spirits do not fit into their worldview. They recognize that there are Satanists but do not believe they are in contact with real evil spirits. They are simply misguided, depraved human beings fascinated by evil.

If all this sounds dreadfully complex and bewildering, it is. I have purposely omitted a great deal in this chapter and tried to summarize what satanic ritual abuse is all about, so that at the very least you can avoid making mistakes. Then, if you are like most of us and not equipped personally to help the victim on a profound level, you can at least refer her to a competent therapist or prayer minister for the help she needs. Remember, too, that many psychiatrists and psychotherapists do not believe in the reality of SRA and will not be able to help beyond a certain point.

If a victim does come and confide in you, it is a singular sign of trust. You may be her only hope of escaping from her spiritual and psychological prison.

He has sent me to bind up the brokenhearted, to proclaim freedom for the captives and release for the prisoners.

Isaiah 61:1

18

Other Kinds of Spirits

Acommon failing among religious people is becoming legalistic. A legalist would read the last four chapters of this book and try to fit every spirit into one of those three categories (trauma, sin and the occult). But there are other kinds of spirits, too.

We do not need to categorize every spirit so long as we realize there are many varieties. Any human behavior that can become driven, addictive, weird or crazy is a fit sphere of action for the influence of demons and other evil spirits. Let's look at just a few examples.

Spirit of False Religion

One demon I encounter fairly often is the spirit of false religion. It is the kind of spirit that drives some good, religious people to overdo their religious activities in compulsive or superstitious ways. This religious spirit influences the person you see in church acting in strange ways—muttering prayers oddly; interrupting a meeting to deliver a false prophecy or message in tongues that is not the gift of tongues inspired by the Holy Spirit; bowing compulsively; lighting too many candles. He may be only an odd person with a psychological problem, but he may also be driven by a religious spirit.

These misdirected individuals are imitating the kind of activity that might be inspired by God in other people, but with them you sense there is something odd. One of the purposes of such a spirit is to give Christianity a bad name, confirming the opinion of some skeptics that deeply religious people are a little nutty.

One man stood up in a large prayer meeting in St. Louis and came out with a long prophecy. The leadership sensed immediately that something was wrong, but several well-meaning people were impressed because some things he said about them were true. They were convinced he had a prophetic gift, so after the meeting they adjourned to a home where he continued for several hours foretelling their futures.

He never returned to the prayer meeting but continued to meet with his followers in their homes, until one evening he took all the furniture out of his house, piled it on his lawn and burned it. After that he packed his family into the car and drove aimlessly around the city, until the police picked him up and took him to a mental hospital.

That is where I went to visit him. I found he had gotten involved with the occult world by praying for a spirit guide. He had learned how to do this by reading a book encouraging people to find their own personal spirit guide. He realized vaguely from his Catholic background that this was dangerous, so he tried to protect himself by setting up a statue of a saint in the room and praying to God before asking to receive his spirit guide. The first night he did this, one of the statues seemed to come alive and turn into a Native American shaman. This was his introduction, through the occult, to a spirit of false religion.

Spirit of Legalism

Sometimes we discover, allied to the spirit of false religion, the spirit of legalism.

I was praying for a Catholic priest, an expert in canon law whose work was applying Church law to decide whether divorced couples could receive an annulment. He found this an anguishing form of ministry, since his own heart and mind sometimes disagreed with the law's application, and he sought prayer to help with his dilemma. While we prayed an amazing thing happened: His hands went up to his throat and his own fingers were reaching to strangle himself.

The spirit was legalism—the very problem Jesus confronted in His day, which had somehow entered this kind-hearted priest.

Spirits that Cause Physical Sickness

The most common spirits I encounter that do not fit under our three main categories are spirits that cause or aggravate human sickness. The spirits that influence physical sickness include *infirmity, pain* and *torment.* We also find spirits that afflict people in specific ways, like *cancer,* and other spirits that infect almost any human infirmity and make it worse.

It is significant that Jesus healed some kinds of physical sickness by casting out demons. The epileptic boy was brought to Jesus by his distraught father, who told Jesus that an evil spirit often threw the boy into convulsions. Jesus rebuked the spirit, healed the boy and returned him to his father (Luke 9:37–43).

Another time Jesus healed a man by casting out a spirit that prevented him from speaking. As soon as the evil spirit left, the dumb man was able to speak again, to the amazement of the crowd (Luke 11:14). This exorcism led to a dramatic confrontation in which Jesus' enemies accused Him of casting out evil spirits by being in league with Beelzebub, the chief of the evil spirits (Luke 11:15).

The Gospel writer attributed the crippled condition of a woman bent over for eighteen years, whom Jesus healed, to a spirit (Luke 13:11). When Jesus defended His action of healing on the Sabbath, He said, "Should not this woman, a daughter of Abraham, whom Satan has kept bound for eighteen long years, be set free on the Sabbath day from what bound her?" (Luke 13:16).

Earlier in Luke Jesus healed Peter's mother-in-law of a high fever by *rebuking* the fever—the same word used in the New King James Version to describe how Jesus cast out the spirit from a man who interrupted Him in the synagogue (Luke 4:39, 35).

Clearly the New Testament writers believed that some physical sicknesses were caused by evil spirits and were healed, therefore, by their expulsion.

Spirits that Cause Mental or Emotional Sickness

Just as we find spirits causing physical sickness, we find spirits (like the spirit of insanity) causing or aggravating mental and emotional sickness. What I wrote in chapter 14 about spirits of trauma will help here, but some crazed spirits seem to descend through family curses.

Those who have seen the movie *The Exorcist* remember the scene in the mental hospital when the priest's mother was locked away. All the haunted faces looking up at the priest as he walked past exhibit the almost animal-like expression that we often see in those infested by spirits. The director was trying to make the point, I imagine, that the priest-exorcist was threatened by demonic forces wherever he went.

I have encountered spirits of insanity when I was praying with psychotic patients, as well as a related spirit called *fear of insanity* that influences some people who are naturally fearful because their families have been plagued by a history of insanity.

I do not imply that all cancer or schizophrenia are demonic in origin, only that physical or emotional sickness is occasionally caused or worsened by evil spirits.

Spirit of Torment

One of the clues that a spirit underlies a sickness or pain is when you pray for the sick person and find that the pain starts moving around the person's body, as if trying to escape. It is an amazing phenomenon that as you follow the pain around—for example, from the stomach to the chest to the arms and then to the hands—it will eventually leave (usually through the hands, mouth or feet).

The following excerpt from a letter from a woman who had been involved in the occult describes what a spirit of torment feels like. Notice that the spirit became agitated when the suffering woman started to receive help, and it proceeded to move around, tormenting her body in an attempt to discourage her from receiving any further prayer:

> After I talked to you I became very ill almost instantly; my feet and ankles became very painful. The next day my calves were extremely painful; the following day the pain moved to my thighs. The day after it moved to my lower back; by that night my upper back and arms were affected. By morning my neck and spine

hurt so badly I could hardly walk or turn my head. Two days later I could hardly breathe and both of my ears became infected.

As the days went by, the pain would come and go. Then I was hit by Crohn's disease, which had been in remission for about nine years. It hit with such a force that I thought I was going to die. The pain was excruciating. I was dehydrated, losing weight, feverish and my hair started falling out. My doctor had me on 24 pills a day. I was ready to give up.

After four years in nursing school, with only fifteen weeks left to go, I was ready to drop out. It seemed that I faced every obstacle that could possibly be put there, while financially we were going right down the tubes.

I am slowly getting better but feel very weak. Two days ago while praying I said, "Lord, I know that the way I have lived my life may not have pleased You, those around me, or even myself, but I did what I had to do in order to survive. Now I am ready for You to take over!"

Almost instantly I started feeling better and my Crohn's disease is under control again, praise God. With God on our side we will survive and win.

As you gain more experience in praying for deliverance, you will discover an amazing assortment of demonic entities impossible to categorize. The important thing to remember is that each name (representing each identity) gives a clue as to how it entered. If you pursue these clues, assisted by the knowledge the Holy Spirit gives you or your team, you will be able to help the suffering person facing you.

Most important, if you are able to identify the door of human weakness that first allowed the spirit to enter, you can help the afflicted person shut that door forever.

19

Deliverance through "Blessed Objects"

God did extraordinary miracles through Paul. Handkerchiefs and aprons that had touched him were taken to the sick, and their illnesses were cured and the evil spirits left them.

Acts 19:11–12

People brought the sick into the streets and laid them on beds and mats so that at least Peter's shadow might fall on some of them as he passed by. . . . And all of them were healed.

Acts 5:15–16

From the earliest days of Christianity, so-called "blessed objects," such as the handkerchiefs touched by Paul, have been used to bless and heal the sick and to drive off evil.

The healing property attached to clothing or objects associated with the apostles reflects the ministry of Jesus Himself. You remember the woman with the issue of blood who was healed by touching the hem of Jesus' cloak (Matthew 9:20–22). You may also remember that people begged Jesus to let them touch the edge of His cloak, and that many were healed in this way (Matthew 14:36). Then there was the man who could not hear or speak, whose speech was healed when Jesus touched his tongue with His own spittle (Mark 7:32–35)—a reflection of the ancient belief that the spittle of a holy man had curative powers.

Traditionally Christians have prayed over various objects (such as oil), asking God to use them as channels of His healing and delivering power. I do not know how it happens, but these objects seem to be extensions of the person who prays for them,[1] much as a piece of inert iron can be magnetized and hold the charge afterward.

In Pentecostal circles people like Oral Roberts pray over little bottles of oil and mail them out; while in the centuries-old Catholic tradition not only oil but water and salt are among the elements often used as helps during exorcism.

Oil

In the early centuries of the life of the Church, and still today, oil is blessed with a forceful prayer based on the letter of James:

> Is any one of you sick? He should call the elders of the church to pray over him and anoint him with oil in the name of the Lord.
>
> James 5:14

Oil is useful not only in healing prayer, but has long been considered a help in casting out evil spirits. It is no coincidence that oil was the universal medicine in Jesus' day; and in using oil during healing prayers, early Christians were simply using the ordinary medicine of the day in conjunction with healing prayer:

> But a Samaritan, as he traveled, came where the man was; and when he saw him, he took pity on him. He went to him and bandaged his wounds, pouring on oil and wine.
>
> Luke 10:33–34

We can simply anoint the sick or oppressed with olive oil, of course, but it seems especially beneficial to use oil that we have prayed for, asking God to use it in healing and driving out evil spirits. The traditional Catholic prayer for oil gives some idea of how early Christians prayed, and of the kind of prayer you yourself might compose to bless the oil. Notice in this prayer that one section asks God to use the oil for healing and another asks Him to use it in freeing the afflicted from evil spirits:

---

1. Catholic tradition refers to them as "sacramental."

Lord God almighty, before whom the hosts of angels stand in awe, and whose heavenly service we acknowledge; may it please you to regard favorably and to bless and hallow this creature, oil, which by your power has been pressed from the juice of olives. You have ordained it for anointing the sick, so that, when they are made well, they may give thanks to you, the living and true God. Grant, we pray, that those who will use this oil, which we are blessing in your name, may be delivered from all suffering, all infirmity, and all wiles of the enemy. Let it be the means of averting any kind of adversity from man, made in your image and redeemed by the precious blood of your Son, so that he may never again suffer the sting of the ancient serpent; through Christ our Lord. Amen.[2]

In later days these prayers of blessing were reserved to bishops or priests, but in the early centuries oil was blessed "either by a bishop or by some charismatic person who might be a bishop or priest or layman or even a laywoman."[3]

Is it superstition to believe that blessed oil could actually accomplish anything (aside from its being a long-standing tradition based on Scripture)? I mentioned in an earlier chapter the time I touched a possessed man on the forehead with oil that had been blessed. Although the oil was room temperature, he screamed and turned aside as if I had touched him with a red-hot poker.

In praying for deliverance, we anoint the afflicted person's forehead and/or her hands, or any other area of her body where she has been suffering.

Salt

Second among the common elements that are blessed and used to exorcise evil is salt. It differs from oil and water in two important ways:

1. If you use it to bless a room or building, it remains for weeks or months, unlike water, which evaporates. (You

---

2. Philip Weller, transl., *The Roman Ritual* (Milwaukee: Bruce, 1964), p. 573, as written in *Prayers and Blessings from the Roman Ritual with Commentary*, edited by Michael Scanlan, T.O.R. (Steubenville, Ohio.: The College of Steubenville, 1978), p. 7.

3. William Clebsch and Charles Jaekle, *Pastoral Care in Historical Perspective* (New York: Harper Torchback, 1967), p. 34.

might compare salt to roach poison, which you need to re-
plenish only occasionally.)
2. Blessed salt can be sprinkled on food—reflecting, again, an
   early Christian tradition.[4]

The person I know with the most experience in using salt in
this way is Father Rick Thomas, S.J., who works with the poor in
El Paso, Texas. Many of the people he works with have been involved in *spiritismo*, and Rick hands out blessed cans of salt for
them to take home. He reports that remarkable deliverances
take place or are helped along simply when people sprinkle
blessed salt on their food (as, for instance, when a wife uses it
to season her cooking for her oppressed husband).

Observe in the following ancient prayer (emphasis added)
the ancient Christian belief that salt can be used in deliverance:

> God's creature, salt, I cast out the demon from you by the living
> God, by the true God, by the holy God, by God who ordered you
> to be thrown into the water-springs by Eliseus to heal it of its bar-
> renness. May you be a purified salt, a means of health for those
> who believe, a medicine for body and soul for all who make use
> of you. *May all evil fancies of the foul fiend, his malice and cun-
> ning, be driven afar from the place where you are sprinkled. And
> let every unclean spirit be repulsed* by Him who is coming to judge
> both the living and the dead and the world by fire. Amen.
>
>   Let us pray.
>
>   Almighty, everlasting God, we humbly appeal to your mercy
> and goodness to graciously bless this creature, salt, which you
> have given for mankind's use. May all who use it find in it a rem-
> edy for body and mind. And may everything that it touches or
> sprinkles *be freed from uncleanness and any influence of the evil
> spirit;* through Christ our Lord. Amen.[5]

My friend the Rev. Matt Linn, S.J., had an unusual experience
in using blessed salt at a time he was not sure he believed in its
value:

> Beth was a religious sister who prayed and received the Eucharist
> daily. She came to me well rested and looking forward to an

4. Ibid., p.34.
5. Ibid., p.3.

eight-day directed retreat. But to her surprise each time she tried to pray, she experienced a tremendous fear and evil presence that made her want to quit the retreat. For four days we tried every spiritual and psychological approach I knew but nothing helped. Finally in desperation I blessed some salt and told her that if this happened again, she should sprinkle the salt in the form of a cross and say simply, "In the name of the Father, Son, and Holy Spirit, I command any evil to leave and only Jesus Christ to be present." She laughed and told me that she didn't really believe in evil spirits and certainly didn't expect this to work. To humor me, she prayed as I instructed, and to her surprise, and, I must confess, to mine, too, she found that the attack immediately broke. She finished the retreat with peace.

I do not think this is an isolated incident since other retreat directors have shared such examples.[6]

Water

Blessed water ("holy water") is still another help in praying for deliverance. It differs from oil in that you can sprinkle it around when you bless a room or house, and it does not stain as oil would. It is used more commonly than oil or salt because of its close association with baptism. (Blessed oil and salt are also used in the traditional baptismal rite.)

The prayer of blessing for water is like the blessing for oil and salt. In the prayer we ask:

> May you be a purified water, empowered to drive afar all power of the enemy, in fact, to root out and banish the enemy himself, along with his fallen angels. We ask this through the power of our Lord Jesus Christ.[7]

Later in the prayer:

> May everything that this water sprinkles in the homes and gatherings of the faithful be delivered from all that is unclean and hurtful; let no breath of contagion hover there, no taint of corruption; let all the wiles of the lurking enemy come to nothing. By the sprinkling of this water may everything opposed to the safety

6. Matthew and Dennis Linn, *Deliverance Prayer* (Ramsey, N.J.: Paulist Press, 1980), p. 9.

7. Ibid., p.4.

and peace of the occupants of these homes be banished, so that in calling on your holy name they may know the well-being they desire, and be protected from every peril; through Christ our Lord. Amen.[8]

All these prayers, written in a medieval style, need not be used as they stand. Nor do we need to use oil, salt and water at all when we pray for deliverance. But they can be a help; and we need to realize that there is a tradition, going back to the earliest days of Christianity, encouraging us to use them. If these prayers are not suitable for you and you wish to use any of these elements, fashion other prayers.

Matt and Denny Linn, who like to experiment and check things out for themselves, wanted to find out about the worth of blessed water and salt:

> Georgia seemed an unlikely candidate for deliverance prayer. She had never heard of deliverance and was a pillar of the Church. As some prayed to heal a disc in Georgia's back, her arms, shoulders, and face began going through contortions. A voice spoke through her twisted lips, "I've got her. Get away, all of you!"
>
> . . . Her behavior was difficult to differentiate from hysteria. But several things indicated to me that this was probably not hysteria. First, when I was behind her, I put a few grains of blessed salt on the back of her sweater. Though she could not feel me do this, nor could she feel the few grains of salt through her sweater, the voice through those trembling lips shouted, "Stop that! It burns!" The same thing happened when I blessed her with holy water, though nothing happened when I used regular water. I was dealing with something that knew the power of blessed salt and could tell the difference between holy water and regular water.[9]

The Linn brothers have, at various times, checked the power of blessed oil, salt and water, comparing them to the same elements that have not been blessed. The evil spirits can tell the difference. The anguished reactions of the demonized do not come from the person—who could not, of course, be tormented by oil at room temperature or by having a grain of salt fall on

8. Ibid.
9. Ibid., p. 23.

them—but rather from the demons reacting against God's spiritual power as if they had been burned.

Remember the anguished cries of the spirits when Jesus came near them, as when He confronted the Gadarene demoniac: "He shouted at the top of his voice, 'What do you want with me, Jesus, Son of the Most High God? Swear to God that you won't torture me!'" (Mark 5:7).

Still Other Helps

Oil, salt and water by no means exhaust all the possibilities of blessed objects that may contain God's power to heal and exorcise. The water used in the traditional Catholic baptism, for example, is a mixture of blessed water and blessed salt. The priest, after blessing the water and salt separately, pours the salt into the water and says yet another prayer asking God to empower the mixture. All we really need to know is that we have many creative possibilities to help us in the deliverance ministry.

One of my friends brings a large Bible with him when he prays for deliverance and, if possible, lays it on the person. Still others light candles that have been blessed or bring crucifixes to be held in the hands of the person they pray for.

These are not merely visual aids, but bring God's healing power in some mysterious way to the afflicted person. These "holy" objects are the opposite of the charms, fetishes and talismans that Satanists use to channel evil into a person or place.

If we rely excessively on these objects, on the other hand, we are getting into superstition.

Remember the bronze serpent that Moses fashioned by God's direction? Anyone bitten by a serpent in the desert could look up at it and be healed (Numbers 21:8–9). Truly the bronze serpent was a blessed object used by God to heal people. But centuries later simple people had come to worship it, and King Hezekiah in his reform smashed the bronze serpent Moses himself had fashioned because the Israelites were offering sacrifices to it (2 Kings 18:4).

Our basic reliance must always be on the power of God, who can use any means He chooses to free prisoners from Satan's grip.

20

Follow-Up

I received a letter from a woman recently suggesting I write an entire book on how to follow up successfully on deliverance. Certainly it is as necessary that we follow up as it is to pray for the actual deliverance. Otherwise, when the house is swept clean, the demons may return.

Yet what we need to know about follow-up is relatively simple. The complications come from the fact that people are different, and that each person's follow-up must likewise be different.

General Follow-Up

First there is the general plan for any follow-up: We must fill the empty spaces with every good gift of God so that the vacuum does not stay empty. These general recommendations include a regular discipline of

Prayer
Scripture and spiritual reading
Church or home group attendance

Beyond this the freed person needs a sponsor (as in AA) who can encourage him and pray for him when he feels weak and in danger of succumbing to temptation again. He also needs someone to give him guidance in how to counteract his weaknesses and grow in the Christian life.

Ideally deliverance is not something that happens once at a prayer meeting; it involves an entire process. It is hard enough for ordinary Christians to receive the spiritual direction they need; but suppose you are a woman who has been the victim of incest committed by your brother, and that since then you have been demonically oppressed. Where do you turn for the help and encouragement you need to grow in love and trust and to develop a love for Jesus? Love for Jesus in His humanity, since we see Him as a man, may be difficult because of your memories of your brother's lust for you.

Sometimes God heals us in a single prayer, but ordinarily it requires a gradual series of prayers, combined with the human advice, love and wisdom of friends, and the spiritual director we all need to mature into the full measure of our life in Christ.

Obviously the person trying to remain free of evil spirits needs to avoid former associations and places that brought about his oppression. But this is not always possible. The person's spouse, for example, may be deeply involved in the occult, in which case the person needs to pray for guidance as to what to do—stay with the spouse or leave? Paul talked about leaving a non-Christian spouse and said it was a personal decision based on the possibility of achieving peace in the family (1 Corinthians 7:12–16).

In addition, the person needs to get rid of any books or objects in his home from which evil spirits might draw power to keep the home oppressed. When occult jewelry is involved, we may need to make a financial sacrifice to get rid of the ring, statue or whatever has been connected with the occult (the opposite of a blessed object)—a price we need to pay in order to remain free. Derek Prince tells of many people set free the moment they took off the bracelet or charm that symbolized their occult involvement.

Specific Follow-Up

Beyond these general recommendations, each person coming out of demonic oppression has a particular area of weakness or sin that opened them up to the demonic. Because for each person this is different, there are no general rules—only specific guidance tailored to each person's needs. The person who suffers from extraordinary fear and is terrified of God needs to change habitual thought patterns in a far different way than the rebellious, furious person who has wounded every person with whom he has ever lived.

To receive the specific guidance to deal with our sins and weaknesses, we need a director or close Christian friend willing to tell us the painful truth when we need to hear it; who can give us practical counsel; and, most important, who will pray for us.

If you have no such director or friend (sad to say, this is only too common), ask the Holy Spirit for direction as to how you can remain free of the spirits that once oppressed you, so that you can

> grasp how wide and long and high and deep is the love of Christ, and to know this love that surpasses knowledge.
>
> Ephesians 3:18–19

Part

Setting Places Free

21

Larger Dimensions
of Deliverance

Two Christian groups call us to consider the larger dimensions of deliverance—two groups in little contact with each other. Each one recognizes a flip side of the truth but sees itself in opposition to the other. We need to merge both views in a larger unity in our work to establish Christianity in the world and to destroy the kingdom of Satan.

The first group comprises those who regard deliverance prayer as far more than prayer for individuals; they see it as prayer against evil principalities and powers that control entire cities, regions and nations. This group is represented by leaders like Peter Wagner,[1] John Dawson,[2] Francis Frangipane,[3] Cindy Jacobs[4] and the novelist Frank Peretti.[5]

The second group comprises those who see evil not so much as evil spirits, but as evil so deeply imbedded in nations, societies and cultures that it blinds people to the evil that operates in their lives. These evils are so enormous (as in Hitler's Germany)

1. As in his book *Wrestling with Dark Angels*, Peter Wagner and F. D. Pennoyer, eds. (Ventura, Calif.: Regal Books, 1990).

2. As in his book *Taking Our Cities for God* (Lake Mary, Fla.: Creation House, 1989).

3. As in his book *The House of the Lord: God's Plan to Liberate Your City from Darkness* (Lake Mary, Fla.: Creation House, 1991).

4. As in her book *Possessing the Gates of the Enemy* (Grand Rapids: Chosen Books, 1991).

5. As in his book *Piercing the Darkness* (Wheaton, Ill.: Crossway Books, 1989).

that they may be called demonic, and their lies must be exposed in order to set the entrapped individuals free. Authors representing this group include the late William Stringfellow[6] and Walter Wink.[7]

Group 1: Those Who Battle Territorial Spirits

This enthusiastic group of Christians, in touch with one another and sharing what they learn through writing and holding large conferences, has rediscovered an ancient Christian belief in the reality of demonic control over cities, countries and regions. Not only are they working to discover the kinds of evil and the names of demons that affect large areas, but they are actively praying to break those demonic strongholds. Much of this emphasis comes from people like Dr. C. Peter Wagner, who teaches at Fuller Seminary in California.

It all began in the late '70s when returning missionaries brought back stories of exorcism from countries in the developing world and how they had learned by desperate necessity to pray for deliverance. Wagner himself, who had been a missionary to Bolivia, realized they were onto something and became friends with John Wimber, who was in the process of founding the Vineyard in Anaheim, California.

Only a minority of the Fuller faculty understood or approved of Wagner's investigation into the need for the charisms of the Spirit in our day, but Wagner got Wimber to co-teach a course on "Signs and Wonders," which became celebrated in the years it was offered (1981–1985). The course was not simply theoretical; at times the students prayed for healing and participated in exorcism.

For years evangelicals had shunned charismatic manifestations such as healing and deliverance, but now they began to investigate these phenomena. Eventually some evangelical leaders and authors (like Dr. Charles Kraft, also of Fuller) accepted the manifest power of the Spirit as essential for Christian revival. They termed themselves the "third wave" of the Holy Spirit

---

6. As in his book *An Ethic for Christians and Other Aliens in a Strange Land* (Waco, Tex.: Word Books, 1973).

7. As in his trilogy *The Powers* (Philadelphia: Fortress Press): Vol. I, *Naming the Powers* (1984); Vol. II, *Unmasking the Powers* (1986); Vol. III, *Engaging the Powers* (1992).

in the twentieth century (the first two being the Pentecostals and the charismatics).

First Wagner learned about the possibility of individuals' needing deliverance. Then, because of his keen interest in missions (he was a professor of church growth and author of more than thirty books on missions), he discovered a further need to identify stronger spirits that influenced entire regions and societies and prevented the Gospel from being preached.

The area of prayer experience is new, and those exploring it are honest enough to admit they are still finding their way, even while they do serious research. More than research, though, they actively engage in spiritual warfare. (They are good examples of theology as a critical reflection on religious experience.)

This spiritual warfare is based on a belief that

Satan delegates high ranking members of the hierarchy of evil spirits to control nations, regions, cities, tribes, people groups, neighborhoods and other significant social networks of human beings throughout the world. Their major assignment is to prevent God from being glorified in their territory, which they do through directing the activity of lower ranking demons.[8]

The scriptural foundation for this lies in the apostle Paul's statement about our wrestling against "the rulers, against the authorities, against the powers of this dark world and against the spiritual forces of evil in the heavenly realms" (Ephesians 6:12). We also hear Jesus talking about tying up the "strong man" and then being free to plunder the strong man's house (Matthew 12:29). "It would seem reasonable," writes Peter Wagner, "that the principle could be applied to a nation or a city or a people group as well as a house."[9]

Then there is the fascinating story in Daniel 10 in which a lesser angel was sent by God to help Daniel, but was delayed for 21 days by "the prince of the Persian kingdom," whom he could not get past until Michael came to his rescue. Obviously no human prince would have been able to hinder the angel of God from his mission. (Incidentally, the archangel Michael is traditionally the angel God assigns to battle Satan, while Raphael

8. C. Peter Wagner, chapter on "Territorial Spirits," *Wrestling with Dark Angels*, p. 77.
9. Ibid., p. 78.

brings healing and Gabriel announces good news. These traditional roles of archangels cover the same three aspects of ministry that Jesus assigned to the disciples: announcing the Good News, casting out evil spirits and healing the sick.)

Then, too, we read about the pagan gods of the tribes bordering on Israel, which seem to have been demonic forces ruling over those cultures and leading them to perform abominable acts such as sacrificing infants to Molech (see Leviticus 18:21; 2 Kings 23:10; etc.). For that reason God called on the Israelites to stay separate or else destroy those cultures.

Those engaged in territorial warfare map out the spiritual dimensions of the cities or regions they are going to pray for. Then they study the history of the area to discover the primary sins and demonic powers to which the places have been dedicated; and they identify, through discernment, the principalities that rule over these areas. Getting involved in this kind of prayer, in contrast to simply praying for demonized individuals, is major spiritual warfare.

For this reason, those who pray for regions have learned not to engage in this ministry until

1. They achieve a certain degree of *unity* among the pastors of an area
2. They are committed to spend considerable *time* in prayer and fasting

Without these two provisos, there is considerable danger. Wagner describes how one of his students reported two tragic incidents involving Presbyterian ministers in Ghana, where various evil spirits had ruled for generations. One minister ordered a tree to be chopped down that had been enshrined by satanic priests. On the day that the last branch of the tree was cut off, the pastor collapsed and died. The second minister ordered a fetish shrine to be destroyed. When it happened, he suffered a stroke.[10]

How can you prove that these calamities occurred because the satanic strongholds were destroyed? You cannot. But so much of this happens that I believe it is no coincidence. So when groups pray to break demonic holds over cities and coun-

10. Ibid., p. 87.

tries, many intercessors are needed, following on much discerning prayer as to whether they should even attempt to get involved in deliverance prayer for the region.

Having offered this caution, let me balance it by mentioning the victories that have taken place through this kind of spiritual warfare. Since this aspect of evangelization is relatively new, we need to read as much as we can and network with others engaged in this work to discover what is happening. Much of what is taking place in this kind of deliverance ministry, regrettably, is unknown to mainline churches and their ministers. This may be why missionaries have achieved so little success in countries like Japan, where fewer than one percent of the people are Christians.

Wagner cites many examples of apparently successful regional deliverance from demonic powers, as contrasted with places where demonic principalities are still in control. The country of Argentina may afford the most illuminating account of regional spiritual warfare.[11]

In the days when Juan Perón ruled the country, he was apparently guided by a warlock (a male witch) named José Lopez Rega, a high priest in Macumba spiritism. Lopez Rega had great influence in the government and in the media, where people testified on national TV how they had been blessed by Macumba. When Lopez Rega left the government, he reputedly put a curse on Argentina, after which an extraordinarily harsh military regime took power and anyone suspected of opposing the generals "disappeared" or was routinely tortured.

Then in 1982, during the aftermath of the Falklands War, a remarkable change took place. The generals left office, and at the same time a number of evangelical Christian leaders (like Omar Cabrera) began to challenge Satan and pray against demonic strongholds from the public platform. Cabrera has been planting churches that now draw over 145,000 adherents. Whenever he moves into a new area to minister, he shuts himself away in a hotel to pray and fast. After several days of personal cleansing preparation, he engages in about a week of spiritual conflict, although it sometimes goes much longer—up to 45 days. At times Cabrera has "seen" territorial spirits. After learning their names,

11. This account is a summary of pp. 198–204 of C. Peter Wagner's *How to Have a Healing Ministry in Any Church* (Ventura, Calif.: Regal Books, 1988).

he asks Jesus to break their power over the city where he is to speak.

Another Argentinean evangelist, Edgardo Silvoso, took a map and drew a circle with a hundred-mile radius around his training center in Rosario, Argentina. In this circle there were 109 towns, but no evangelical churches. Then they discovered that a warlock named Merigildo, who lived in one of the towns, exercised great power and had trained twelve disciples. Silvoso invited a number of Christian leaders to gather in that town to pray and take dominion in the name of Jesus Christ. Then they went to Merigildo's headquarters and announced that his power had been broken. Less than three years later, 82 of the 109 towns had an evangelical church, with more planned.[12]

Some people I respect who pray for deliverance question whether we should become involved in deliverance on this scale. Even the archangel Michael, when disputing with Satan over the body of Moses, would not get into a direct fight, but said, "The Lord rebuke you!" (Jude 1:9).

The evidence is anecdotal; you cannot *prove* that whole regions have been evangelized because the evangelists said fervent prayers to free the region from demonic principalities. But I believe these Christian pioneers are discovering an important dimension of intercession that needs to be taken seriously, and I encourage you to read some of the books mentioned in the footnotes to this chapter, as well as others that are sure to follow in years to come.

Group 2: Unmasking Societal Evil

The second group, perhaps best represented by Walter Wink, shows how invisible evil forces determine our human existence. They see these evil forces—"principalities and powers"—not as personal evil spirits but as belief systems with an energy of their own. This powerful hidden energy makes them *like* demons in

12. It is significant, and sad, too, I think, that in evangelical literature, Catholic churches in the area are not usually counted as being Christian. Part of the reason is surely that many priests in Argentina and Brazil do not confront Macumba openly but accept the popular religion, which combines Christianity with witchcraft without much protest. But I personally know priests in those countries who do confront *spiritismo* and pray for deliverance for individuals, although usually not on this larger scale.

their need to be exorcised from our society so that we can truly live as Christians:

> The demonic in our time has a peculiar proclivity for institutional structures. It is as if the demons of the Bible grew up along with us and, while leaving some of their smaller cousins to continue harassing individuals, swelled to the gigantic proportions of our transnational corporations, military establishments, university systems, and governmental bureaucracies. [13]

In this view (which I believe is true), we are all influenced unconsciously toward evil choices because of the evil embedded in the very institutions in which we live. The function of the prophet is to bring these hidden evils into the light where we are free to make a choice. This is, in some sense, an exorcism.

Because we are blind to what we have always accepted (like breathing in air), we think we are doing good when we may actually be doing evil. The clearest example in recent times is Nazi Germany led by Adolf Hitler. Not only was Hitler in some sense possessed, but the German nation was blinded and marched off to war with the blessing of most church leaders. The majority of Germans were either Catholic or Lutheran, yet with a few exceptions (like Dietrich Bonhoefer and Franz Jagerstätter, a Catholic farmer whose conscience told him he could not serve in the German Army, as a result of which he was shot), most Christians fought as loyal soldiers and made no protest when the Jews were slaughtered. This kind of group thinking, with its power to blind people and influence them to do evil, is a massive force that is in the broad sense of the term demonic. It tempts, deceives, drives us to bow down and worship the idols of this world.

While we find it easy to recognize the evils of the past and the sins of other nations, we tend to be blind to the present evils that hold us in bondage. I remember a book I read many years ago, *Protestant, Catholic and Jew: An Essay in American Religious Sociology*,[14] in which sociologist Will Herberg claimed that these three major religions, which see themselves as different from one another, are alike in a way they do not suspect. When he analyzed these three major Judeo-Christian religions not by

13. Walter Wink, *Unmasking the Powers* (Philadelphia: Fortress Press, 1986), p. 69.
14. Will Herberg, *Protestant, Catholic and Jew: An Essay in American Religious Sociology* (Chicago: University of Chicago Press, 1983).

what they taught but by how they acted, he found they were basically alike in that they really worship the American way of life. America has become an idol.

My friend Father Richard Rohr suggests that adults who want to return to college and spend two years getting a graduate degree would learn more if they spent six months in the developing world, not as a tourist but by living and working in a poor mission. Then, when they came back to their own country, they would see old, familiar things in a new light.

After my experience traveling extensively in Latin America, Asia and Africa, I agree. Imagine that you are spending time in Bolivia or India where a large percentage of the people are starving. You see them dying on the streets; then you return to the United States where dieting to get rid of excess weight is a multibillion dollar business. Suddenly your values are challenged: What do we really worship? Do we live according to Jesus' demand that we share what we have with the needy? Is gluttony an idol in my life?

Writes Walter Wink, "As members of a society suicidally ravishing the environment and arming ourselves to oblivion, we are perplexed at the high rate of suicides."[15] I think any thoughtful student of evil in our world will agree that Wink's three books are, in Morton Kelsey's words, "a must for anyone who would understand the seductive and destructive aspects of evil which are so much a part of human life."[16]

The great value of this second school, which I believe has a prophetic vision, lies in its uncovering the lies and evil that deceive us and lead us into acquiescing to evil unwittingly. Again Wink writes, "Martin Luther King Jr.'s prophetic declaration in 1967 that the United States is the greatest purveyor of violence in the world is even truer now than when it was uttered."[17] These evil structures and pervasive seductions of our society are enormous and are like energy fields in their own right. These flawed human institutions are created by our own fallen human nature, but I believe they are also molded and influenced by the demonic world. We need prophets who will confront the evil in our institutions. (Instead they are usually punished or jailed for

15. Wink, *Unmasking the Powers*, p. 51.
16. Morton Kelsey on the cover of the above-mentioned book by Walter Wink.
17. Wink, p. 51.

their stand.) Jesus did this when He strode into the Temple and turned over the tables of the moneychangers, in order to illustrate what had happened to true worship in His day: It had turned into a den of thieves.

What is missing among those who take a stand for social justice and against institutional injustice is that they do not, for the most part, recognize that demons and evil spirits really exist, and that, until we deal with them, we cannot successfully destroy the kingdom of Satan.

Unfortunately, many of those who are keenly aware of aspects of societal evil ("institutional injustice," as Pope John Paul II termed it) know little about deliverance from evil spirits, as distinct from simply unmasking evil forces or energies. Their experience has been that certain Christians have used their belief in demons as a ploy to avoid taking personal responsibility for evil ("The devil made me do it!").

> Priests in Brazil described to my wife and me how belief in possession merely reinforced the fatalism of people who believed that God had already planned everything. The church there is trying to teach people that they can make their own history, that they can be responsible, that they need not blame demons when their child's illness is worms caught because their family cannot afford to buy shoes for her. What is *really* demonic so often is the way religion and popular superstition conspire together to mystify the true causes of distress under a fog of demonology.[18]

These critics have also seen the excesses of well-meaning but misguided exorcists:

> Jesus does not subscribe to the opinion that our emotions or habits can or should be cast out by exorcism. To attempt to cast out something essential to the self is like performing castration to deal with lust. Great harm is done by well-intended, self-appointed "exorcists," largely in neo-Pentecostal circles, by exorcising people who are not genuinely possessed.[19]

I can agree completely with this criticism but disagree with the same author's later conclusion:

18. Ibid., p. 54.
19. Ibid., p. 52.

It is my hope that the somewhat demythologized understanding of the demonic that I have proposed here will counteract the tendency to personify demons as little beings in the sky, and help us to identify the demonic as the psychic or spiritual power emanated by societies or institutions or individuals . . . whose energies are bent on overpowering others.[20]

This is one more example of the perpetual tragedy of Christians discovering a profound aspect of Christian truth that has been obscured for centuries, then making the leap to deny *another* aspect of Christian truth. I do not see demons as "little beings in the sky," but I do believe they are real. It is the old "two ships passing in the night" story all over again.

Why can't we have not an either-or but a both-and situation, believing

1. that there are demonic, personal powers that control regions, societies, political systems and institutions (including those that influence churches);
2. that there are also evils to which we are blind that influence the same regions, nations and societies, in which our human greed and selfishness become institutionalized and larger than life, beyond the ability of any one individual to reform and, therefore, "demonic" in the sense of being an evil that has a kind of life of its own.

Both-And: An Example of Social Exorcism

Here I want to share with you a remarkable account of a social exorcism—a deliverance from evil spirits worked by an unlikely source: a social activist from the Methodist Federation for Social Action. Its director, the Rev. George McClain, had been continually frustrated by the refusal of the national United Methodist Board of Pensions to get rid of its investments in South Africa, even though the United Methodist Church had called for divestment in order to protest apartheid. In fact, George had been arrested, with 36 of his colleagues, for blockading the Board of Pensions' offices in Evanston.

20. Ibid., p. 68.

Then George sat in on several exorcisms that his wife, Tilda (also a minister), had conducted. George found all his rationalistic ideas about evil ("the absence of good") "blown to pieces" as he came to realize that exorcism was a reality, not just an "embarrassing aspect of the New Testament's witness."

He began to sense that the Board of Pensions, though its members were dedicated Christians, was held captive by evil powers; and he gathered seven friends to pray for the Board's exorcism (at a distance, of course). In prayer they discerned the names of the oppressing spirits—fear and intimidation being the principal ones. They held a Communion service, then performed the exorcism:

"Spirit of fear and intimidation, in the name of Jesus Christ, we order you to depart from the Board of Pensions and go to Jesus. . . ."

So it went for several hours until they felt their prayer mission had been accomplished. At the end they felt exhausted.

Several weeks later came the first big surprise: The general secretary of the Board, their strongest opposition, resigned unexpectedly. Three months later, when the Board met at the historic Seelback Hotel in Louisville, George noticed a great change in their attitude when they met with him once again to hear his position on South Africa. Afterward, while the Board was deliberating, George and 25 others held still another exorcism service in the chill November wind outside the hotel.

Then came the announcements: A new, open-minded secretary had been elected, and the Board voted to pull their investments out of South Africa. A change of attitude took place in the Social Action group, too (the group that George headed). Instead of seeing the Board of Pensions as a faceless bureaucracy, they began to love, even like, them. George realized that he, too, had been caught up in a spirit of fear and arrogance.

Since then several more social exorcism services have been held when there were church conflicts filled with "spiritual poison." Each time positive changes took place, with some remarkable surprises.

So here we have a new discovery: the possibility of group exorcism, not to further our own desires but—only after true discernment—whenever a group is held captive by the forces of evil.

A good example of the study of group evil that takes on a life of its own is contained in Dr. Scott Peck's masterly *People of the Lie*. He investigates, as one example, the MyLai massacre in 1968 in which U.S. troops in Vietnam massacred about six hundred unarmed villagers:

> How is it that approximately five hundred men, the majority of whom were undoubtedly not evil as individuals, could all have participated in an act as monstrously evil as that of MyLai? Clearly, to understand MyLai, our focus must not be limited solely to individual evil and individual choice.[21]

Dr. Peck concludes that institutional evil affected not only those five hundred men but our entire nation during the time of the Vietnam War, in which we engaged in massive lying (as in the MyLai cover-up) and violence.

It is not a question of human, institutional evil as contrasted with a struggle against territorial evil spirits. Situations can involve both: enormous institutional evil compounded by the influence of evil spirits. Unfortunately, many conservative Christians have little sense of social injustice (they tend, as Will Herberg observed, to idolize our nation), while social justice activists have little understanding of the reality of evil spirits and the value of deliverance. Conservative Christians often excoriate social activists as "bleeding-heart liberals" and call for a stronger military, while social activist Christians scorn conservatives who seem to come down on the side of the wealthy and ignore how unjust structures oppress the poor.

The truth about evil lies in the balance.

---

21. Ibid., p. 216.

22

Deliverance of Places

J ust last week I was informed that five chairs were found on our property arranged in a circle around a voodoo doll. In fact, this happened twice last week. The chairs were found once in our chapel and once on the grounds outside our chapel. Whoever did this wanted to make sure we knew they were praying against us.

So I asked a member of our staff who has good discernment to go over to the chapel and see if any spirit had been summoned up and, as it were, left behind. Half an hour later she reported that there was indeed a "large" spirit right behind the altar. She had been praying and the spirit had gotten "smaller," but would I please come over and pray to get rid of it. (The spirits themselves do not get smaller, of course, but the space they occupy and influence can grow smaller.) She asked another member of our staff, who discerns spirits, too, to check it out. It fascinated me to see how they both agreed as to the place the spirit occupied: They knew where it was because of denser air pressure in that place. Also, when they moved into that place, they felt oppressed and one actually got a headache, which disappeared when she moved out of the space.

So the three of us prayed. Each time the space got smaller. Finally, after about twenty minutes it left.

That same day last week my secretary, who has been putting this book (which I write out by hand) onto the computer, told me that every day when she was driving to work, she developed a headache. She also felt oppressed while she was typing, although she loves her work here. So we prayed for her office and especially the corner of the room where she was typing. Within a few minutes the headache and oppression lifted and she was feeling fine.

One morning last month the computer flat-out "refused" to write out a particular sentence on how to break a curse, until we prayed for it. After that the computer worked fine.

Later, when the manuscript for this book went to Jane Campbell, who was editing it for Chosen Books, further startling problems developed. I asked her to write up her own description of what took place:

> First my computer started giving me messages that "an unrecoverable disk error had occurred." Then I found I was unable to save what I had been working on for the last fifteen minutes. So I got rid of the text (sacrificing fifteen minutes' worth of editing), brought it back, made a change and tried to save it. I couldn't. I repeated this cycle for fifteen minutes or so. Then the text disappeared altogether and the screen went white.
>
> At that point *I* went white. I was afraid the whole chapter had been lost. Next I was unable to access any chapter in the book and feared that the four chapters I had already edited were gone, too. Later I was relieved when the "Tools" function on my Macintosh told me there were 3,639 words in chapter 5, but I was utterly unable to access them. The support man from Microsoft called my problem "strange" and "weird," and told me it was at a level deeper than the software and that he couldn't help me.
>
> I clung to Colossians 2:15: "Having disarmed the powers and authorities, [Christ] made a public spectacle of them, triumphing over them by the cross." "Even if this computer screen remains white," I said, "Jesus triumphed over you by the cross!" And I bound spirits and praised God.
>
> And five hours later the text returned (for no apparent reason) and every glitch disappeared.

These bizarre experiences reflect the ancient Christian tradition that places, buildings, rooms and objects need to be exorcised and blessed. These blessings follow the familiar pattern that we find in blessing oil, salt and water. First we pray to drive away any evil that may reside in the place. This is the *exorcism* of evil. Then we bless the place, asking God to fill it with His goodness, the power of the Holy Spirit and the presence of His holy angels. This is the *blessing*.

Sometimes the evil that dwells in a place (like our chapel) arrived through a curse, which needs to be broken. At other times a crime has been committed in the place. Many haunted houses, for example, have a history of some murder or violent deed that took place on the premises. When a crime has been committed, you need to do something, in addition to exorcising and blessing the place, to rectify the crime and set any restless spirits at rest.[1]

Dr. Ken McAll, who has studied these phenomena for years, believes that the tragedies of lost ships and downed airplanes that have disappeared mysteriously in the Bermuda Triangle were caused by the thousands of slaves dumped overboard and drowned in this area of the Atlantic, when the slavers decided they were too weak to finish the voyage. Their souls were crying out, as it were, for revenge. Dr. Ken prayed intently with friends ten years ago over the situation, then arranged to have a minister lead a special service asking Jesus to take care of all the murdered victims of the slave trade. Since then the mysterious tragedies in the Bermuda Triangle seem to have ceased.

If a particularly nefarious crime has been committed in a site that was previously dedicated to God, the building or place also needs to be *rededicated*. In Catholic tradition, for example, if a murder has been committed in a cathedral, the cathedral needs not only to be spiritually cleansed but rededicated.

At other times various rooms need to be cleansed because people afflicted by evil spirits seem to leave something behind in places they have visited. Our waiting rooms at Christian Healing Ministries need to be cleansed and blessed every so often because so many hurting people come for help. It is something like a hospital, where extra precautions have to be taken against the spread of infectious diseases that the sick bring with them.

In summary, we need to pray for rooms, buildings, churches and other properties under the following circumstances:

1. For those from a Catholic tradition, this means celebrating a liturgy, asking God in His mercy to set these wandering souls at rest.

1. when they have been targeted by curses, hexes and spells by satanic groups;
2. when crimes or other serious sins have been committed there;
3. when people infested by demons have lived or spent time visiting a place.

Also, of course, when we first move into a new home or apartment (or place of business, if we are in charge), or when a minister moves into a new church assignment, it is wise to bless the place and pray through it. We should ask God to pour out His blessing on the property and protect it from evil.

If you have not had experience in these things, what I have written here may sound extreme. Certainly you cannot prove that some tragic event occurred because someone cursed you, or that you avoided harm because you prayed for protection. Yet if you add up the number of times you have experienced something like this, you will find the chance that it is mere coincidence too great. Nothing can be proven by a single instance, but an inductive proof from many instances can readily be made.

Is it just coincidence that my secretary, about whom I wrote earlier in this chapter, arrived at work this morning to say she has felt no oppression and had no headaches since we prayed four days ago, even though headaches and inexplicable depression had bothered her at work for the previous three weeks?

There are many practical applications you can make from this teaching about blessing and exorcising places. As just one example, some of my friends who are spiritually sensitive are always careful about the motel or hotel rooms in which they stay. If they sense something spiritually oppressive or evil about the room, they ask for a change, or pray in the room until the oppression lifts.

The people I trust enough to ask to come and pray through our home and ministry center are not extremists; they are mature, thoughtful and balanced. But they have learned to discriminate and sense the presence of evil when it is there, without going overboard and becoming overly fearful. Then they pray calmly.

We all need friends like that.

Part 7

Final Words

23

Baptism in the Holy Spirit

In August 1967 during a conference at Maryville College in Tennessee, my life changed radically when I asked for prayer to receive baptism in the Holy Spirit. When a group prayed for me as if I were to receive the Spirit for the first time, nothing much happened. But the next afternoon, when a few friends prayed for a release in me of the gifts of the Spirit (which I had already received in baptism, confirmation and ordination), I was overwhelmed with joy, and a wave of laughter swept over me.

My life has never been the same. Since then I have prayed for hundreds of people whose lives have also been transformed as they asked to receive the fullness of the Holy Spirit. There are many explanations—and disagreements—about baptism in the Spirit and what it has caused to happen to millions of Christians in the Pentecostal, Charismatic and Third Wave renewals in this century. If you are unfamiliar with this extraordinary outpouring of the Spirit, I encourage you to read one of the many fine books that have been published.[1]

1. Among these are Dennis Bennett's *Nine O'Clock in the Morning* (S. Plainfield, N.J.: Bridge Publishing, 1970). I also recommend his complementary books, *The Holy Spirit and You* (co-authored with Rita Bennett) and *How to Pray for the Release of the Spirit*. These books, also published by Bridge, are two of the many excellent books on the subject. If you are interested in the scriptural and historical background for baptism in the Spirit, I recommend *Christian Initiation and Baptism in the Holy Spirit* (or its abbreviated version, *Fanning the Flame*) by Killian McDonnell and George Montague (Collegeville, Minn.: Liturgical Press, 1991).

One of the purposes of this immersion in the Spirit is empowered ministry, as Jesus promised His disciples after His resurrec-
tion:

> I am going to send you what my Father has promised; but stay in
> the city until you have been clothed with power from on high.
>
> Luke 24:49

This promise (*promise* in Luke usually refers to the Holy
Spirit) was fulfilled, as we know, at Pentecost. Up to that point,
the disciples were Christian believers and had, to a degree, received the Holy Spirit. But something was still missing; they
were in hiding, praying and waiting for the promised Holy
Spirit. But after the Spirit descended on them like a rushing
wind, they burst out of doors, eager to preach.

What first drew me to ask for baptism in the Spirit back in
1967 was meeting some remarkable Christians who healed the
sick and were filled with enthusiasm to share their life in Christ.
This desire to evangelize was something I believed in but had
not seen much of in the Christians I knew, including many
priests and ministers. Our religion was private, reserved for formal occasions when we were expected to speak about religion
or pray formal prayers according to the book.

As for healing, I had read about it in the lives of the saints of
old, but saw little evidence of it around me. So when I met Christians who routinely prayed for the sick and cast out evil spirits,
I was curious, to say the least. And when I asked how they got
that way, they told me it had started after they were baptized in
the Spirit.

Even Jesus in His human nature needed to be empowered by
the Spirit before He began His public ministry, preaching, healing and casting out evil spirits. At that time, when John the Baptist baptized Him in the Jordan, the Spirit descended on Him.

> More than any of the gospels, however, Luke portrays Jesus' pub-
> lic ministry of healing and deliverance as empowered by the Holy
> Spirit, stemming from the Spirit's anointing at his baptism. In
> Acts 10:38, Luke notes "how God anointed him with the Holy
> Spirit and with power": a reference to Jesus' baptism which em-
> powered him to perform healings and exorcisms.

It is obvious here (Lk 4:18–19) that Jesus, who will later send the Holy Spirit upon the community (Lk 24:49; Acts 2:33), himself receives the Spirit at his baptism, or at the very least a new manifestation of the Spirit upon him since his conception, and that the Spirit endows him with prophetic and healing charisms for his ministry. For Luke the baptism of Jesus is a paradigm of the baptism of the community at Pentecost.[2]

We know that the Spirit was present to Jesus in His humanity from the very beginning at His conception, when Mary was overshadowed by the Spirit (Luke 1:35). Often when I speak to priests about praying for Christians to receive the Holy Spirit, they object, "Our people have already received the Holy Spirit at baptism and confirmation. What are you trying to do, call into question the fact that they have been confirmed? Don't you believe in baptism?" Evangelicals object, "These people are saved. They have already made their decision for Christ. Don't you believe they received the Holy Spirit then?"

The answer is simply to look at the example of Jesus, who walked with God for thirty years, then needed a new dimension of union with the Spirit to empower Him for ministry. I need that empowering, too.

I remember a talk that Padre Salvador Carillo, a respected theologian, gave to a group of priests in Mexico City. He told them they should not get trapped into trying to figure out too much theoretically. The main thing they should ask themselves was *whether what happened to the apostles at Pentecost had happened to them.* Were they eager to preach the Gospel? Were they healing the sick and casting out evil spirits? As for their already having received the Spirit through the sacraments, the answer was yes. But they were something like the apostles before Pentecost.

Were the apostles already Christians? Yes. They had followed Jesus for three years and believed His teaching. Were they already ordained? Nobody knows when it happened, but tradition says they were ordained at the Last Supper, almost two months before Pentecost. Yet they were not ready for ministry until the Spirit descended on them at Pentecost.

So the question we need to answer is, "Has what happened to the apostles happened to us yet?"

2. McDonnell and Montague, pp. 25–26.

I was blessed in that I did not experience anything in Tennessee when that first group prayed as if I were receiving the Holy Spirit for the first time. It was only the next afternoon when friends prayed for me to experience the release of the power of the Spirit (whom I had already received) that it really happened and I was overwhelmed with joy. There are many explanations and demands that good Christians make, such as, "You must pray in tongues to show that you've been baptized in the Spirit." But I encourage you to approach this on the simplest basis possible. Ask yourself if you have truly received the fullness of the Spirit, attended by all the gifts that you need for ministry. Certainly if you pray for deliverance, you need the power of the Holy Spirit in the greatest measure you can receive it, including discernment, the gifts of healing and the spiritual authority to cast out evil spirits.

Perhaps this is why there is such a strong conviction in the Catholic tradition that exorcists usually get chewed up spiritually and physically in their ministry. (We talked about this in chapter 9.) Without a release of the Spirit's power, we are out of our spiritual depth; and exorcism is a ministry any sane person would avoid! Recall Malachi Martin's warning:

> The exorcist is the centerpiece of every exorcism. On him depends everything. He has nothing personal to gain. But in each exorcism he risks literally everything that he values. . . . And no matter what the outcome, the contact is in part fatal for the exorcist. He must consent to a dreadful and irreparable pillage of his deepest self. Something dies in him. Some part of his humanness will wither from such close contact with the opposite of all humanness—the essence of evil; and it is rarely if ever revitalized. No return will be made to him for his loss.[3]

Admittedly there are dangers, especially when we confront the occult demonic realm. But I have already suggested that the reason priests have lost so much vitality may be that they need more of the power of the Spirit in their ministry. These torn-up ministers remind us of the seven sons of Sceva, who invoked the name of Jesus over a man who had an evil spirit, until he "jumped on them and . . . gave them such a beating that they ran out of the

3. Malachi Martin, *Hostage to the Devil* (New York: Reader's Digest Press, 1976), p. 10.

house naked and bleeding" (Acts 19:16). Those exorcists believed in Jesus to a certain extent, but did not have a personal relationship with Him and were not empowered by the Spirit.

That seems to be the point—not that we should be afraid that the fate of the sons of Sceva be ours, but rather that we should become like Paul and the other apostles. They did not seek out conflict with evil spirits, but did not shrink from it when it came up:

> Elymas the sorcerer (for that is what his name means) opposed them and tried to turn the proconsul from the faith. Then Saul, who was also called Paul, filled with the Holy Spirit, looked straight at Elymas and said, "You are a child of the devil and an enemy of everything that is right!"
>
> Acts 13:8–10

Paul hardly sounds like a man afraid he will be forced to "consent to a dreadful and irreparable pillage of his deepest self"! I think the problem with the fearful approach to exorcism is that too much confidence is placed in the faithful recitation of the words of the formal rite. If we made sure everyone who attempted exorcism was baptized in the Spirit, the exorcists would have much less to worry about.

Early Christians had a lively confidence that they would overcome demonic powers, as we see in the comments of Lactantius (who lived around the year A.D. 300):

> The [evil spirits] do indeed injure, but those only by whom they are feared, whom the powerful and lofty hand of God does not protect, who are uninitiated in the mystery of truth.
>
> But they fear the righteous, that is, the worshippers of God, adjured by whose name they depart from the bodies of the possessed: for, being lashed by their words as though by scourges . . . therefore oftimes having uttered the greatest howlings, they cry out that they are beaten, and are on fire, and that they are just on the point of coming forth: so much power has the knowledge of God, and righteousness! Whom, therefore, can they injure, except those whom they have in their power?[4]

4. Lactantius, *Divine Institutes*, Book V, chapter XXII, as contained in *Biblical Healing, Hebrew and Christian Roots* by Frank Darling (Boulder, Col.: Vista Publications, 1989), p. 169. This is the first of three fine books Darling has authored documenting the history of Christian healing up to the present.

The early Church had the attitude that if *anyone* was to be afraid or shrink from combat, it was the demons. Not that we should not have a prudent hesitation about getting into deliverance, but if we are protected by the weapons the Holy Spirit gives us—which are increased through the baptism of the Spirit—we are shielded by God's power, which is immeasurably greater than that of Satan. The strong man has been tied up. And among the Spirit's gifts, we are endowed with discernment and the word of knowledge to guide us, together with the power and authority to heal and cast out evil spirits.

As for the "dreadful and irreparable pillage of [our] deepest self," I think of the courageous example of Derek Prince, still traveling around the world in his late seventies to preach and exorcise, even after some forty years of strenuous deliverance ministry. Of all the people I know, he has probably done the most speaking and prayer for deliverance.

If you accept the belief that you will be destroyed spiritually as well as physically if you get into deliverance, you end up buying into the destructive myth propagated by Satan to keep the Christian community from destroying his evil empire. This myth honors Satan by lifting his power to God's level and even beyond, while we, God's followers, fear to enter the arena of spiritual combat.

But with baptism in the Spirit we receive power for ministry, and many wonderful things happen. My friend the Rev. Tommy Tyson once defined baptism in the Spirit as "an event in our lives by which we become more constantly aware of the presence, the Person and the power of the risen Christ." Each of these words carries significant meaning.

As to the *presence* of Christ, many people I know are aware of Jesus' presence almost constantly, with little effort of their own, ever since they prayed to receive baptism in the Spirit. Some have seen visions of Jesus or heard Him speak to them.

As to His *Person*, their love becomes more concentrated on Jesus as their Friend and Brother, rather than merely as Lord and Master (although he remains, of course, their Lord and Master). Rather than solely use the formal title *Christ*, they now feel more comfortable using the more personal *Jesus*.

> You are my friends if you do what I command. I no longer call you servants, because a servant does not know his master's business.

Instead, I have called you friends, for everything that I learned from my Father I have made known to you.

John 15:14–15

You have been adopted into the very family circle of God and you can say with a full heart, "Father, my Father." The Spirit himself endorses our inward conviction that we really are the children of God. Think what that means.

Romans 8:15–16, Phillips

As for receiving the *power* of the risen Christ, it means that we receive the gifts (1 Corinthians 12:8–11) beyond our unaided humanity,

To *know*, prophesy, discern, interpret tongues, teach, preach and understand;
To *heal*, cast out evil spirits and work miracles;
To *pray* in tongues.

All these gifts are an immeasurable help in the deliverance ministry. So to be fully equipped for this difficult ministry, it is wisdom for us to seek to be filled with God's Holy Spirit.

When the apostles in Jerusalem heard that Samaria had accepted the Word of God, they sent Peter and John down to them. When these two had arrived they prayed for the Samaritans that they might receive the Holy Spirit for as yet he had not fallen upon any of them. They were living simply as men and women who had been baptized in the name of the Lord Jesus. So then and there they laid their hands on them and they received the Holy Spirit.

Acts 8:14–17, Phillips[5]

---

5. Notice that these Samaritans were already believers and had been baptized, yet something was missing. In the following paragraph Simon the magician offered Peter money to buy the ability to impart this power, this baptism in the Spirit, so it must have been accompanied by startling manifestations. (The Samaritans had come to believe in the first place because they saw Philip the deacon healing the sick and casting out demons.)

Sample Prayers

Following are some of the prayers that appear in the text of this book. I offer them not as *the* prayers to pray, but as examples of the kinds of prayers you can pray in different situations. Please be guided by the Holy Spirit, by the particular situation and by your own personality.

Sinner's Prayer (see chapter 16)

Lord Jesus, I confess that I have sinned against You, and I ask that You forgive me for all my sins. I believe that Jesus Christ is the Son of God, who shed His blood on the cross for the remission of my sins. I give my life to You and ask that You come into my heart, that I may live with You eternally. In Jesus' name. Amen.

Prayer for Protection (see chapter 7)

Lord Jesus, I ask You to protect my family [mention by name] from sickness, from all harm and from accidents. If any of us has been subjected to any curses, hexes or spells, I declare these curses, hexes or spells null and void in the name of Jesus Christ. If any evil spirits have been sent against us, I decommission you in the name of Jesus Christ and I send you to Jesus to deal with as He will. Then, Lord, I ask You to send Your holy angels to guard and protect all of us.

Prayer for Deliverance (see chapter 13)

In the name of Jesus Christ I command you, you spirit of [name], to depart without doing harm to [name of counselee] or anyone else in this house, or in her family, and without making any noise or disturbance; and I command you to go straight to Jesus Christ to dispose of as He will. Furthermore, I command you never again to return.

Cleansing Prayer for Deliverance Minister for Cleansing (see chapter 13)

Lord Jesus, thank You for sharing with me Your wonderful ministry of healing and deliverance. Thank You for the healings I have seen and experienced today. But I realize that the sickness and evil I encounter are more than my humanity can bear. So cleanse me of any sadness, negativity or despair that I may have picked up.

If my ministry has tempted me to anger, impatience or lust, cleanse me of those temptations and replace them with love, joy and peace. If any evil spirits have attached themselves to me or oppress me in any way, I command you, spirits of earth, air, fire or water, of the netherworld or of nature, to depart now and go straight to Jesus Christ, for Him to deal with as He will.

Come, Holy Spirit, renew me, fill me anew with Your power, love and joy. Strengthen me where I have felt weak and clothe me with Your light. Fill me with life.

And Lord Jesus, please send Your holy angels to minister to me and my family, and to guard and protect us from all sickness, harm and accidents (and guard me on a safe trip home, and grant us a peaceful night's rest).

I praise You now and forever, Father, Son and Holy Spirit! Amen.

Prayer to Break a False Judgment (see chapter 8)

In the name of Jesus Christ and by the sword of the Spirit, I cut you free from this false judgment of _____ and declare it null and void.

Prayer to Break a False Vow (see chapter 8)

In the name of Jesus Christ I break this vow of _____ and declare it null and void, no longer able to influence you. By the sword of the Spirit I cut you free from this vow and all its effects.

Prayer to Break a Seal (see chapter 16)

In the name of Jesus Christ [or *in the name of the Father, and of the Son and of the Holy Spirit*], I break every seal of Satan and I set you free by the sword of the Holy Spirit. (Repeat three times.)

Binding Prayer Prior to Prayer for Inner Healing (see chapter 14)

In the name of Jesus Christ I command you, spirit of [name], not to interfere with this prayer. I bind you off from influencing _____'s will, from his mind, from his imagination or emotions, from his memories and from his body. I cut you off by the sword of the Spirit from stirring up _____'s grief [or fear or any other primary emotional problems]. I command you to be quiet and to leave when we finish our prayer for healing.

Appendix **2**

An Interview
with Father Rufus Pereira

In this book I have tried to share with you the urgency for restoring the ministry of deliverance—not just in the abstract or as it affects the lives of missionaries and people in the developing world, but as it touches our own lives in the West. Prayer for deliverance is just as important for us in North America or Europe as it is in Africa or Asia, but we do not seem to realize it. For some of your friends, perhaps even for you, it may be a matter of life and death.

If you travel almost anywhere in Africa, Latin America or Asia, you will see firsthand the people's desperate need for deliverance from the power of evil spirits. One vivid glimpse of that third world experience is contained in an interview I had with Father Rufus Pereira in India in 1978 (from which I quoted in chapter 7).

Father Rufus continues to be one of the most prominent leaders in the Roman Catholic charismatic renewal and was commissioned in 1976 by the late Cardinal Gracidas to work full-time in the renewal. He is well-educated in philosophy and theology, having finished his studies in Rome, followed by three years of biblical studies. This sophisticated background makes his experiences in freeing people from evil spirits all the more impressive.

In the interview you cannot help but notice the acceptance of supernatural phenomena (except among the clergy) that would immediately impress you if you visited India, Nigeria, Venezuela or almost any country as yet untouched by our own scientific rationalism.

My very first case of deliverance took place on the 7th of March, 1976. It happened during a prayer meeting held in Bombay where between two hundred and three hundred people were present and we were on our break time. Suddenly we heard a shout and screaming, and we all went over to see what was happening. I saw there a young girl on a chair who was screeching and flinging her arms all about. I asked someone what was happening and was told that she was possessed. It was the first time I had ever met such a person, said to be possessed.

Something inside me inspired me to say, "I command you in the name of Jesus to leave her." At that very moment she stopped doing all those things; her eyes opened and she gave me a beautiful smile. I absolutely didn't know what I was doing! Later she told me how for ten years she had been afflicted by evil spirits and that she had been going to a Muslim shrine, but now she felt freed.

In the two years since that time I have prayed for between four hundred and five hundred cases of deliverance. About one-third of these were deliverances from so-called Hindu gods and goddesses.

I love my country very much and have a great respect for Indian religion and philosophy, but perhaps there is no religion that has within itself such a wide spectrum, all the way from the highest form of religious endeavor to the lowest degradation of humanity—all in the name of religion. I have been led to believe from my experiences that many of these gods and goddesses in Hindu mythology are nothing other than demons. The reason I think this is that in a third of the cases, when we asked the demons to identify themselves, they gave their names as Hindu gods or goddesses. On one occasion a woman even gave me the name of Krishna, which was a shock to me.[1] (I'm not saying that Krishna is a demon; I'm just saying that in this one woman who was brought before the cross, the spirit identified itself as Krishna.)

There are certain gods and goddesses who turn up frequently in these cases of deliverance. One in particular is a god called Andarvar. He's a god who, according to popular belief, is a very evil spirit who possesses women; he is very lustful and wants to rape women. These afflicted women actually experience this god coming during the nighttime and raping them. They all say it was not a dream. They say it was as if they were awake—that it actually happened while they were awake. Speaking to their husbands, I have been led to believe that what they say may be true.[2]

Another thing I would like to share with you is that many people get possessed on the festival days of these gods and goddesses. My own cousin was an officer in the army many, many years ago. He went out on a Hindu festival day, and when he came back he fell sick with a fever—the doctors couldn't diagnose it—and within one week's time he died. Another cousin also died in the same mysterious circumstances. (My mother used to warn us when we were small never to go out of the house on the day of Hindu festivals.) I've also found that in many cases of possession, the attacks of the evil spirit become far more intense on festival days.

Q: Can you share something about the dancing god that was inhabiting the young woman whom you showed us stretched out in a dancing posture during last week's conference?

A: Yes. We had at least five cases of possession by Hindu gods and goddesses during the last three days of the national convention, and I made it a point to ask the members of your team to come and gather firsthand knowledge of what takes place in these cases. You will remember what she looked like: The girl was taking on the poses of the Hindu god who is called Lataranjan—the dancing god. (This dancing god is an aspect of the god Shiva.)

1. In Hindu mythology Krishna is one of the three main deities and is a benevolent being, very different from Kali, who is malevolent.

2. In Western literature we find such sexual demons, too. Those who take the male sexual role are *incubi*, from the Latin meaning "the one who lies on top," while their female counterparts are the *succubi*, from the Latin meaning "the one who lies underneath."

What is really remarkable is that this girl knows nothing about Indian dancing. She is actually in many ways alien to Indian culture because she was brought up in a Western culture home. Yet here she was, taking the absolutely correct dancing poses in her fingers, her wrists, her hands and her feet—the exact poses of this very god. We took one photo, but I wish more photos had been taken of the different poses. It was just something fantastic to watch, if it were not also something very cruel, very abominable. Even her face—her eyes and mouth—were all changed into the features of this Hindu god.

After commanding the spirit to identify itself, I found that it got into her because of a spell cast by a Hindu doctor (who perhaps had lustful motives when he was treating her). Probably he called upon his favorite god, who happened to be Lataranjan, to possess her so that he could gain power over her.

Another fascinating case came to light during the second day of our healing seminar when a college girl told me that when she was a young girl, she went to a Hindu temple and there observed the image of a god with six hands—it's called Mahakali. It is the most terrible goddess in Hindu mythology, a goddess who is bloodthirsty and wants to kill. Hindus try to pacify this goddess by frequently offering human sacrifices, even in our own day.

Q: Is she the same as Kali, the one who appears in some of our movies that are set in India?

A: Yes, Kali. They call her Mahakali out of respect; it means "great Kali." Tens of thousands of people have been sacrificed in the past two hundred years to propitiate her. This girl told me she went to the temple and saw this goddess there. Then one night during these days of conference she had a dream—she was half-awake—and saw this goddess coming toward her. She described her as a huge, fat, ugly woman with big eyes and six hands coming to throttle her.

When we prayed for deliverance she started to suffocate and was tormented in her throat. Finally she could not speak at all; she became dumb. After prayer she was able to speak again, but the irritation in her throat remained. On the last day of the healing seminar, when she came forward and was anointed with the oil that you blessed, the irritation in her throat left immediately. She also felt, when the oil was applied to her forehead, a great sense of peace.

Hers is perhaps the most interesting case I've had in India—in many ways a beautiful case, but also in many ways a terrifying case. She told me that she now realizes she was afflicted because her grandfather—he's supposed to be a Catholic—used to do this work of exorcism in his spare time through the power of a god called Hanuman. He's the monkey god, very popular in India. He would free a person through Hanuman's help and then transfer the spell somewhere else.[3] He would say to the spirit, "Now go on the road, and let the first person who comes your way come under your spell." She was telling me that her grandfather had hurt many people that way, and that's why all this backlash has come into her whole family. She further told me that her father has been getting up every night during the past month screaming that someone was choking him. Anyone who stays overnight at their home also feels someone choking them.

I think this is another thing worth noting: Very often when there is some member of the family—a father or grandfather—who does this work of casting

---

3. Non-Christian healers and exorcists do effect healings and exorcisms. But if they do this through the power of spirits other than the Holy Spirit, the last state of the person may prove worse than the first.

out evil spirits through the power of a Hindu god or goddess, then the third generation seems especially to get affected.

Q: Is she a Catholic?
A: Yes, she is.

Q: Why do you think she fell under this demonic influence—just through her grandfather's involvement? How can this be?
A: Now this is a very, very strange thing. I believe that if a father or grandfather is in league with Satan, all the members of the family will be affected to a greater or lesser extent.[4] I don't know why this particular little girl was affected more than the others, but it does seem to be true.

Later on she revealed to me that when she was in college she felt very lonely because her father was an alcoholic and everybody made fun of her. Then one day walking on her way to college she met three girls, and she became very friendly with them. They used to come into the college just to sit next to her. These friends were the only ones she went out with, and after class was out, they would take her to places where many evil things happened, and they would try to force her to do these wrong things. They would force her to masturbate with them. Finally they wanted to give her a stone, promising that the stone would give her power: "If only you invoke Satan and ask him for anything, you'll get it." They said that if she would do that, then she would get everything she asked for.

Q: They gave her a stone?
A: A big, black stone about three inches in diameter. She was supposed to keep it with her and say the formula: "Satan, Satan, come into me; give me all I need," or something of that sort. Of course, she didn't exactly know what she was doing. She also told me the names of these girls, but when I went to the college to verify their names I couldn't find them in the registry. From all that she told me, I guessed that they were not real girls; that they were spirits who took on this guise and began to lead her the wrong way.

The first time I came to her town and they brought her to me to pray for her physical healing, she told me that the previous day these girls had met her and told her, "Don't go anywhere near that priest called Rufus from Bombay. He's short and he's wearing a blue shirt and black pants; don't go anywhere near him!" She also told me that when her mother brought her to the place where I was, she looked in through the window and saw Jesus sitting in the chair, but when she came into the room she was surprised to find me sitting down in the same chair. That was the beginning of her whole story, and then marvelous things started to happen in that town. She was one of the five from among our five hundred cases that took a long time to pray for.

Q: What do you think of transcendental meditation?
A: Regarding TM, I believe very strongly that they give the beginner the name of a Hindu god or goddess to be recited as a mantra. [A mantra is a name that is recited until it becomes part of you.] Last year in Toronto, Canada, I met a girl who came into contact with the charismatic renewal and was doing wonderfully well, and then she got involved in TM, and that affected her to such an extent that she often tried to commit suicide, and now for three years she's been committed in a psychiatric hospital. She's from India, and when her friends learned that I was in

4. This bears out what I wrote in chapter 7 on curses.

Canada they brought her to see me in a parish rectory. When we prayed over her nothing happened. I said, "Go to church on Sunday, and at the same time we'll be saying mass for you." On Thursday when she came to the prayer meeting, I could see from her face that something had happened, and she told me that for the first time she could sleep without taking a sleeping pill. Later she wrote me to say that there is great danger in TM.

Q: What mantra was she using?
A: I don't remember now, but it was the name of a Hindu god.

Q: Is TM strong here in India, or is it just influential in the U.S.?
A: It's quite strong, especially among the educated intellectuals. Very often they're business executives who take to it because they're under stress—as a sort of meditation. And I'm afraid that many Catholics, including sisters and priests, are also using TM.

Q: What some people in the U.S. say is that they feel better and are more at peace when they use TM. If someone said something like that to you, how would you respond?
A: If somebody told me that he felt better after TM or after going to a Muslim *faquir* or a Hindu *pujari*, one of those people who seem to have the power of freeing people from evil spirits, I'd tell them two things. I've not met a single case where the improvement has lasted more than a week, or a month at most. Often for three or four days they feel better, and then they become worse. Every case I've met of people who have gone to these people—they become worse after going.
   The first thing I'd like to say, then, is that they become better for a short time. The second thing is that they become worse afterward.

Q: One more thing about TM. Its initiation features a *puja* ceremony in which the devotees offer fruit before the picture of the guru. Is that a Hindu ceremony?
A: It is strictly a Hindu ceremony, but in those areas of India where the Christians have not been well catechized, they often continue to perform it quietly and privately. I'll tell you of one authentic case in a certain convent in India. When the sisters began to get sick, the mother superior called on the Hindu *pujari* to deliver all the sisters from these evil spirits. The *pujari* went to the convent and asked each nun to cut a bit of hair from her head, together with a bit of fingernail, to put in the *puja*. Then she performed a *puja*, and after that all of them became worse. (The mother provincial has asked me to go there to free them, but so far I haven't gone to that part of India.) Yes. These things are happening.

Q: You told me about another convent where you did go to pray for the sisters.
A: Yes. You know, sometimes people wonder how Christians, especially nuns and priests, can become possessed. I myself wonder, but facts are facts. I remember once a mother provincial invited me to give a retreat to the nuns, but she warned me, "Father, please don't frighten my innocent nuns with stories of devils." This is the protective attitude they have, and they don't seem to realize that these things are happening.
   One of the most difficult cases of deliverance I had was of a nun who was attacked and for three hours was under the power of an evil spirit called Lambdi. This spirit is not a Hindu god or goddess, but comes from a wandering tribe in India who are like the gypsies and dabble in the occult. They specialize in casting spells on people, and it was one of these spirits that came into the sister. (She was prayed for and delivered.) I've come across many cases of nuns being possessed

in a very dramatic way. As for priests—I haven't come across any cases so far of them being possessed in a vile and dramatic way, but to a smaller extent, yes.

Q: What about yoga?

A: This was one of the topics the National Service Team discussed at length, because we have two different groups in India. One group is conservative and believes that anything that smacks of Hinduism must be diabolic; they are therefore against having anything to do with yoga. I feel that is a bit extreme. The other group is composed of many people, even priests and nuns, who somehow feel that things like yoga are even more helpful in some ways than Christianity. So we have these two extremes.

We came to a decision in which we formulated a statement declaring that, on the one hand, the emotional and spiritual elements of yoga need to be avoided; at times they can even be diabolic and make us vulnerable to the forces of evil. Nevertheless, the purely practical aspects of yoga can be accepted so long as they are deliberately placed under the Lordship of Jesus.[5]

Q: What would those practical aspects be?

A: In yoga the practical aspects consist of the breathing exercises and the bodily postures. When I see people using these exercises combined with a strong Christian life, nothing wrong happens; the persons benefit. But when they do it with a kind of longing for the emotional and spiritual aspects of yoga, I find that wrong things start to develop in their lives.

Q: Do you deal a lot with people having spells cast on them? How do you break those?

A: Like the rest of my ministry, I walked into this by accident. I stumbled into it; I had not read any books or heard about it before. I found that just by praying, things started to happen. I would simply pray in this way: "In the name of Jesus I break the spell that has been cast upon you and every member of your family." And then I'd begin praying in tongues and things would happen. I've not come across a single case where a spell was not broken, sometimes instantaneously. Sometimes every member of the family, wherever they were, even in the countryside, would report later that at the very moment we prayed, they felt something happen.

Q: One of the things you also mentioned was that some of the priests traditionally beat the people to exorcise them.

A: Oh, they perform exorcisms in an awful way. They tie up possessed people and whip them all day. They pull people by the hair and beat them until they are black and blue all over their bodies. Often they also pour boiling wax upon them. That's how they do it, accompanied by a lot of shrieking and screaming. Terrible things happen to people in this traditional way—that's why there's so much antipathy to exorcism, because the only thing educated Indian people hear about exorcism is that these exorcists are hurting people.

Q: What are some of the ways you can tell the difference between when a person just suffers a psychological problem and when he needs deliverance?

5. The best person to make a decision in such a controversy, I believe, is the ardent Christian who understands the culture where the practice takes place—in this instance, a native of India.

A: People often ask how I can tell the difference. I don't have any special system; probably I have a gift of discernment of spirits. But when I see a person I know at once what's wrong, and so far I've not had a single case where we've made a mistake. I know almost immediately whether it's a case of deliverance or not.

There are also various external signs that indicate when you are dealing with a need for deliverance. Most of the time, for example, demonized people will tell you they've been to every possible doctor and psychiatrist and they've experienced no improvement. The doctors themselves will say to this person, "We cannot find any cause for your illness." Often even Hindu doctors will say, "Only prayer can help you; you go to your priest and he'll pray for you." Already that gives you some hint about what's wrong.

Then when you begin to pray, if you see various signs such as the person displaying hatred for you, or reacting very adversely to the name of Jesus—often they put their hands over their ears—that will indicate the presence of evil spirits.

Another thing: I will bring them blessed water to drink and a demonized person will refuse to drink it. Even if I secretly place my finger in the water and ask them to drink it they will say, "But you put your finger in that water." Then I'll bring a third glass of water which I haven't touched, and they'll drink that water. So these are some of the signs that I've discovered. People also may feel intense pains, which were not there before they came into my presence; that's another sign. Often if a demonized person is in a room and I just pass in front of that room, they will scream with pain at that moment.

Yet even with all these signs I am very, very careful; I take a long time before I finally decide it's a case of deliverance. Usually I go on the premise that it's not a case of deliverance; only when there is clearly a need for deliverance do I act upon it.

Q: Would you like to say a word about ancestral spirits?
A: There are many cases of this happening. I myself am not completely sure as a point of doctrine whether they are really ancestral spirits or whether they are demons pretending to be ancestral spirits. I'm not one hundred percent sure which is the correct answer. But from all that I've seen, there are familiar spirits—whatever they are—and they are very, very common in India. There are many cases in which a spirit gets into a person selecting a victim who has a similar personality as to the ancestral, familiar spirit.

One case we had in Bandra last year was a girl ten years old. She was oppressed by the spirit of a deceased girl who came from the same school, who was the same age, who used to sit in the same place in the girl's favorite tree, and who had a similar moral problem. She would speak to the girl. And when I asked her, "Why did you come into her?" she said, "Because she was like me. She was so depressed she would sit down in that tree; she hated her father just as I did." That's why she came into her. Of course we prayed for her, and this girl was never again troubled.

Q: Of the four to five hundred people you've prayed for, how many do you feel have been released?
A: I would say that, of all the cases I know of, all except four or five have been freed. But I would say that three-fourths of these cases were minor deliverances. "Minor" is to say that they took little time and they were not violent. But there were some powerful deliverances as well.

Q: Have you performed formal exorcisms?
A: No, I've never performed any formal exorcism because—well, actually, I never even thought about it. That's because when I begin to pray I feel that within five

minutes the person will probably be freed. So I've never done a formal exorcism, ever.

As I told you, I almost stumbled into this deliverance work just two years ago. I've been going around, especially in India, preaching to priests—I feel that is my particular calling and charism—preaching retreats to priests. My bishop, Cardinal Gracidas,[6] was the first bishop in India to release two of his priests for full-time work in the charismatic renewal. Although he himself was not particularly involved in the renewal, I believe he was led by the Spirit to release us for this work. I came into this ministry of deliverance at just about the same time he released me for this work.

For the first year I used to pray that the Lord would take this ministry away from me, because after every case I wouldn't be able to sleep the whole following night. I used to put a light on; I used to be afraid because the evil spirits would threaten that they would come and torture me at night. When I visited Ann Arbor last year I asked them to pray over me to be freed from this fear. From that time on, not only do I have no fear, but I have a great confidence to just go and confront Satan wherever he is.[7]

Q: What response have you met with from priests and bishops as a result of your work?
A: Most of the priests and bishops I've met don't like this subject at all. They don't even believe in it. But one thing I'm pleasantly surprised at is that many of the bishops I know send cases to me. That's because I have a good reputation as being a very quiet, unemotional and theologically sound person; therefore, they accept what is happening in my life.

I realize that many descriptions in this interview may come as a shock to those of us from North America or Europe—but that's the point! Those of us who pride ourselves in our scientific, rational worldview are a minority on our globe. Other cultures that we may regard as primitive are ahead of us in many ways; they are more in touch with spiritual reality and the world of the supernatural.

I taped this interview back in 1978 when I brought a team to India and gave a number of conferences, including two retreats for priests (attended by about four hundred priests and thirteen bishops), as well as the healing conference mentioned by Father Rufus, concluding with a healing service in Bombay for about twenty thousand people. It was a remarkable evening in which two hundred priests participated, each going out with a team of laypersons to pray for healing among those thousands of people, which included many Hindus.

The happy outcome of all the startup pains mentioned by Father Rufus— the lack of acceptance and understanding among clergy—has changed to such an extent that there are now about a million Catholic charismatics in India organized into ten thousand prayer groups. One of Father Pereira's disciples, Father Matthew Naik-amparampilil, now conducts healing services throughout India, and his crowds sometimes exceed one hundred thousand!

6. This was in the 1970s.
7. In view of the popular belief (shown in Malachi Martin's book *Hostage to the Devil*) that the exorcist dies a bit with each exorcism performed, Father Rufus shares what I believe is the true teaching on this subject of danger to the exorcist.